KATIZA'S JOURNEY

BENEATH THE SURFACE OF SOUTH AFRICA'S SHAME

Fred Bridgland

KATIZA'S JOURNEY

BENEATH THE SURFACE OF SOUTH AFRICA'S SHAME

Foreword by Emma Nicholson

Sidgwick & Jackson

First published 1997 by Sidgwick & Jackson

an imprint of Macmillan Publishers Ltd
25 Eccleston Place, London SW1W 9NF
and Basingstoke

Associated companies throughout the world

0 333 72737 1 Hardback
0 333 73047 X Trade Paperback

1 3 5 7 9 8 6 4 2

A CIP catalogue record for this book is available from
the British Library.

Typeset by SX Composing DTP, Rayleigh, Essex
Printed and bound in Great Britain by
Mackays of Chatham plc, Chatham, Kent

Contents

CONTENTS

CONTENTS

vii

Abbreviations

ANC   African National Congress

AZAPO   Azanian People's Organization

Capp   Co-ordinated Anti-Poverty Programme

Codesa Convention for a Democratic South Africa

Fedtraw Federation of Transvaal Women

KZP   KwaZulu Police

MMD   Movement for Multi-Party Democracy (Zambia)

MUFC   Mandela United Football Club

SACC   South African Council of Churches

SAP   South African Police

UDF   United Democratic Front

UNIP   United Independent Party (Zambia)

UNHCR   United Nations High Commission for Refugees

WTN   World TV News

Foreword

EMMA NICHOLSON

Katiza's journey has been one of sorrow, a pilgrim's progress towards redemption. Those who have helped him along the way, for whom he has much gratitude, include Nathi Watiwane, Nathi Nene and Bongane Mfeka, his childhood friends; Linda Malek and her mother and Kenneth Kaunda's son Kambaranja of Zambia; UNHCR's Philippe Lavanchy and Abu Moussa, both Commissioners; Stephen Digby, lawyer, and his colleagues at Withers; friends in Sierre Leone, particularly Georgie Omoro, his landlady and Patricia Harding of UNHCR; together with Sam Norman, deputy minister of defence; and Derek Johns of AP Watts, literary agents, Georgina Morley of Macmillans, Nicholas Claxton and author Fred Bridgland. His deepest gratitude is for President Frederick Chiluba of Zambia, without whose intervention he would not have remained alive beyond November 1991.

*

I have always felt at home in Zambia. Since my first visit to the country when it gained independence in 1964 (I was designing computer software for the first national government), Zambians and I had been fully at ease with each other. The new

President elected in 1991, Frederick Chiluba, became a friend. We had met in the election-campaign heat. As a Commonwealth Secretariat election monitor from the UK House of Commons I had urged the electorate to take the chance to vote. It might not come again. Chiluba's opponent, Zambia's founder and President, Kenneth Kaunda, had failed his people.

The morning after Chiluba was declared president, mine was his first appointment, at nine o'clock. Now we were facing a problem together, one that I had forced upon him; his first decision as the new President now confronted him.

The prisoner sat on a sofa in the President's study. The afternoon sun came through the window behind him. He was small and thin, dressed in clean, brown-striped cotton pyjamas. His black skin seemed to bear a white mask, the gloss of health powdered over by the pale-grey pallor of starvation. He was almost too tired to speak. The President sat upright in front of the fireplace in a carved wooden chair. Three large and vigorous uniformed men seated near by made the prisoner seem even smaller. But when he spoke, his story swelled to fill the room. We were all pushed back, to become invisible auditors to a murder story – indeed, to several murder stories, and of a great man's betrayal by his wife.

Clustered together we, five outsiders, were peering through an unexpectedly opened window into South Africa's domestic tensions. The curtain drew back and we stared, horrified, into the inner turmoil of the bloody struggle waged by the African National Congress movement against apartheid. The mesmeric beauty of Winnie Mandela, wife of the imprisoned leader Nelson, was lit up for a brief moment. Then her heroic public image crumbled to dust and ashes before us as the self-styled Mother of the Nation was revealed as the black mamba of the

ANC. She turned into a witch as we listened.

She was the threat to the prisoner's survival. I vowed to help him live against this powerful opponent.

This was Katiza Cebekhulu. I had been asked to search for him by the eminent British journalist based in South Africa, Fred Bridgland. And I had now found him. He was the so-called 'missing witness' of Winnie Mandela's 1991 trial for murder. He had disappeared. President Chiluba and I both now knew where to. Worse, we knew who had caused his forced departure from South Africa; we knew who had made space in jail in Zambia and thrown him into it; and, above all, we knew the reasons why. Katiza Cebekhulu had seen and understood too much; and he had spoken out. He had to be gagged, bound and deported to another nation's prison.

I did not doubt the prisoner's tale. Nor did the others in the room.

What could we do? Zambia had no right – nor did the President desire – to jail kangaroo-court victims from other countries. But if the prisoner were released, he would be killed by fellow countrymen protecting Mrs Mandela's reputation. His story should be told for reasons of natural justice; but what of the stability of the ANC, the only national hammer against apartheid? And how would the story impact upon Nelson Mandela? Nelson was the international freedom fighter, hero to all who believed in liberty and equality. What was his real part in this? His reputation was of vast importance. Was it essential to involve Nelson in the attempt that I must now make to quench his wife's bloodlust?

Later, when Katiza Cebekhulu unburdened himself to me privately, in anguish and over a period of years, I concluded that he had been the court jester in Winnie's household. Like a medieval monarch she had to be kept amused, and he had filled that role. His natural talent for mimicry and uneducated but sharp wit had earned him his household place – his food and clothes and schooling. He was a member of the Football Club (her notorious gang), but like all court jesters he saw much, kept silent and mourned her victims' fates. Until he became one himself. It was in this unhappy guise, as a victim, that the new President of Lusaka and I had met with him. Much work lay ahead of me as a result of our encounter.

After the prisoner had been taken away by his grand, three-man guard and we were alone, President Chiluba and I made a pact. He would keep Katiza Cebekhulu in Zambia while I would work with different governments, my own the first, to find him a safer country to live in.

Six years later, in the late summer of 1997, I am still looking for that haven. During that time Katiza Cebekhulu has nearly died several times. Apartheid has been vanquished in South Africa, the new First Lady unwillingly divorced and re-elected President of the ANC Women's League. President Nelson Mandela has paid one state visit and several informal ones to Britain. The Truth and Reconciliation Commission has been set up and has examined the evidence of others, but there has been a curious reluctance to take an interest in Katiza Cebekhulu's witness. I hold full power of attorney for him as a friend. I stand ready to give evidence on his behalf, but I am not summoned. Although I have spoken plainly to high-ranking ANC members now in government, the block on his settling in any other country as a refugee has not been lifted. The UN High Commission for Refugees has approached government after government at my request, but the answer has been the same: no, Katiza Cebekhulu cannot be given asylum in their country as the South African government has indicated conclusively that this would harm the bilateral, official relationship between their nations. My lobbying in Britain led me to the then Prime Minister's office. John Major gave the British 'no' to me himself.

Nelson Mandela's close colleagues have worked throughout that time to protect him. In 1991 Mandela was the leader in a fight to the death that was not yet won. His emotional stability (he loved Mrs Mandela throughout his long imprisonment) was vital. Katiza Cebekhulu's story included inner-household knowledge of Mrs Mandela's rampant adultery. There had been visual evidence, pictures he had removed from a bedroom. They were not pretty ones. In addition, lengthy loss of physical freedom such as Nelson Mandela had endured drains the will, tires the spirit and shrivels the emotions of even the strongest prisoner. He had had too much to bear. More might have destroyed him. And, without him, everything would be lost. Nelson's close colleagues therefore wanted Katiza Cebekhulu kept quiet. He was the watcher in the night. He knew too much. He would have to be gagged.

For Winnie Mandela's supporters, Katiza Cebekhulu has remained from 1991 until today a traitor to be silenced, by death if possible or by global political manoeuvres if not. He has held the knowledge which would demolish their goddess's international power. They have depended upon their illusions about her to justify their own past violent behaviour, even towards other members of the ANC, most carried out on her instructions or with her involvement. Katiza Cebekhulu also threatened their future positions in the new South Africa. As long as they could shield her, their past was invincible and their present power-base secure.

For politicians, police and journalists Katiza Cebekhulu has been a tool which, if they were able to find and use it, would enable them to bring down Mrs Mandela. His existence has been of short-term interest to them only.

I wanted him to stay alive and have a future, a wife and a family. He had a Zambian girlfriend, but could not remain safe in her country. We had to find somewhere for him to live in peace. Eventually a temporary place was found in Sierra Leone. The government would eject him if anyone discovered he was there. Katiza rapidly became very ill. Almost at death's door he sent me a slender notebook. This was his story. I must publish it, and let him die. By fax and telephone I urged him to hold on to life. Unwillingly he resumed eating and survived. Publication of the story was the key to his morale. I set to work.

After strenuous new arguments with an implacable Home Secretary, Michael Howard, I squeezed out a few weeks' UK visit for Katiza Cebekhulu in 1995. Michael Howard was adamant that Katiza's visit should not be discovered, lest his reputation for being tough on refugees should be impaired. I called Fred Bridgland to meet us both; he was the right man to write Katiza's story. He sometimes paled with horror at the diet of violence he was recording in peaceful Devon. I allowed the South African Police an informal session with Katiza and myself. We followed that up with an affidavit. Stephen Digby of my lawyers, Withers, became a friend.

Katiza remained profoundly unwell through malnutrition and malaria. Eating was a problem, because so many of his teeth had been forcibly removed. On his last night in the United Kingdom we ate in an Italian restaurant in Westminster. Sombrely, he wondered if we would ever meet again, or he enjoy so carefree a meal with close friends and away from fear. I promised that he would. Our hearts were heavy as he flew back to Sierra Leone.

Nelson Mandela paid his first state visit to the United Kingdom in July 1996. I could not speak with him; his officials would not allow it. They knew my subject and told me he was not to hear me on it.

Cyril Ramaphosa, the ANC negotiator for the new South African constitution in 1996, visited Britain too. He turned away on hearing Katiza's name. They all did.

But telling his story to the South African authorities formally would not be easy either. As he could not visit the country, I would have to act for him, with the full power of attorney he had already authorized. What if he died of sickness? Or was wiped out by Winnie Mandela's vengeful followers? Or extradited – legally or otherwise – by South Africa's police, placed in a South African prison and had his evidence demolished and discarded again? A letter from National Commissioner of Police J. G. Fivaz of June 1996 had already declared his evidence to be unreliable on the false premise of several police interviews supposedly carried out with him in London. No such interviews had taken place. And the notarized affidavit I had supplied to the South African police officer Major Moodley was completely accurate. I had to clear Katiza's name completely.

Perhaps the Truth and Reconciliation Commission offered us hope. Katiza had bared his soul to me early on, so that I knew it all: good, bad, reprehensible and laudable. He deserved amnesty. His words were all recorded on tape and stored in the bank. We could offer them the evidence to prove it.

I had been contacting the TRC since its inception. I was nervous that its spotlight might disclose Katiza's location, or bring other unwelcome attention. Privacy is impossible for refugees, whose lives are owned by others. And the Truth and Reconciliation Commission's trawl of misery and overload of work was huge. For many months its telephone was rarely answered. I was reluctant to press its officials hard in case they had reacted fast and subpoenaed Katiza without providing protection for him in South Africa. And there was an outstanding warrant for his arrest. I found an ally in Archbishop Desmond Tutu's secretary, Lavinia Browne. Calm, efficient, thoughtful, she passed on faxes and messages to those in charge – but they never replied. They did not have time – or was there some other reason? Was Winnie Mandela's influence still so large? The women of the ANC re-elected her as their President. Had they all been brainwashed? Katiza was right. His story must come out. It was the only way to make a future for him.

In late spring 1997 my eye was caught by chance by a three-line announcement in the London *Times*. Amnesty applications to the South African Truth and Reconciliation Commission would cease to be accepted at midnight the following day. I set to work. This would be kill or cure. We had to apply. I telephoned Katiza and got his agreement. But it was a high-risk step. If this flushed Katiza out of his hiding place, all would be lost. Yet, although he would probably never be safe in South Africa, amnesty would allow another country to accept him.

It was a struggle to obtain the required documents in time. I faxed them, and Lavinia Browne confirmed their arrival; we'd been in time. But we had drawn attention to ourselves. Now there was no way back. We had to go on.

Unexpectedly a Mr Pigou, of the Johannesburg office of the TRC, contacted me a week later. His unhappiness was evident from his calls. He was collecting evidence on Mrs Mandela, but was doing so against heavy political pressure in her favour from inside the TRC. I undertook to visit him while in the region later in June 1997 to discuss a framework within which Katiza could give evidence in, say, September. I hoped that his health might have improved by then. I could go with him to South Africa, if the Witness Protection Scheme could make it safe for him to enter. Otherwise, I could go alone as his volunteer attorney.

The newly promoted Senior Superintendent Moodley joined me for lunch in London in late June. It was good to learn of the rise in responsibilities under the new South Africa of non-white officers. Of Indian blood, Moodley would have been kept down for ever under apartheid. What a gigantic maelstrom of good and bad South Africa was now. I knew Katiza and I were right – although those with bitter past experience did not agree – to work with the new South Africa's formal institutions. Theirs was the responsibility; mine was to help them discharge it properly. I took Moodley to the Westminster restaurant Katiza had liked so much. He explained how we could find a way out of the outstanding warrant problem. I could pay the Johannesburg court fine or seek to have the warrant set aside. It was a small matter. I would need to give reasons.

But TRC's Mr Pigou was in despair. His superiors wanted the Winnie Mandela case dealt with rapidly. He could not get the required data together before the autumn of 1997. He feared that a cover-up was under way. His calls ceased. A Johannesburg *City Press* article of 1 June fully exposed our conversations. I called Pigou's boss. Pigou had left the day before. I got through to the Truth and Reconciliation Commission Headquarters in Cape Town. Yes, please come urgently. A Commissioner would interview me. My offer was never taken up. Further worrying newspaper reports appeared.

Winnie Mandela was to be subpoenaed to appear before the Truth and Reconciliation Commission, but *in camera* and very soon. Pigou's worst fears had been realized.

Fred Bridgland's first draft of Katiza's story was long finished. He had clearly and unequivocally exposed the whole horror. Filming had begun, with Nicholas Claxton for the BBC. In
June I led the media team to Sierra Leone. From the hot and
steamy airport we took a ship across the sunset sea into
Freetown. Clowns came on board to amuse the passengers.
Their mournfulness behind the painted laughter was real. The
country's economy had collapsed. How would it ever revive?
Rebels were now firing bush villages; half a million displaced
villagers were roaming Freetown.

Rats scuttled across the bleak restaurant floor in our
crumbling hotel, the Cape Sierra. Katiza Cebekhulu slipped in
quietly, and the next three days were taken up with recording
his intricate testimony. The effort dragged him back to a past he
hoped he had put behind him. Filming was a miserable
experience for him, trudging again through a hall of past horrors, bringing corpses back to life. At the end of the first day he
sat alone with me, gathering his strength to get through the next
day's sessions without collapsing through grief and misery. He
saw again the faces of dead Lolo Sono, little Stompie and the
other friends lost through violence. Bitter tears came privately.
But with the team he showed quiet dignity.

I spent time strengthening Katiza's local position. I had sent
him money regularly. Some of it, meant to buy a house, was
stolen from him. I had to work quietly, or Katiza would be
deported. I sought citizenship. He had a possible future in
Sierra Leone with that, although the climate was undermining
his health badly. Heavy and constant malaria dragged him
down; he had become pale and thin again.

Our brief film trip had been successful. A Russian helicopter
delivered us to the airport. Our aeroplane rose into the sky and

Freetown dwindled beneath us. We settled into a cramped international flight. Night fell and our aeroplane, the Flying Dutchman, flew through a sky of Wagnerian drama. The electrical system became disabled. We were grounded in nearby Côte d'Ivoire.

Freetown during those few hours had exploded. Bubbling since November 1996, when the democratically elected government had taken over, the political cauldron now overflowed. Violent anarchy prevailed.

I talked to Katiza by telephone. After the first violent hours had passed he changed houses regularly, particularly at night, as he had been lodging on a main street. Darkness triggered armed raids everywhere; all household belongings were being taken by force from even the poorest residents and their houses burned. Through the telephone receiver I could hear the rattle of machine-gun fire and the thuds of bombs landing followed by deep explosions. I did not think Katiza Cebekhulu, as a foreigner, could survive the coming blood bath.

Death stared us in the face. No papers, no money, the wrong nationality: what action could be taken? Embassies had been hastily vacated. Katiza's simple, UNHCR-created papers, giving him identification as a refugee, were lost for ever in the rebels' destruction of civil service paperwork. Even his bank account had gone; computer systems in all the banks were destroyed early in the targeted rampage and the Central Bank headquarters building razed to the ground. To all intents and purposes, Katiza Cebekhulu did not exist.

This was our chance to start again. I suggested a Sierra Leonese *nom de plume*. Katiza found a willing seller. I pledged him money by telephone. The man accepted my word as my bond as he had seen and heard me regularly on BBC World

Service. Genuine new documents were very difficult to obtain.

An approximation for an identity card emerged. We took a metaphorical deep breath and Katiza Cebekhulu disappeared from public view. He re-emerged under a different name, and with a different nationality and personal history. We did it again. A third identity was created. Since his photograph had never been published I felt we had found true anonymity at last.

We were back at square one. But now that I had the knowledge I could surely do better in the next round than in the first one. I was determined to win.

I sought and gained thoughtful advice from Foreign Office officials in London. The new Labour ministers, following Tony Blair's victory at the May 1997 general election, were more concerned and more serious than their predecessors. I flew to Zambia. I saw President Chiluba privately and we spoke off the record. We discussed many things and renewed ties of personal friendship. Next, Kenneth Kaunda's story unfolded as I questioned him.

I now knew by whom and why Katiza Cebekhulu had been hunted for so long. The puzzle had come together. His story could now be told.

The Preamble to South Africa's new Constitution states that her people will 'honour those who suffered for justice and freedom in our land'. It is now time for Katiza's great burden to be lifted, for his suffering to be recognized and honoured too.

I sent a new signal to him from Zambia in careful code, and he started the long walk home.

Emma Nicholson
July 1997

Prologue

At Pietermaritzburg, the gateway from the land of the Zulus into Africa's vast interior, Katiza Cebekhulu boarded the train for Egoli – the City of Gold, known to non-Zulus as Johannesburg. Katiza was beginning a journey made hundreds of thousands of times through earlier decades by young Zulu men from the rolling hills of Natal, where in the nineteenth century the warrior-chief Shaka Zulu had built a mighty African kingdom.

Most of these young Zulus were drawn by the possibility of adventure and enrichment in the white man's city fringed by gold mines. Many were escaping something, perhaps a girl-friend made pregnant, often a crime – a robbery, a rape, a murder. Most were simply fleeing the modern poverty, in South Africa's racially divided society, of their home villages and townships. Many were secretly glad to be shedding the tight restrictions of Zulu custom – secretly, because few Zulus publicly admit flaws in the great tribe's proud, but authoritarian, martial culture.

Katiza's journey resembled that made by Absalom Kumalo, the tragic son of the fictional central figure in Alan Paton's novel *Cry, the Beloved Country*. Absalom left from Ixopo, a rural area of green hills 'lovely beyond any singing of it', and passed through Pietermaritzburg before his train began the climb through the great Drakensberg Mountains towards the high veld and Egoli. Katiza, however, left from the teeming urban township of Mpumalanga – not a long way from Ixopo's rolling hills as the snake eagle flies, but wounded and grim beyond any telling of it.

Absalom's dreams turned to dust. He met his town cousin, made 'bad' friends, got a girl pregnant, saw murder, murdered and faced trial. Absalom went to the gallows and never returned to Zululand.

Katiza's hopes too were dashed. But there was nothing fictional about his personal tragedy. He met Nomzamo Winifred Zanyiwe Mandela, Stompie Seipei Moeketsi, the President of Zambia and Nelson Rolihlahla Mandela. He committed assault, stole, saw murder and came close to being murdered. He achieved celebrity as a defendant in a famous trial. He was kidnapped from Johannesburg and thrown into a foreign prison for years without charge or trial. He did not return to Zululand. But, unlike Absalom Kumalo, he has survived. And now he has emerged to tell his story which will possibly shake South Africa to its foundations and reverberate far beyond the Beloved Country.

CHAPTER ONE

Mpumalanga

1970–1988

Katiza Cebekhulu was born in the troubled township of Mpumalanga in Zululand, part of the South African province of Natal, a tropical region of rippling grassy hills, precipitous mountains and rivers tumbling to forests, swamps and white-owned sugar estates on a narrow coastal plain alongside the Indian Ocean.

Katiza was almost born for misfortune. His unmarried, illiterate mother, Joyce Cebekhulu, told him he was rotten in the womb and that she had given birth to a dog. He barely knew his father, Joseph Bengu, a car thief, now dead, who spent long periods in prison and never lived with Joyce. He never liked his mother's common-law husband, Mandla Sebese, and dislike became hatred when he discovered that one of his small step-sisters was being sexually abused by Sebese.

Katiza was born on 12 February 1970 in Joyce's township house, a typical tiny matchbox dwelling rented from the municipality. Fourteen family members from three generations, including Joyce's mother Gladys, crowded into one scullery, a living room and two small bedrooms. Katiza slept wrapped in blankets on the concrete floor under the scullery table. All fourteen were supported by the Rand 100 (then worth

3

£18) that Joyce Cebekhulu earned as a labourer at a white-owned chicken factory farm.

Mpumalanga, the black township for Hammarsdale, a white town between Durban, South Africa's greatest port, and Pieter-maritzburg, Natal's capital, became one of the most violent places on earth as opposition to white rule grew from the mid-1970s. Rival supporters of the United Democratic Front (UDF), a front organization for the banned and exiled African National Congress (ANC), and the Zulu nationalist Inkatha Freedom Party fought turf wars which took thousands of lives. 'Political cleansing' went on that harbingered Bosnian-style ethnic cleansing. People, including babies and grandmothers, were knifed, clubbed, strangled and burned to death as ANC/UDF and Inkatha gangs sought to impose their wills on territories. Housewives were forced to drink cooking oil by young militants of either side if they declined to pledge the 'correct' allegiance. Once an area was politically cleansed of supporters of a rival group, all other inhabitants were forced to fall in line. Warlordism and fear divided families. Violence transcended politics and became a habit, a whole dismal lifestyle, practised by bored, ill-educated, unemployed and often hungry township youths who rarely knew much about their leaders' policies.

The sheer bestiality of the violence made good men despair. 'We have savagery in Natal which puts us right back into the Dark Ages,' wrote Aggrey Klaaste, one of black South Africa's most distinguished journalists, after an ANC gang beheaded a township infant. Klaaste said historic clan fighting among the Zulus had been used to excuse the new barbarism, but went on: 'How can we possibly point a finger at faceless [white] butchers when we murder children, chop their heads off with an axe, in broad daylight?'

The township war was a fact of life which youngsters like Katiza Cebekhulu could scarcely avoid. His time was spent on the streets of Mpumalanga, home to nearly half a million people. There was no privacy in the small brick house, one of thousands all built to the same design laid out in uniform, barrack-like blocks along straight dirt roads which white soldiers and riot police could patrol with ease in their armoured vehicles. The house had a corrugated-iron roof but no interior ceiling. There was no bathroom. The Cebekhulu family washed and bathed with cold water from an outside standpipe. Their toilet was a 'long drop' surrounded by rough planks in the outside yard. Rubbish was piled on street corners where it was overrun by rats and pye-dogs. Food was cooked over small coal-burning clay stoves which blackened the walls of the kitchen where Katiza slept. In the short but sharp winter the fumes from thousands of clay stoves hung over Mpumalanga like a pall and there was a background sound of countless wheezing lungs. In places there were rows of homes which had been burned out in the ANC–Inkatha warfare, and 'struggle' graffiti covered every available wall. 'There is a self-created desolation about the houses and the people – especially the youngsters – that desecrates life and empties it of meaning,' observed one black writer.

Against this background, Katiza grew up wild and barely educated. He was truly feral, but also intelligent and streetwise. As he entered his teens he spent more and more of his time among the violent township thieves known as *tsotsis* on Mpumalanga's teeming streets and in its shebeens, the drinking dens established when blacks were forbidden by law to consume alcohol. He became a petty thief, and when a neighbour accused him of stealing a radio-cassette player, Joyce, rather than report the incident to the hated apartheid-era police, called in Mpumalanga's community 'punishment men' to administer instant justice.

Years later Katiza wept at the memory of the humiliation and his mother's rejection of him as he told me: 'I was sitting at home with my stepfather. The punishment men enter. They wanted me. My mother said: "I'm fed up. Do what you want to do with him." They took me. They tied my hands. They removed all my clothes. They leave me naked. They beat me with a sjambok [a reinforced rubber whip] and sticks. They stepped on my fingers with their boots. They beat me until I collapsed. One of the neighbours came and said: "Stop, he shouldn't be beaten like that, it's too much." I went to hospital and was admitted for about a week.'

As his tears fell, I told Katiza it was a terrible thing to happen to anyone. I asked him if in those times he had felt very lonely. He nodded and recalled that he was well past the age of seven before he attended a local Zulu-language primary school. He soon became an habitual truant yet his mother seemed unbothered, which upset Katiza profoundly. 'My mother never paid me much attention,' he told me. 'She used to curse me because she said she'd given birth to a dog. She used to tell me like that, even when I was small. But she was the one who born me, and it was her job to love me and show concern, wasn't it?'

Throughout his life, it seems that Katiza has been all too aware of how much had gone wrong for him and how profoundly he had gone astray, that awareness counterbalanced by a real insight that in other circumstances his life could have been different. After one particularly gruelling interview session, he said to me: 'You know, Mr Fred, I think there is a better Katiza inside me trying to get out.'

Katiza spent less and less time at home. He slept out at night in drainage pipes and sometimes up trees in the bush beyond the township. He consolidated a friendship with his great-grandmother who lived in another area of Mpumalanga and survived by selling snuff and roll-up cigarettes. She fed him on mealie pap (a maize porridge, the staple food of most black South Africans) and boiled cabbage and collected cast-off clothes and repaired them to replace his own rags. Smiling at the memory, Katiza recalled how he liked to sit outside with her in the sunshine or help her weed her small patch of sweet potatoes.

Katiza had no political loyalties beyond those of convenience. His main commitment was to survive through small-time thievery. He crossed regularly from the ANC/UDF-dominated area of Mpumalanga, where his mother lived, to the Inkatha-controlled area where his great-grandmother grew her sweet potatoes. At sixteen, now grown up, he was a small man, less than five-and-a-half feet tall with short legs and a thin face animated with a wide range of expressions. A natural astuteness and a gift as a skilled mimic and raconteur in the African oral tradition boosted him in the battle for survival. Old men in Mpumalanga, still steeped in the customs of village lives they had left behind, held story-telling competitions under a tree and Katiza was a regular winner. Daughters of a senior official in the Inkatha-controlled KwaZulu homeland government, which managed housing and education in Mpumalanga, semi-adopted him and gave him clothes because he made them laugh, perhaps by miming a local hunchback or telling the convoluted tale of the Protestant pastor who seduced his elders' wives and stole the congregation's money.

However Katiza soon drifted into an ANC/UDF gang led by a local warlord called Bruce Buthelezi. No one knew how Bruce had become the ANC leader because the people had never been consulted: no election had ever been held. At the beginning of 1987 Inkatha marauders crossed into Bruce Buthelezi's territory and burned down three houses, in which six people died. 'So Buthelezi called a special meeting and he said we should make a revenge attack,' said Katiza. 'He targeted individuals. I was among the boys who took part. When they came to my house to pick me up they were carrying petrol bombs and sticks. At that time we didn't have guns. I had no choice. I could not refuse. I didn't carry any petrol bombs, I was just part of the crowd. We burned houses on the Inkatha side. Several people were killed.'

The attack was reported in *Ilanga*, a mass-circulation Zulu-language newspaper owned by Inkatha. Inevitably there was a revenge counter-attack, for the Zulu equivalent of 'an eye for an eye' is 'two eyes for one eye'.

It came as about ninety ANC supporters gathered at a garage to be told by Bruce Buthelezi of another action planned against an Inkatha stronghold. The meeting was meant to be secret and all the men summoned were ordered to come dressed as women in an attempt to throw Inkatha snoopers off the scent. Katiza dressed in one of his sister's skirts and high-heeled shoes. But despite the drag, the ANC men were still spotted and armed Inkatha *impis* (warriors) quietly surrounded the garage.

'They opened fire without warning,' Katiza told me. 'Everyone ran for their lives and I slept the night in the bush. The next day we counted thirteen dead and seventeen injured.' They also found a KwaZulu Police cap and a standard-issue police boot at the scene of the attack, suggesting that the homeland police had collaborated with the assailants. The KwaZulu Police (KZP) force, made up of Zulus with whites as senior officers, was answerable to the KwaZulu Chief Minister Chief Mangosuthu Buthelezi, the Inkatha leader who posed as the true guardian of Zulu heritage and tradition. The KZP regarded the ANC as a 'Marxist terrorist' organization and gave the banned movement's loyalists no protection against Inkatha attacks. KwaZulu was one of the tribal homelands or bantustans established as the centrepiece of the apartheid (apartness) system erected in South Africa after the National Party came to power in 1948. Blacks were herded into these homelands and, deprived of South African citizenship, had to obtain special passes if they wanted to commute to or live in white areas in order to work. These Pass Laws reinforced the principle that blacks in white South Africa were only visiting from their homelands. KwaZulu comprised a dozen or more jigsaw-shaped pieces of tribal land scattered through white-administered Natal, the most British of all apartheid South Africa's provinces, which the English-speaking whites proclaimed as 'The Last Outpost' (of the British Empire) on their Union Jack car stickers. Mpumalanga was in a tongue of KwaZulu territory which nestled beside Hammarsdale in Natal. Zulus in employment had to cross the boundary into white Hammarsdale, where the factories were located. The KZP were helped by the South African Police (SAP) in Hammarsdale when picking up suspected ANC supporters for questioning; the suspects could be held for up to six months at a time, without charge or trial, under any one of the many Orwellian pieces of legislation designed to enforce apartheid. Many of those detained were routinely tortured. Most talked. Some did not come out alive.

On arrival home from his night in the open, Katiza's grandmother, Gladys, handed him a police summons which had been delivered ordering him to report to SAP headquarters in

Hammarsdale for questioning about the UDF/ANC attack. A friend of Katiza's had already been arrested in connection with a panga (machete) assault on a suspected rapist and police informant, Bhekumuzi Nqobo, who later died from his wounds. Katiza, who had participated in the attack on Nqobo, quickly decided not to report to the SAP, fearing that he would be beaten and imprisoned.

His immediate course of action was decided for him when he saw clouds of dust approaching his house – number A1298 in Mpumalanga's Unit 1 South – along the dirt road. Snatching his Okapi hunting knife from his blanket roll, he ran out of the back door, leaped over the fence and ran between houses until he reached the open bush. He ran and ran before plunging into a river to hide in thick reeds. Police with alsatian dogs later began moving through the bush. Katiza stood in water up to his neck armed only with the Okapi knife and a stick he had picked up and sharpened.

'I heard the dogs barking and the police calling on me to give up or be shot.' Then he was horrified to hear his mother's voice over a loudhailer urging him to surrender. 'A police dog appeared growling on the river bank near me. I hit it with the sharpened stick and my knife. It bled and it died. I moved down river as I heard more police coming with dogs. I reached some forest and got out of the water and climbed high into a tree.'

The police called off the search when darkness fell. Katiza climbed down from the tree and made his way to Mpumalanga's Engogeni section, where the UDF/ANC had a safe house. He met Bruce Buthelezi and said he felt the time had come to move to Johannesburg to seek a new life. His mother didn't like him. His father had deserted him at conception. His stepfather was unbearable. Mpumalanga had become too tough, too violent, too complicated, too 'hot'. The next evening Katiza slipped home to pack a few things. He told his grandmother where he intended going, and Gladys wailed: 'If you go to Johannesburg you'll never return. My husband went to Johannesburg and he never came back.'

Grandmother Gladys was virtually repeating the words of the wife of the Reverend Stephen Kumalo about their son Absalom in *Cry, the Beloved Country*, a refrain reprised countless times by other Zulu mothers, grandmothers, wives, sisters, girlfriends, daughters who had watched as their menfolk departed for far-off Egoli – 'When people go to Johannesburg, they do not come back . . . There they are lost, and no one hears of them at all.'

*

All Katiza's worldly possessions were packed in one plastic bag as he trudged the night streets of Mpumalanga to wait for a bus to take him to Pietermaritzburg to catch a train for Johannesburg. It was raining heavily. As he waited at a bus stop, a car drew up. One of the four men in it asked if they could give him a lift. Katiza stepped in gratefully but soon realized the car was heading in the opposite direction to Pietermaritzburg. Soon he was standing before Sipho Mlamba, a rich businessman and the most powerful Inkatha leader in Mpumalanga.

Mlamba shook hands with Katiza and said: 'You will now have to join Inkatha. If you refuse you will be killed. If you run away we will burn your mother's home with everyone inside.' Men were commonly press-ganged – and still are – to fight for one side or other in the war for control of the Zulus. Katiza accepted his fate: the car had chosen for him.

The next evening Katiza was taken to a big Inkatha meeting and introduced as a former UDF/ANC activist who had seen the error of his ways. Mlamba gave the house of his second wife to Katiza as a temporary home – Mlamba had banished the wife to her home village after he caught her in bed with another man, who was then arrested by the KZP on the warlord's orders. The house was carpeted. There was a TV and video and other luxuries and comforts, such as an inside toilet, that the young Zulu had never before known.

Katiza was debriefed about the locations of houses belonging to key UDF/ANC activists, including the Engogeni safe house. Inkatha attacked soon afterwards. The Engogeni hideout and three other houses were burned to the ground. Three UDF/ANC men and a number of women and children were killed. Katiza did not take part in the attack, but word quickly spread that he had defected to Inkatha and provided the intelligence for the raid. Revenge was inevitable. Two evenings later Katiza was dropped late at night at his house by Sipho Mlamba's driver. He unlocked the iron security gate shielding the front door, then the door itself, relocked both, made a cup of tea and went to bed and quickly fell asleep.

Some time later he woke up and smelt smoke and heard a crackling noise – 'The sitting room was on fire and then petrol bombs came through other windows. I heard gunshots and heard someone shout: "Hey you, burn alive and die!" I broke a window but there was an iron burglar grille over it. I was screaming through the window for someone to help me and I could feel the heat of the fire behind me getting nearer and nearer. That night I didn't know whether I was going to heaven or hell. I pushed and pushed on the grille and at last it gave way and fell out. It was like a miracle.' The UDF/ANC attack force had by now been beaten back by Inkatha supporters and someone led him away to spend the night in a neighbouring house.

Police arrived in the morning and refused to believe Katiza had been in the house. It had been totally razed and it seemed impossible that anyone could have survived the blaze. Katiza was handcuffed and taken to Hammarsdale police headquarters for questioning by Colonel Steenkamp, the area SAP commander. A prolonged period of interrogation, provocation and torture followed. Katiza kept silent as Steenkamp accused him of a variety of offences, including participation in at least two attacks on township houses, murdering the residents of the houses, burning down Sipho Mlamba's house, murdering Bhekumuzi Nqobo and killing a police dog. Steenkamp showed him photographs of Bruce Buthelezi and other UDF/ANC members, but Katiza denied knowing them. Steenkamp, who knew he had been an ANC gang member before turning up in the Inkatha house, taunted him with being a double agent.

Steenkamp ordered him to be taken away for interrogation. He was gagged and masked with inner-tube rubber and beaten with a heavy-duty sjambok. Electrodes were attached to his body for electric-shock torture. Hot needles were applied to various parts of his body. When all this failed he was taken to the police morgue and shown the broken corpse of a former UDF/ANC friend, Mandla Shange, who Katiza knew had been arrested several months earlier under one of the draconian laws permitting detention without trial. Katiza asked who killed Mandla and was told he had 'committed suicide' by throwing himself from a seventh-floor window of the Hammarsdale police HQ.

The interrogators repeatedly told Katiza he was a liar and double agent until eventually he broke and made a tape-recorded confession of the main allegations. He was taken to court, where he was remanded for treatment in hospital in

Hammarsdale for injuries sustained during his interrogation. 'They took me to the hospital in handcuffs, but an Indian doctor refused to begin examining me until the police removed them. A policeman stayed with me all the time. I knew it was the end for me in Mpumalanga. I had to escape. After a few days I went to the toilet and climbed through a window as the policeman waited at the door.'

He went straight to a girlfriend in Mpumalanga called Nomandla and told her of the trouble he was in, with the ANC, Inkatha and the police all after him. 'I felt I was going mad wondering what I could do now. She said I had no choice, the only way was to leave. "They will kill you," she said. She gave me some money. I can't remember how much, but it was not more than Rand 50. I went straight to Pietermaritzburg and slept the night in the railway station. All I had was that money and the T-shirt, shorts and slippers I was wearing.'

The Johannesburg train left late the next afternoon. The journey would take fifteen hours overnight. He had no food to eat and, after buying his ticket, only 50 cents in his pocket. It had been raining and he was cold. 'When the train came it was a bad day for me, as if it were a funeral. It seemed as though it was somebody else's life, as though someone else was playing my part, because I had no power over my life. I cried as the train pulled out. I didn't know where my life was going, believe me. I was hungry, but I had no food. All around me people on the train were eating. I hadn't eaten since running from the hospital. I just lay down and one song by Marvin Gaye kept going through my head – that wherever you lay your head, that is your home, like a musician on the road. I liked that song.'

CHAPTER TWO

Johannesburg

1988

The train thundered 'through the night, over the battlefields of long ago', and climbed over the Drakensberg Mountains on to the African plateau known as the high veld.

The seventeen-year-old Katiza Cebekhulu arrived at central Johannesburg's Park Station, as had Absalom Kumalo and numberless hopeful real-life Zulus before him. It was January or February 1988 – he does not remember which. He was cold and very hungry. All he owned in the world were his rubber slippers, T-shirt and shorts with 50 cents in one of the pockets. He raised another 50 cents by begging in the station and a further 50 cents by stealing coins from a blind beggar's cup while pretending to drop in some money.

He had no idea what he was going to do next – 'I had nowhere to go and nobody had time for other persons.' So he hung around a queue at the fare counter and heard black people asking the Afrikaner clerk for tickets to a variety of places whose names he had never heard before – Naledi, Mzimlophe, Pfeni, Leeukop, Krugersdorp, Springs. When one old man asked for a ticket to somewhere called Orlando East and paid 80 cents, Katiza dipped into his newly acquired wealth and bought a ticket to the same destination.

But first he wanted to ease his gnawing hunger. He left the station and with the remainder of his cash bought a loaf of bread. He could not afford anything else to eat with the bread, so he took the loaf behind a fast-food restaurant selling chicken, fish and chips and began to eat ravenously. 'I took in the smells of frying food coming from the kitchen and when I ate my bread I imagined I was eating chicken with it.'

With his hunger partly satisfied, Katiza returned to the station, saw the old man from the queue and followed him on to a train. Forty-five minutes later it stopped at Orlando East station, in the shadow of a giant hospital, Baragwanath, on the edge of the great sprawling black township of Soweto, home to more than a million people from every tribe in southern Africa. 'I sat on the station for the rest of the day. It was a problem for me where to go now, where to start to move. What could I ask anyone? I was in trouble. I spent the next night on that station and the next morning I came out.'

Emerging from the station, Katiza wandered along the pot-holed roads of Orlando East until he saw a modern two-storey office building, surrounded by a tall razor-wire fence, standing incongruously among tiny single-storey matchbox houses like those back in Mpumalanga. There was a sign outside identifying it as 'Community House'. A passer-by told him it was the headquarters of a social-work organization which helped the homeless.

'Ohh, I said, let me go in and cry to the social workers. I pressed the bell and the woman inside said: "What can I do for you?" I explained to the woman I was Katiza. I came from Natal, there is violence, I left for safety reasons. I didn't say I left because I stole.' The receptionist asked Katiza to follow her upstairs and showed him into an office where a woman was sitting behind a desk. 'She was there. Winnie Mandela.'

*

Winnie Mandela. At that time she was perhaps the most famous woman in the world. Tall, strikingly handsome and aged fifty-three, she was widely revered at home and abroad as the 'Mother of the Nation', the wife of one of the world's few authentic political heroes, Nelson Mandela, who was still serving a life sentence imposed at the Rivonia Treason Trial in 1964 for his leadership of the black struggle against apartheid. (He had been in prison since 1962.) Both Mandelas were Xhosas, the southernmost Bantu tribe of Africa, which had settled the Eastern Cape and Transkei coastlines. The richly expressive Xhosa language incorporates a repertoire of clicks of the Cape's original Bushmen and Khoi peoples, who were pushed out by the Xhosas moving south and European colonists moving north.

Winnie had suffered harsh reprisals for the beliefs of her husband, with whom she had lived for only five weeks in broken spells in their first four years of marriage before he was arrested and imprisoned. She too was imprisoned, on one occasion for seventeen months mainly in solitary confinement: for one period of 160 days she was not allowed a bath or a shower. Later, in 1977, the security police sent her into a long internal exile in the bleak Orange Free State town of Brandfort, South Africa's equivalent of the Soviet Gulag.

The eight years spent in Brandfort were intended to render Winnie Mandela a 'non-person', but the apartheid authorities' game-plan backfired spectacularly. Instead it focused worldwide attention upon her as a symbol of white oppression of the black majority. She was widely seen as a heroic one-woman resistance army at a time when Umkhonto we Sizwe (Spear of the Nation), the military wing of the outlawed and exiled ANC, was largely ineffective. She was described by various authors as 'a hero, a living martyr to the black liberation cause', 'a woman of regal presence', of 'warmth and generosity . . . a leader in her own right'; a woman who impressed by 'her very pleasant disposition, her calmness and complete composure, her charm, her singing laughter, her unchanging face and her ever-present dignity'. The author Rian Malan noted she had been the subject of ten thousand hagiographic newspaper and magazine profiles, several sycophantic books and at least three prospective Hollywood movies. American Senator Edward Kennedy met her and said he was deeply moved by Mrs Mandela's 'gentleness and firmness, in a touching but meaningful way'.

In early 1985 Winnie returned permanently to Soweto when the South African Appeal Court ruled that the banning orders which exiled her to Brandfort were not legally valid. During her long absence an alliance of more than 600 independent organizations had joined together as a surrogate ANC under the title of the United Democratic Front (UDF) to fight apartheid.

Winnie early on decided to have nothing to do with the UDF and instead formed her own personal vigilante group – the Mandela United Football Club (MUFC). The Football Club soon started behaving menacingly towards members of the community. Because black activists were unwilling to provide the apartheid government with ammunition which depicted Winnie Mandela as anything much less than a saint, public criticism of her rarely surfaced. But one young Sowetan activist and former detainee lamented to a foreign correspondent: 'She is not accountable to anyone, that's the problem. There is tension as a result.'

She upset many activists at home, and alarmed millions of people abroad, when she overrode UDF policy by publicly approving necklacing, the barbaric method used in townships of killing suspected 'sell-outs' and police informers. Necklacing involved jamming a car tyre over the shoulders of the victim and then filling it with petrol before setting it ablaze. Hundreds had died this way. Some, perhaps many, were innocent of any betrayal. Their murderers used the political volatility and injustice of the times to settle personal scores which had nothing to do with politics, or just to kill for killing's sake. The ANC's exiled President, Oliver Tambo, was ambivalent about the necklace. While he felt unable to condemn it because of the government's own brutality, he was clearly unhappy about the message each necklacing sent to the world about the nature of the ANC.

'We have no guns. We have only stones, boxes of matches and petrol,' Winnie told a rally on 13 April 1986 in Munsieville, the black township for the West Rand town of Krugersdorp. 'Together, hand in hand, with our boxes of matches and our necklaces, we shall liberate this country.' Law and Order Minister Louis le Grange was so delighted by the potential damage to the ANC of her utterance that he relaxed the harsh media law forbidding the quoting inside the country of ANC leaders and allowed portions of the speech to be reported.

A brave Sowetan journalist, Nomavenda Mathiane, was the first black writer to suggest, in 1987, that all was not well between Winnie Mandela and the Soweto community itself. 'Many people have become uneasy that Mrs Mandela is taking her role as "First Lady" too heavily,' wrote Mathiane a year after Mrs Mandela returned to Soweto. 'They want to know: is she still an ordinary mortal at heart?'

Mathiane, who for some time had tried unsuccessfully to obtain an interview with the 'First Lady', was suddenly summoned to accompany the Football Club to Zondi, in Soweto, where Winnie was to preside at a 'people's trial'. Few understood how Winnie had so quickly acquired this power to act as prosecutor and judge in myriad cases; equally, few people were brave enough to question the authority of the Mother of the Nation. At the Zondi 'trial' a nineteen-year-old girl named Ntsiki protested that an old male relative who had paid for her to come from the countryside to live in Johannesburg had reprimanded her unnecessarily harshly for the way she moved freely in and out of his house. The old man addressed the kangaroo court judge, Winnie, in a soft voice as 'madam' and then testified: 'I find this very hurtful that I have lived with you, Ntsiki, for so many years and treated you like my own child and when today we have a difference you call a gang for me.'

Winnie, assisted by her 'assessors', all members of the Football Club, asked Ntsiki what she wanted done. She said she was no longer prepared to stay at the old man's house. Winnie ordered her 'boys' to carry Ntsiki's belongings to the Football Club minibus. Throngs of people watched, and as the minibus left Mathiane heard one woman in the crowd remark: 'Where will all this end?'

One month after Mathiane witnessed the Zondi trial two teenage brothers, Peter and Philip Makanda, were woken in their uncle's house in Soweto by a banging on the front door. When their uncle opened the door three men wearing stocking masks stormed in; one carried a gun. The invaders abducted the Makanda brothers at gunpoint to a waiting car. One of the three men, subsequently identified as John Morgan, driver of the Mandela United Football Club minibus, drove to Winnie

Mandela's small house in Orlando West, the matchbox dwelling in which she and Nelson had set up home after their marriage in 1958 and from which she was removed in 1977 to enforced exile in Brandfort.

The Makandas were forced into a shack in the back yard where they saw a third youth tied to a chair: he had been beaten and was bleeding. Winnie Mandela was summoned. She entered the room, gestured towards the third youth (who has never been named or found) and told the Makandas: 'If you don't want to be hurt like this boy, you must tell the truth.' Winnie left and an assault began on the Makanda brothers by Football Club members, some of whom were carrying guns. The brothers were accused of being 'sell-outs' and 'informers' whose actions had caused deaths among 'comrades'.

Peter Makanda denied the accusations. He was struck and then hung by the neck with a rope from a rafter. The rope broke and he fell to the ground, still alive. The Football Club then placed a plastic bag over his head and repeatedly dipped his head into a bucket of water. Philip Makanda was beaten too. When threats to shoot the brothers failed to elicit confessions, one Football Club member said: 'Let's stoep [carve] them.' Peter was forced to sit on a mattress and watch as Philip went first.

Philip was seized and made to sit on a chair with his hands tied behind his back. A Football Club member produced a penknife and cut a big 'M' for Mandela into his chest. 'Viva ANC' was carved along one of Philip's thighs before car-battery acid was smeared into the wounds so that the slogans were etched permanently into the flesh. Peter was then pinned down while 'Viva ANC' was sliced across his back.

The brothers were beaten some more before being ordered to

lie down and sleep. Grotesquely, Winnie Mandela entered the room later with tea and cakes for the mutilated Makandas. The third youth, meanwhile, had told the Football Club about someone else he said was a 'sell-out'. A Football Club raiding party left to bring in the 'fourth man', who was soon thrust into the room and warned he must tell the truth unless he wanted to end up looking like the Makandas and the third youth.

A Football Club guard entered with a warning that a police car was patrolling the area and it was probably no longer safe to keep the quartet in Winnie's house. They were loaded into a van, driven to John Morgan's house and locked in his garage. Peter and Philip Makanda deduced how to open the garage door from the inside and escaped. They left the other two youths behind and never saw them again.

From John Morgan's house the Makandas went straight to a police station and gave statements about what had happened to them. Morgan and the two men who helped him abduct the brothers were charged with kidnap and assault and the case came to court the following year. One of the lawyers who gathered evidence saw the brothers before the trial and observed that their scars were still eye-catching.

Peter and Philip Makanda were asked to pick out their attackers at an identity parade without the protection of a two-way mirror. They had to sit in front of a line-up and point to anyone they recognized while being watched and listened to by both police and potential suspects. Their nerves cracked under the intimidating circumstances and they gave such contradictory testimony that the magistrate concluded it would be impossible to obtain convictions. Dismissing the case, the magistrate commented: 'The experience must have been so frightening that their powers of observation were affected and their minds were more on how to get through the ordeal alive.'

The case brought by the police had involved alleged serious assault by members of Winnie Mandela's Football Club, in her own home and with her knowledge. According to the Makandas' statements, she had made threats and at least twice entered the room where they were beaten and carved up. Strangely, she was never charged in connection with the assault, nor listed as a witness nor even questioned by the police.

'Lack of police action against Winnie made her extremely suspect in the eyes of Soweto residents,' wrote one of her biographers. 'But it also made her appear invincible.'

*

Katiza Cebekhulu knew none of this as he told Winnie Mandela his story at Community House.

'I felt she understood. I told her I was not ANC and I was not Inkatha. She said she felt pity for me and she would keep me in her house. She said there was nowhere else for me to go because Soweto was politically divided, like Mpumalanga. She said I'd be safe in her house. In the office she introduced me to other people, Slash and Shoes, who were staying with Winnie. I didn't know anything about them.'

I asked Katiza if she seemed a kind woman. 'Yes, she was good,' he said. 'I can't lie. She was good.'

Katiza was taken to one of Winnie Mandela's three Soweto homes, a luxury bungalow with an open-air jacuzzi in the back courtyard in a suburb for the black upper-middle class called Diepkloof Extension, just across the main road from Orlando East. He was introduced to Shakes, one of Winnie's drivers, and other members of the Football Club.

Although Katiza was never a footballer, he was given a Mandela United Football Club tracksuit, in the gold, green and black colours of the ANC, and a school uniform, grey slacks and a white shirt, of the nearby Silelekele High School. Using her friendship with the headmaster, Winnie enrolled Katiza in a class four years above the one he had last attended in Mpumalanga. But Katiza was soon in trouble with his form mistress at Silelekele because he kept falling asleep in class. 'I was exhausted. I was doing guard duty, patrolling around the house through the night, cleaning the yard, washing cars, cooking.' Winnie clearly expected her protégés to earn their keep.

The most glamorous member of the Football Club at that time was a man named David Themba. While other MUFC 'players' slept together like rows of sardines on the floors of back rooms in Winnie's Diepkloof Extension and Orlando West houses, Themba had his own bedroom in the Diepkloof house. Others with bedrooms in the house were Winnie; Zindzi, the youngest daughter of Nelson and Winnie; and Zindzi's four children by different fathers. Katiza's duties included cleaning shoes for Zindzi's children, preparing their breakfasts and cleaning Winnie's and Zindzi's bedrooms.

Themba's activities were shrouded in mystery, but Football Club members knew his main responsibility to Winnie was to smuggle ANC guerrillas into South Africa from Zambia and escort youths out of the country for military training. 'Themba was the most powerful man in Winnie's house,' said Katiza. 'He knew all the safe routes in and out of the country.'

Although Katiza slept in one of the two outside rooms at the back of the courtyard beyond the jacuzzi, he began spending more and more time in the main house because of a growing friendship with Zindzi. They shared an interest in soul and pop music. Zindzi let him listen to her Kenny Gee records and tapes, and the pair frequently went to the cinema together. Katiza also came to regard Zindzi's boyfriend, Sizwe Sithole, the father of her latest child and an ANC underground gunman, as his best friend. Although Katiza's English at that time was poor, his wit and articulacy in Zulu, which had won him story-telling prizes from township elders, had made him one of Winnie's favourites among her MUFC boys. He was the 'little clown' of the Mandela household. Winnie liked to sit and laugh at his fund of stories from his days as a ragamuffin-turned-hoodlum on the streets of Mpumalanga.

One day in 1988 – he believes it was in either June or July – Katiza had returned from school and entered the Diepkloof house to get some food and see if there were any instructions for his evening duties. As he stood preparing a snack in the kitchen, he saw through the open door Winnie leave her bedroom with her friend Dali Mpofu, a twenty-five-year-old lawyer who worked for Kathy Satchwell, whose Johannesburg legal firm represented most of the Mandela United Football Club. Handsome and personable, Mpofu also had a white British-born girlfriend, Teresa Oakley-Smith, who in 1988 gave birth to his son. A feud began between the two women, who sometimes turned up together at Mpofu's central Johannesburg apartment and quarrelled about who would stay the night. Oakley-Smith, a lecturer at the University of the Witwatersrand in Johannesburg, began receiving telephoned death threats, mainly at night. She told friends that Winnie warned her, in a voice slurred from heavy drinking, to stay away from Dali.

Katiza watched Winnie and Dali leave the house and heard them drive away. Shortly afterwards, David Themba emerged from his bedroom, carrying a briefcase, and entered Winnie's.

Katiza, still sitting in the kitchen, thought Themba looked furtive – 'He opened Winnie's room like, you know, someone who wanted to steal' – but he pretended not to notice him. Themba left Winnie's bedroom a few minutes later, still carrying the briefcase, and immediately walked out of the house and drove away.

Themba had acted so suspiciously that Katiza decided to go into his room and look around. He looked under the mattress and then, using a *skelm* key (a 'thief' or, more literally, 'scoundrel' key, made from a filed-down piece of metal), he opened locked bedside drawers. 'I found photographs – there were so many of them – of Winnie making love to Dali Mpofu.'

I asked Katiza whether they were all just of Winnie and Dali.

'Yes. I was so afraid. I took one. I closed the drawer.'

Were they making love in all the photos?

'Yes. So I took one.'

Katiza said it was smaller than a postcard. It was in colour, apparently taken from above, of Winnie naked on her back looking upwards with Mpofu between her legs.

So, I asked, you now had this photograph and you didn't know what you were going to do with it?

'Yes. I locked everything. I can't say what I was thinking. I just keep it. I didn't know what to do. I was confused.'

Katiza slipped the photograph inside his underpants. 'I was wondering: can I tell Mrs Mandela? Aaah, no. I didn't know what to do.'

Themba returned to the house soon afterwards. Katiza was back in the kitchen. 'Themba entered his room. When he came out he looked changed, as though he had lost something. He asked Winnie's servant: "Who was here in the house?" She said: "Only Katiza was here in the house."'

Katiza said he got the feeling Themba wanted to question him. But what could he possibly have asked? 'If he'd said: "Did you see the picture?" I would have said: "Of what?" What could he say? So Themba left the house.'

The next day Winnie Mandela received a phone call ordering her to report to Protea, Soweto's main police station. She went in one of the Football Club's minibuses, a blue Volkswagen donated by the West German Embassy, with Shakes, one of her drivers, and Katiza. 'Shakes and I stayed outside. She was in there for about an hour. When she came out she looked deeply sad and worried. She said: "Themba is dead."

'Something had touched her deeply. Now I was really worried, but already I had wrapped the photo in plastic and hidden it under the floorboards of the dog kennel in Winnie's courtyard. We drove back to the house. I didn't know what to do.'

The stolen photograph would one day destroy another life. As Katiza was rapidly to discover, the true sport of the MUFC was violence.

CHAPTER THREE

The Fate of Lolo Sono

NOVEMBER 1988

Katiza, on arrival from Mpumalanga, had soon been introduced to Jerry Vusi Richardson, the 'chief coach' of the Mandela United Football Club. It was a football club in name only: it never played a match. Richardson was Mrs Mandela's lieutenant in charge of what, in fact, was her bodyguard and personal vigilante group.

When he was first appointed MUFC chief coach, Richardson was living in his matchbox home in Mzimlophe, a particularly tough area of Soweto, several blocks away from Winnie's upmarket Diepkloof house. Richardson idealized Winnie and always called her 'Mummy'.

He felt less affection for his own wife, a local girl he had married at the age of seventeen. Virginia Richardson eventually left her husband, taking with her their two daughters. She later alleged that Jerry Richardson had attempted to kill her several times. Richardson used to bring other women home and would banish Virginia from their bedroom so he could sleep with them. It was one such occasion, when she had to move out of the bedroom, which finally triggered her decision to leave. 'One night he came into the lounge where I was sleeping. Luckily I heard his footsteps and woke just before he stabbed me. I pleaded with him to spare my life so I could leave the following morning. He agreed. But he emphasized that I was not to come back.'

Katiza Cebekhulu said he and all the other Football Club members feared Jerry Richardson – 'The system was that Winnie instructed Jerry and then he gave us orders. He was a rough man who wouldn't take advice from anyone but Winnie. I always did what he told me: I was afraid of him. On his instructions, I once led a Football Club raid on a truck. We stole many cartons of orange juice and took them back to Winnie's.'

Richardson's attorney would later say of his client that he was poorly educated and mildly retarded, and that the Football Club, the 'struggle' and Winnie Mandela were what gave his life meaning. Admitting that the Football Club's chief coach had 'terrible qualities', the attorney said these were 'easily exploited by people involved in the struggle, people like Mrs Mandela'.

On 9 November 1988 police attacked Jerry Richardson's house and killed two ANC guerrillas who were sleeping there. A policeman was also killed in the shoot-out. Richardson's house was burned to the ground and he moved into the back rooms of Winnie's house with the rank-and-file Football Club members. In Katiza's account to me, he said Winnie Mandela told the Football Club she believed two youths, Lolo Sono and Siboniso Tshabalala, had 'sold out' the guerrillas to the police. She ordered the Football Club to find Sono and Tshabalala and bring them in.

Katiza was present when on 12 November Richardson and other Football Club members brought twenty-one-year-old Sono to the garage of Winnie's Diepkloof house. Katiza said Sono was beaten up by the Football Club and by Winnie, who wielded a sjambok. 'I watched,' said Katiza. 'It was the first time I had seen Lolo. He was beaten and kicked until he admitted he worked with the police. Then he said he had a paper which proved he worked with the police. Mrs Mandela said that was the paper she wanted.

'Mrs Mandela took Lolo in the minibus to his parents' home the same day. I went with her. I was in the back seat. Lolo was in the middle seat – his eyes were swollen. The father for Lolo begged Winnie to give his son back and said there were no documents. Winnie said, "No, the movement will decide what to do with him." We went back to Winnie's house. Because the documents were not found, Winnie ordered Lolo to be killed. Winnie said, "Take him away" – it was her order to kill. Richardson and the others took him away. He has never been seen since.'

Katiza added: 'I think Winnie needs to tell a court where she wanted Lolo Sono taken away to. I believe he was killed. He had been beaten really badly, so I don't think they would have taken him to hospital . . .'

*

Katiza Cebekhulu's new evidence about the fates of Lolo Sono and Siboniso Tshabalala will be news that is both terrible and perhaps also welcome to Nicodemus Sono, who has fought a long, lonely and courageous campaign to discover the fate of his son since he last saw him in Winnie Mandela's minibus on the evening of Sunday 13 November 1988.

As part of my own need to seek corroboration of Katiza's story, I sought out Nicodemus Sono at his home in Meadowlands, on the northern edge of Soweto's fifty sprawling square miles. He confirmed Katiza's story, but added more detail and gave reasons for his belief that the apartheid South African Police were protecting Winnie Mandela.

Nicodemus owned a small fleet of minibuses, but was also an underground ANC operator: his role was to use his legitimate business as cover to move guerrillas returning from training abroad deep into the country. The guerrillas were given fare invoices to prove their bona fides, but sometimes they travelled disguised as nuns or priests. Guns and ammunition for operations were sealed in door panels of Nicodemus' vehicles. Nicodemus also distributed money smuggled in from the ANC's exile headquarters in Lusaka, Zambia.

Nicodemus had known Winnie Mandela since he began attending clandestine ANC meetings with her in 1970. At the funeral of thirteen-year-old Hector Peterson, the first child to die under a hail of police bullets in the 1976 Soweto uprising, Nicodemus stood at the graveside between Winnie and Desmond Tutu, the future Anglican Archbishop of Cape Town and Nobel Peace Prize winner, who was then Dean of Johannesburg.

In 1988 Nicodemus' cousin, Franz-Peter Maluleke, who had fled the country in 1977 for guerrilla training abroad, sent a message saying he would return to Soweto in July of that year with two guerrillas. One fighter would stay only briefly and the orders were for Nicodemus to drive him to the Eastern Cape, the heartland of ANC resistance outside the Johannesburg region. The other guerrilla, whose name was Tsepho, would remain in Soweto, pending his assignment to a mission with Franz-Peter. 'Lolo had his own small business selling vegetables and pottery from our house and making peri-peri sauce,' Nicodemus told me. 'I'd kept Lolo out of my ANC work. I wanted something different for him. But while I was away he started talking to Franz-Peter.'

Franz-Peter ignited Lolo's sense of adventure and romance

31

and sent him to bring a small group of guerrillas by public transport bus to Soweto from near the Botswana border, which they had crossed on foot during the night. By the time Nicodemus returned home from the Eastern Cape, one of Winnie Mandela's drivers called Mike was visiting Lolo, Franz-Peter and Tsepho regularly in a red MUFC minibus.

Early one Sunday Franz-Peter, Tsepho and Mike drove back to the Sono house from an all-night party. All three were heavily drunk. Mike crashed the minibus into the gate of neighbours of Nicodemus Sono. The family remonstrated. 'Tsepho became irritated and began threatening to shoot them,' said Nicodemus. 'I calmed him down and went to assess the damage. Franz-Peter said he would pay for it. But one of the daughters in the house told her policeman boyfriend about the incident.

'I was working all day the following Saturday, but when I came home all the house doors were unlocked and wide open. The police had been there. Tsepho had been taken to Meadowlands police station, but Franz-Peter had escaped and run away to Krugersdorp to shelter with his younger brother. I sent Lolo with one of my own drivers to bail Tsepho.' Tsepho was ordered to appear in court within three weeks on a charge of threatening behaviour. Nicodemus sent a message telling Franz-Peter to stay away from Soweto.

Tsepho returned to court. He was remanded on bail, but within hours Nicodemus Sono's house was again raided by police. Nineteen vehicles drew up outside and Tsepho was arrested. His fingerprints had been found by the security police to match those of a suspected ANC underground activist.

Nicodemus' worries intensified when he discovered from Lolo that he and a boy next door called Richmond had begun storing weapons in the house – automatic rifles, bullets, land mines and hand grenades. He questioned Lolo, who told him they had been delivered in a red Toyota car hired by Winnie Mandela. 'I wanted those weapons out of the house,' Nicodemus told me. 'I loaded them in one of my vehicles and drove to Winnie's. She told me to park in the garage, where Football Club boys unloaded the weapons. I had to leave quickly because I'd received a note ordering me to go to Protea police station, where Tsepho was being questioned by Special Branch [the state security agency responsible for counter-terrorism]. Winnie told me to go to Ismail Ayob [her lawyer and Nelson's] for help. I got to the police station and was interrogated. The police said Tsepho had confessed he had come from Zambia. They released me but said I would have to return for more questioning.'

From Protea Nicodemus raced to cover his tracks. He sent instructions for the ANC to cancel the next scheduled delivery of eight guerrillas from Zambia through Mafeking, near the Botswana border. He also warned Lolo to break all contact with Franz-Peter.

Nicodemus left Soweto again to take passengers to the Transkei homeland in the south on a purely commercial journey. His minibus broke down and he was stuck in the Transkei for a week. When he returned home he learned that four notes had been delivered instructing Lolo, Richmond and another boy who had become involved with them, Siboniso Tshabalala, to report to Special Branch at Protea police station. 'Lolo told me he had taken the notes to Mrs Mandela to show her that the police were after them,' said Nicodemus. 'Winnie said they should refuse to go and she tore up all the notes.'

Lolo Sono and Siboniso Tshabalala had now become so

deeply involved with Winnie and the Football Club that on the nights of Monday 7 November and Tuesday 8 November 1988 they slept in the back rooms of her Diepkloof house. Nicodemus said that during his absence in Transkei Winnie had also found shelter for Franz-Peter and another newly arrived guerrilla at Jerry Richardson's Mzimlophe house. 'Lolo wanted to speak to Franz-Peter,' said Nicodemus. 'One of Winnie's drivers took Lolo and Siboniso to Richardson's place. Franz-Peter asked them to leave their cigarettes with him and warned them to disappear because there was going to be trouble.'

It was Wednesday 9 November, and within minutes of Lolo and Siboniso leaving Richardson's house a police helicopter appeared overhead. A shoot-out followed which was witnessed by Richardson's neighbours and Lolo and Siboniso. The neighbours estimated that the fight lasted two hours. They said that as the helicopter hovered overhead Richardson emerged with his arms raised, signalling surrender to the police, who had approached the house in cars. Policemen handcuffed him and pushed him into the back seat of a car; he was driven away by two white officers. Police marksmen then began pouring grenade and rifle fire into the house. Franz-Peter and the other guerrilla returned the fire. By the end the two Umkhonto we Sizwe guerrillas and a white police officer lay dead and Richardson's house was virtually destroyed.

At the subsequent inquest, Jerry Richardson testified that Winnie Mandela had brought the two guerrillas to his house. They had shown him an AK-47 rifle wrapped in a yellow towel and hand-grenade detonators. They had talked about hitting 'suitable targets' in Johannesburg and Krugersdorp.

Richardson was briefly detained and released without being

charged. With his own house destroyed, he moved into Winnie's Diepkloof house. Winnie Mandela was never questioned by police in connection with Richardson's evidence.

Immediately after the attack on Richardson's house Nicodemus received a fifth note ordering him and Lolo to report to Special Branch at Protea police station. 'They showed me photographs of Franz-Peter's body and asked me to bring his parents to identify the corpse. They said they had no time to question us that day, but told us to return on Monday 14 November.'

In the days following the 9 November police assault on Richardson's house, Lolo Sono continued to move between his parents' Meadowlands home and Winnie's Diepkloof house. Lolo was not at home on the night of Saturday 12 November, but the following day Nicodemus was visited at about 8pm by Mike, Winnie's driver, who said: 'Someone in the combi [minibus] wants to see you.'

Nicodemus knew immediately that it must be Winnie. He went outside and saw a blue minibus in the road. 'I opened the sliding door and went in. Winnie was in the front passenger seat. Lolo was further back being held by the collar by a big Football Club member who had a gun in his other hand. I saw Lolo had been badly beaten. He was shaking and his eyes were swollen. I tried to speak to him, but Winnie told him to shut up.

'Winnie ordered Mike to drive off. She told me she was taking Lolo away because he was a spy and that two comrades had been killed because of him. I pleaded with her that she'd got it wrong and that Lolo was an activist. She didn't want to listen. Mike drove around the block and Winnie ordered him to stop again outside my front gate. The big man with the gun pushed Lolo out of the combi, still holding him by his collar. Lolo sent a message to Richmond, who came and gave photos of Tsepho, Franz-Peter and some other local boys to Winnie. The big man with the gun insisted that the "documents" be handed over as well, but Lolo said there were no documents, only photos.

'I asked Winnie if I could give Lolo a sweater because he was shaking so badly. His mother brought one and I passed it to him. I spoke to him quickly. He said he had gone to Winnie's of his own free will because he wanted to be smuggled out of the country to train for the struggle. Instead, he had been beaten up.

'I pleaded with Winnie to return my son. She totally refused. She said: "I'm taking him with me. The movement will see what to do with him." I assumed she meant she would send him across the border to the ANC camps. It never crossed my mind that he was going to be killed, because Winnie and I had done so many other things together in the past. I was seeing another Winnie altogether.'

Nicodemus watched Winnie drive away with Lolo in the MUFC minibus. He never saw his son again. He went into his garage and sat down to think. A short time later he saw Shadrack Tshabalala, Siboniso's father, approaching. He was highly distressed. Jerry Richardson and other members of the Football Club had come to his house and said they wanted to take Siboniso away to become a member of the team. Siboniso packed his clothes and told Shadrack and his wife, Nomsa, he was going to Winnie's house in the belief that he too was going to be taken across the border to join Umkhonto we Sizwe. Mr and Mrs Tshabalala were grief-stricken at the thought they would not see their son for many years as he set off for Zambia or perhaps one of the ANC's other military camps in Angola, Tanzania or Uganda. In fact, they too never saw their son again.

Although Nicodemus never imagined then that Lolo might be murdered, he did realize that something very odd was going on inside the MUFC. 'I had been ordered earlier to report with Lolo to Special Branch at Protea police station [on Monday 14 November]. I went and told them why Lolo was not with me. I told them exactly what had happened and said I wanted to make a statement about Winnie, the Football Club and Lolo's condition.' Special Branch refused to take the statement and told Nicodemus to lay his complaint at Meadowlands police station. A Captain Kleynhans took the statement, but Nicodemus heard nothing until two months later when police collected him and Nomsa Tshabalala and took them to Diepkloof morgue.

Nicodemus and Mrs Tshabalala found the experience entirely weird and frightening. They were asked to examine bodies in the morgue and to say if they recognized anyone. The police refused to explain why they had been brought to the morgue or to answer any other questions. Lolo Sono's father and Siboniso Tshabalala's mother recognized no bodies and heard nothing subsequently from the police.

*

The Tshabalalas were half paralysed with fear and overcome by depression. They retreated into their home and did little to discover their son's fate. But Nicodemus confronted Winnie Mandela five times in 1989 to ask what had happened to Lolo. 'She told me the Football Club had dropped him off at a place where he asked after the combi left my house [on 13 November 1988]. I asked her: where? She didn't reply or look me in the eye. I clearly became a nuisance because two weeks before [Nelson] Mandela was released from prison [on Saturday 11 February

1990] I called at her house three times in one day and each time she refused to admit me. I've never spoken to her from that time, and when we've bumped into each other she's been surrounded by her bodyguards and she hasn't greeted me.'

In the next turbulent five years – spanning Nelson Mandela's sweet walk to freedom in 1990 after nearly thirty years of imprisonment, long-drawn-out constitutional negotiations and the establishment of majority rule in 1994 through all-race elections – Nicodemus and his wife Caroline made no progress in finding out what had happened to Lolo.

In Cape Town in March 1995 Tony Leon, leader of the small liberal Democratic Party, made a statement in the new South African Parliament on the disappearance of Lolo Sono and Siboniso Tshabalala and asked for police investigations to be reopened.

On 14 March 1995 Nicodemus and Caroline Sono were summoned to Cape Town by General George Fivaz – appointed South Africa's new Police Commissioner by President Nelson Mandela – to tell him the stories of the disappearances of both Lolo and Siboniso. However, on 5 October 1994 Nomsa Tshabalala had received an extraordinary visit at four in the morning from police attached to the Soweto Murder and Robbery Squad, tasked with investigating crimes linked to Winnie Mandela's MUFC. 'They demanded that I open the door,' she told me. 'Then they demanded to see Shadrack. I told them he had been shot dead in his car two months ago. [The assailant has never been found.] They showed me a photo of a youth. I was shocked. I said, "That's my son. Have you found him?" They said no, only that he had "passed away". Nothing else at all, not how he died or where he was buried. They didn't explain where they got Siboniso's picture. It was heartless. The last time I had heard from Siboniso was almost six years earlier when he phoned me and said, "Mummy, I'm here with Lolo." I said, "Where are you?" but he dropped the phone and it went dead. Then the police said if I wanted to know about my son I must go to Pretoria and pay Rand 4,000 to exhume him. They didn't say the address I should go to or who I should pay the money to. We are still waiting for Siboniso.'

General Fivaz told the Sonos that the Lolo Sono and Siboniso Tshabalala cases would be reopened. On their return from Cape Town the Sonos were visited at their Meadowlands home by officers of a special police unit in Pretoria working on unsolved cases. They asked for the original numbers of police dockets opened in 1988 on Lolo and Siboniso.

Nicodemus still had the numbers, so he gave them to the men from Pretoria. A few days later the Sonos received a strange visit from a man they had never met before, Captain Fred Dempsey, who for the past four years had led the Murder and Robbery Squad's MUFC investigations. 'Dempsey acted as though I would remember him,' said Nicodemus. 'He asked why the Pretoria men wanted the case numbers when he was already conducting the investigation. And he demanded to know why we had gone to see Fivaz when we knew the efforts he was making. I told him we knew no such things and that he had never troubled to find us before.

'After Dempsey's visit I went to see Mrs Tshabalala. She was in a terrible state.' She had been visited by an Indian officer called Major H. T. Moodley, who said he was Dempsey's deputy. 'She told me he had shouted: "Why are you investigating your son when we've already told you he has passed away?" He took away the photo of Siboniso that the Murder and Robbery Squad had left earlier.'

Nicodemus Sono said he telephoned Dempsey several times after these incidents, but he never replied. 'Then we discovered that several members of the Football Club had been incorporated into the South African Army. We concluded that Dempsey must be working with Winnie and the Football Club in some way – otherwise, why has she never been questioned? Why does nothing happen? Why does he browbeat us for trying to reopen the case? Since Fivaz saw me, and Dempsey and Moodley made their visits, I've gone on TV to say that what hurts me most is that the police only ever ask questions, they never give any answers.'

The last time I saw Caroline Sono she took my hand and wept as she said: 'You know, Mr Bridgland, I hoped for so many years that my son was still alive in some foreign country. Now I know he is dead. What we want is our minds put at rest. We don't want anyone put on trial because we know justice is never done for people like us in South Africa. We just want someone to tell us where Lolo's bones are, so that we can bury him properly and his spirit can be with us, and for Winnie to say she's sorry. She is not the Mother of the Nation, she is the killer of the nation.'

CHAPTER FOUR

A Sting

DECEMBER 1988

Within three weeks of Lolo Sono's disappearance, Katiza moved from observer to participant in Winnie Mandela's sinister activities. Towards the end of November 1988 Winnie summoned him and gave him a special task – a 'sting' operation, designed to lure a white priest into a sexual honeytrap.

The Reverend Paul Verryn, a radical young Methodist minister, was the target. Katiza was to go to the Central Methodist Church in Johannesburg's Pritchard Street, a stone's throw from the Rand Supreme Court, and present himself to Verryn, a stocky, red-haired, bespectacled man with a formidable record of opposition to apartheid.

He was to tell Verryn he was a destitute boy from Zululand, newly arrived in Johannesburg, who needed accommodation in the Methodist Church shelter run by the white minister at his manse in Soweto. If Verryn, a bachelor, accepted him, Katiza's orders were to try to sleep in the minister's bed. Katiza said Winnie instructed him: 'If he lets you sleep in the bed and sodomizes you, you should tell the housekeeper.' If Verryn did not violate him, Katiza was to use his initiative and choose a moment to act as though he had been raped – and still alert the housekeeper.

Verryn was the first white minister to be placed in a black township by the Methodist Church. He had a courageous record, preaching against apartheid and police brutality, and was popular with the black community in which he lived and among his liberal white friends. He spoke his defiance of apartheid by conducting funerals of blacks and whites who had died at the hands of the police and covert government death squads. After Dave Webster, a popular Witwatersrand University lecturer and ANC supporter, was assassinated by a Military Intelligence death squad in May 1989, I watched in awe as Verryn conducted a stunningly moving memorial service in Johannesburg's St Mary's Anglican Cathedral where thousands of people of every colour defied a government ban on the singing of ANC anthems and the parading of ANC colours: it was enough to make him a possible target of the government's licensed killers.

In Soweto Verryn managed five parishes, including the Orlando West Methodist church, just a short distance from Winnie Mandela's Orlando West matchbox house. His flock totalled about 3,000 parishioners; he was helped by seventy-seven local preachers and two women who cared for the elderly. In a time when it took guts for a white to identify with the vote-less black majority, Verryn's commitment to the liberation cause was beyond doubt.

Winnie Mandela did not doubt it either. Verryn gave shelter at his Orlando West manse to as many as forty youths at a time who were on the run from police in their home townships, mainly because of their anti-government activism. The manse was small and, as in nearly every Soweto home, the residents slept packed together like tinned anchovies – on beds, sofas and tables, under tables, in armchairs and on floors. Verryn had friends who owned a farmhouse in the Magaliesburg

Mountains, to the north of Johannesburg, where twenty to
thirty particularly vulnerable youths sent by the minister were
in hiding at any one time, sometimes prior to being smuggled
out of the country.

Winnie often referred youths from her Community House
social work centre to Verryn for shelter. Superficially, the relationship between the two establishments, sharing the same
ideals, was easygoing and relaxed. Why she now launched the
sting against Verryn in the shape of Katiza Cebekhulu is not
known, but there are two main possibilities – either she
genuinely believed that black youths were being abused by a
white homosexual in priest's garb; or – more likely – she simply
became envious of Verryn's popularity and success among the
people of Soweto and the funding he was attracting from local
and international Church organizations.

Rumours had been circulating in the township that Verryn
was making sexual advances to some of the boys at his manse.
These began after Verryn expelled one teenager, Maxwell
Rabolou, who had moved to and fro between the Methodist
manse and Winnie's Orlando West home. Verryn first asked
Rabolou to leave in 1987 because he persisted in staying out
overnight without telling the minister where he was. It was one
of Verryn's strict house rules that the youths keep him informed
of their whereabouts and report in each night because people
were disappearing and being detained all the time in the conflict
with the white government. Masses of children were on the run,
hiding from the police, and it was important to act quickly if it
was known someone had been detained by the security forces: it
was often a matter of life or death. Rabolou went to Winnie, who
said the youth complained to her of sexual advances by Verryn
and claimed that he was too frightened to return to the manse.

What transpired subsequently is not absolutely clear. But Rabolou certainly stayed with the Football Club in Winnie's back rooms for about two months before disappearing into the township and then returning to Verryn's manse at the beginning of 1988. According to a close friend of the priest, Rabolou continued to irk Verryn by vanishing for days at a time without giving notice. 'On one occasion he came back to Paul's and said he had been beaten at Winnie's house,' Verryn's friend told me. Eventually Verryn became so exasperated by Rabolou's disappearances that he again ordered him to leave. Rabolou warned Verryn as he left: 'I will make you pay for this.'

By mid-September 1988 Rabolou had returned to Winnie's and complained again about sexual advances by Verryn. Winnie raised the matter with her close friend the Secretary-General of the South African Council of Churches, the Reverend Frank Chikane, who called Verryn to tell him about the allegation. Verryn immediately informed Bishop Peter Storey, head of the Methodist Church in the Johannesburg region. Storey investigated and concluded that the allegation was unfounded, but he suggested that Verryn put his bedroom out of bounds to other occupants of the manse. Verryn rejected the advice as impractical: his bedroom, the biggest and most comfortable, would have to continue to be used because there were always fifteen or more youths seeking shelter who would otherwise all have to sleep uncomfortably in the lounge and two other tiny bedrooms.

Winnie's biographer Emma Gilbey, who knew about Mrs Mandela's allegations against Verryn but not about the sting, argued: 'As her neighbour, Verryn was impossible for Winnie to ignore: it may have been that he seemed like a galling rival with his own houseful of youths. As a white Methodist priest he may have appeared to represent the influence of the Establishment on young blacks. His manse might have been thought of as an opposing power base rather than a place of refuge.'

Katiza Cebekhulu, however, believes the real reason Winnie launched the sting against the priest was simple envy of the growing success of Verryn's project: he was very popular and was attracting more and more finance, particularly from Europe and through the radical South African Council of Churches. For years, as the tragic wife of Nelson, the great imprisoned leader, Winnie herself had brought in massive sums from foreign organizations and individuals who saw her as the supreme symbol of opposition to apartheid. 'I think Mrs Mandela wanted to destroy Paul because she was jealous,' said Katiza.

One close friend of Verryn's concurred with Katiza. 'Her obsession with Paul was weird,' she told me. 'Was it really the homosexual thing? Was it because he was white? Or maybe even because he was a Methodist? Whatever it was, Winnie seems to have been jealous of a rival operation in areas where she had gained credibility and power. Somebody was challenging her constituency with strong backing from the South African Council of Churches. She could not have failed to notice that Paul's operation went unscathed when her own house was being burned down.'

This was a reference to an attack, on 28 July 1988, by pupils from Soweto's Daliwonga High School on Winnie's Orlando West matchbox house: her small home was set ablaze and completely destroyed, along with all Winnie's letters from Nelson, most of her photographs and the slice of cake from their 1958 wedding she had been saving for the past thirty years for his eventual release from prison. Mrs Albertina Sisulu, the wife of Nelson's imprisoned friend in the freedom struggle, Walter Sisulu, went to see the damage and found many scorched and uncashed cheques from overseas donors strewn among the ruins.

The dispute between Winnie and the pupils had begun in 1987 when members of the Mandela United Football Club arrived at a soccer pitch where a match involving Daliwonga School was in progress. The MUFC peremptorily ordered Daliwonga from the field, which Winnie's 'team' wanted for practice. A fight broke out which was settled when the MUFC produced guns and forced the schoolboys to flee. Daliwonga players and their friends launched a revenge attack: they stoned Winnie's house, causing Rand 1,000 worth of damage, and captured two MUFC members, whom they took to their school and beat up until teachers intervened. Discord continued until July 1988 when a girl who was close to the MUFC was gang-raped by Daliwonga High youths. She told the MUFC what had happened, and revenge followed. The Daliwonga rapists were identified, caught and taken to Winnie's Orlando West house, where they were tried, found guilty and beaten up before being released. The MUFC raped one of the Daliwonga schoolgirls as part of the Football Club revenge.

Daliwonga prepared for counter-revenge against the MUFC enemy. On Thursday 28 July 1988 a mob of teenage schoolboys climbed the wall surrounding Winnie Mandela's house, smashed all its windows and doors and in broad daylight set the building on fire. Neither Winnie nor any MUFC members were there at the time. None of Winnie's neighbours tried to prevent the attack: as the fire intensified they did nothing to stop the blaze, none bothering to throw even a bucket of water on to the flames. Fire brigade, ambulance and police arrived, but they too did nothing, joining other Sowetans who gathered to watch indifferently as Winnie's house was totally destroyed.

The burning of Winnie Mandela's house was barely reported at the time, although many journalists knew the grisly details. Rian Malan reckons white reporters and editors did not want to be branded racists while black reporters were paralysed by fear. 'If you lived in Soweto, there are some things you dared not say for fear of being labelled a sell-out. Sell-outs did not live long,' wrote Malan in *My Traitor's Heart*, perhaps the finest and most honest book ever written about South Africa. 'One of the township's most prominent black journalists chuckled bleakly when I asked why the full story of the arson attack on Winnie Mandela's home hadn't yet been written. "You write it," he said. "You're white, you might get away with it."'

*

If the 'Mother of the Nation' was meant to heed the blaze as a warning to curb the excesses of her football team, the ploy did not work. Following her instructions, Katiza Cebekhulu packed a small bag with a few clothes at Winnie's house on 17 December 1988 and left to catch a train to central Johannesburg. Somewhere along the way he was joined by Eric Ngelisa, a fieldworker for the Justice and Reconciliation Commission of the South African Council of Churches, with whom Verryn had worked in squatter camps around Johannesburg.

Katiza accepted his mission willingly, with no moral qualms – 'I was attending school properly for the first time. I was being fed and clothed, so I respected Winnie. I did as I was told. I never knew at that stage how things were going to develop. If I had known, I wouldn't have done it.'

At Pritchard Street, Verryn asked Katiza what he could do for him – 'I told him I had nowhere to sleep. I know nobody, and I'm coming from Natal. Paul said his house was too full. So I begged him and asked him where else I should go. At last he accepted.' Verryn's judgement was that Katiza was deeply traumatized and irrational, but not unintelligent. He was reluctant to give him shelter, and was convinced only by the special pleading of Eric Ngelisa, who it later emerged was one of Winnie's close confidants. That evening Verryn drove Katiza back to Soweto to take up residence in the Orlando West manse.

There he introduced Katiza to the other fugitives sheltering in the small single-storey manse, in the shadow of Orlando West's big and airy Methodist church. Among them were Xoliswa Falati, Kenneth Kgase, Thabiso Mono, Pelo Mekgwe and Stompie Seipei Moeketsi.

Falati, a thirty-five-year-old woman whose house had been burned down in KwaThema, a township thirty miles east of Johannesburg, had arrived at the manse only recently with her teenage son and daughter. Kenneth Kgase dreamed of becoming a writer and, unlike the others – political activists of one kind or another – had moved into the manse to collaborate with Verryn on a gospel play to be performed by the Orlando West Methodist Church. Thabiso Mono was from Ikageng, the black township of Potchefstroom, an Afrikaner university town seventy miles west of Johannesburg. He had arrived just two months earlier with his friend Pelo Mekgwe after spending a year and a half in prison for illegal ANC activism.

Stompie Moeketsi, a fourteen-year-old boy small for his age, had achieved cult status for his leadership of resistance by children to the apartheid police in the small Orange Free State

town of Parys, 100 miles to the south-west of Johannesburg.
His reputation stemmed from the period of township turmoil
in 1986 when, according to newspaper reports, he mobilized an
army of 1,500 child activists aged between eight and fourteen in
Tumahole, Parys' black township. The area was a stronghold of
diehard white right-wingers whose Nazi-style 'A-team' vigi-
lantes staged periodic raids, ignored by the police, on
Tumahole to intimidate and control the black population.
Stories abounded of how Stompie, then aged twelve, acted as a
general of his army and beat back the whites. The legend was
enhanced by colourful tales of his powers of oratory and his
ability to recite in full the Freedom Charter, the ANC's 1956 call
for the abolition of apartheid and the restoration of South
Africa's wealth to all of its peoples.

That he led a teenage gang and that he had a magnetic personality are not in question, but there are doubts about other
elements of the legend. 'Knowing Tumahole as I do, I doubt
that anyone could muster 1,500 children there for any purpose,
and the idea of an "army" and a "general" with those images of
order and discipline is simply ridiculous,' wrote the Sowetan
journalist Nomavenda Mathiane at the time. 'Watching little
Stompie do the toyi-toyi [an ANC guerrilla dance] on TV, I
could only see a youngster being paraded by the big boys [of the
ANC] to depict a struggle that has become a plaything.'

I am sure Mathiane was right. I visited Stompie's unmarried
mother, Joyce Seipei, in Tumahole. The Moeketsi part of her
son's name came from his father, who died when Stompie was
five years old. Joyce Seipei was an uneducated, impoverished
woman who lived, and still lives, in a corrugated-iron shed
without running water and electricity on a bleak, windswept
plateau on the edge of Tumahole, which probably housed only

5,000 people and would have had to perform miracles to raise any kind of army let alone one made up of 1,500 children. Joyce Seipei's grim section of Tumahole was named Mandela Village, in honour of Nelson Mandela.

Joyce described to me how Stompie had a 'big brain' and how, as a very small boy, 'he used to be a little clown full of fun. He was very talkative and cheery. He liked school very much and wanted to be a lawyer, but I used to tell him lowly people like us couldn't do that kind of thing. He grew up a poor boy. I couldn't afford to buy him lots of things.' She said Stompie's vocal opposition to the Nationalist government inevitably got him into trouble. On 9 July 1986 he was arrested for the first time. 'The police came to my place and roughed me up and tore the place apart looking for Stompie. They said he was so small that he could hide anywhere and that they would kill him when they found him.'

Joyce eventually persuaded them that Stompie was out of the house buying bread. They waited, and when Stompie returned from the errand they told him he was very troublesome. 'They asked if he was aware that he was putting me in trouble. He laughed – he never got angry – and told them: "No, I am only fighting for the freedom of the black people. I will never turn back from fighting for the struggle." . . . He used to talk like a grown-up. Then the police told him to get lots of clothes together because they were taking him to the cells and it would be cold. They took him to the police car . . . I cried and tried to talk to him, asking him whether he was scared. He said "No." The police said he must say goodbye to me because he would not see me for a long time: but he just laughed at them.'

Stompie, then aged twelve, was taken to Potchefstroom Prison, fifty miles from Parys, and Joyce did not see him again for nearly a year. When he was brought back to Parys and released on 25 June 1987 his face was swollen, as though he had been beaten. Stompie left for Johannesburg and became a celebrity in the black community for his speech making and his courage in defying the police: he even gave a lecture at the University of the Witwatersrand, a bastion of Johannesburg white liberalism. But he was soon rearrested and imprisoned for a short time at Koppies, near Parys. A few months after his release he went back to Johannesburg, telling his mother he needed to get away from the police and that he would not return to Tumahole until he had obtained an education. 'I was scared when he left,' said Joyce. 'I thought he would be detained again or killed by the police.'

There were allegations that Stompie had become a police informer under torture during his spell of almost a year in prison during 1986–7. Some people doubted the allegations, including Thabiso Mono, who was already in prison in Potchefstroom when Stompie arrived – 'My comrades and I used to meet Stompie in Tumahole. I liked him and I never thought he was an informer. He was a small boy and people under torture give information. But Stompie was not someone who deliberately collaborated.'

Priscilla Jana, a senior partner in the law firm which represented Nelson and Winnie Mandela, also doubted the allegations. She took on Stompie's case when he was arrested for the second time, fought for his release from prison in Koppies and took him to Johannesburg from Tumahole in early 1988. He spent much of his time in Jana's office, where the women workers doted on him, gave him a Mickey Mouse watch, a toy camera and other presents, made him sandwiches and took him to and from school.

Stompie stayed for a while in Johannesburg's white northern suburbs with one of Jana's junior lawyers, Matthew Chaskalson, son of human rights lawyer Arthur Chaskalson, who represented Nelson Mandela at his 1964 trial for sabotage and plotting the violent overthrow of the state. In November 1988 Chaskalson left Johannesburg for an extended holiday and asked Paul Verryn if he would let Stompie stay at the Orlando West manse. As far as Verryn was concerned, the boy would be given only temporary accommodation until Chaskalson returned. Stompie had few clothes, so Verryn gave him two T-shirts, one of them red and blue striped with a sea-side scene on the chest. Verryn noted the boy's leadership qualities, but also considered him boastful, argumentative and reluctant to wash. Soon Stompie was clashing with Xoliswa Falati, who had appointed herself housekeeper of the manse.

Verryn arrived home one evening to find Stompie cowering in terror after Falati had interrogated the boy, accused him of being a police informer and beaten him after he got into a fight with her son, Mlaxndo. Verryn lost his temper with Falati and told her to leave Stompie alone. Soon afterwards the boy ran away and was brought back by one of Verryn's lay deacons.

Verryn was never quite sure how Falati became a member of his household. She moved in uninvited with her two children during the first week of December 1988, Verryn's friends told me, and was there when the minister got home from work. Verryn had earlier met her briefly in KwaThema when he visited the township for a counselling session with children on the run from police. He did not feel at peace with her. Falati said she had fled KwaThema when her house was bombed and burned to the ground by the 'system'. But confidants informed him that she had a reputation for unreliability in the 'struggle' and that young 'comrades' had possibly bombed her house on suspicion that she was a police informant.

When Falati first left KwaThema she stayed with a relative in Hillbrow in central Johannesburg. It was theoretically out of bounds to blacks under the Group Areas Act, which defined Hillbrow as a whites-only locality. But it had become a 'grey area' under a government policy of turning a blind eye to illegal multi-racial living in a few areas of South Africa. Nevertheless, Falati feared a possible police raid and moved into Verryn's Soweto refuge. She pushily took over responsibilities for buying food and for cooking, administered money for transport and organized the cleaning. She also threatened those who did not help clean the house with 'discipline' from the Mandela United Football Club, though the other residents did not understand what Falati's connection was with Winnie's bodyguard. But she obviously knew Winnie quite well. Verryn grew weary of her story of advice given by Winnie's personal physician, Dr Abu-Baker Asvat, to his famous patient – that a woman who did not have frequent sex would suffer from high blood pressure. The minister regarded Falati as moody and disruptive and tried unsuccessfully to find accommodation for her with one of the women members of his congregation.

Katiza Cebekhulu's arrival at the manse increased the tension. Verryn's friends told me he was temperamental and nervous and constantly told the minister he was afraid the other youths would attack him. Because of his fear, Verryn agreed to Katiza's plea to be allowed to sleep in the minister's own bed. Yet even in that haven, Katiza slept with a knife under his pillow.

During his time at the manse Katiza made a real friend of only one person – eighteen-year-old Nompumelelo Falati, a tall, strikingly pretty girl. Nompumelelo used to sing for him Teddy Prendergass's 'We Can Be Lovers' and Natalie Cole's 'I Need Your Love Every Minute', while Katiza made her laugh with his fund of Zulu songs and anecdotes.

Nompumelelo would be killed in due course in strange circumstances. Years later, when I told him of his friend's death, he wept and sighed: 'Ah, sometimes I ask why God made us to be born.'

*

The first part of Winnie Mandela's plan for Katiza Cebekhulu at Paul Verryn's manse did not work out. Verryn and Katiza, with his knife, slept in the same double bed. It was hot and humid at the height of the South African summer and rainy season, so both slept only in their underpants.

'Obviously, we touched,' said Katiza. 'But it wasn't deliberate. He didn't do anything.'

Did he suggest anything?

'No, no, no, no, no, no, no,' Katiza told me. There was nothing resembling or suggesting a sexual advance.

Verryn was due to leave Soweto on Thursday 22 December 1988 to spend a two-week holiday with family and friends in Pretoria and Potchefstroom. That morning he decided to leave early for his office because he had a lot of work to complete before he could relax; among his tasks that day was helping make arrangements for an ANC activist, who was one of his church fieldworkers, to be smuggled out of the country.

Katiza realized he could wait no longer to implement Winnie's alternative plan. In the early hours of 22 December, before sunrise, he leaped from his bed, screamed and ran outside crying. Verryn followed and found Katiza sitting sullenly on the back doorstep. 'Paul asked me what was wrong. I didn't answer him. He asked me to come back to bed,' Katiza told me. 'I shouted at him to leave me alone.' Verryn went back indoors, packed his holiday bag and left to help the church worker begin his escape.

A week later, on Thursday 29 December, Xoliswa Falati asked Katiza what had happened that night. He told her that before going to bed he had not felt well and that he had told Verryn, who gave him a sleeping pill. 'I told Xoliswa: "I don't know exactly what happened, but when I woke up in the morning I found myself smeared with sperms [semen], particularly around my anus. Paul, he raped me while I was sleeping."'

Katiza said Falati immediately left the manse and went to see Winnie. 'When she came back she said Winnie wanted to see me. She had told Winnie Paul was a gay who had raped me in the night.' (In another statement, Falati said she had found Katiza trembling after his 'rape' and that he vowed to stab Verryn to death in revenge. Her main evidence, she said, for allegations of homosexual rape against Verryn came from stories Katiza had told her.)

John Morgan drove Katiza to Mrs Mandela's house in a minibus. 'When we reached the house, Mrs Mandela asked me: "What happened?" I told Mrs Mandela Paul Verryn he raped me. Mrs Mandela said: "What?" I said: "Paul Verryn, he raped me."'

'She said: "Xoliswa, do you suspect other people in that church they can be sodomized by Paul Verryn?" Xoliswa said yes. Mrs Mandela said: "Who are those?" Xoliswa said: "Stompie, Pelo Mekgwe, Kenny Kgase and Thabiso Mono, they are being sodomized by that white man, I'm telling you."'

'Falati also said: "Mrs Mandela, Stompie is working with the police."'

Katiza said Winnie decided to organize a raiding party to the Methodist manse to 'rescue' Moeketsi, Mekgwe, Kgase and Mono. Katiza was part of the Mandela United Football Club rescue mission which left at sunset on Thursday 29 December 1988 in the Club minibus to collect the four boys. Chief coach Jerry Richardson led the group. John Morgan was the driver.

'Winnie said we should get Paul as well if he was there,' Katiza told me. 'She wanted to question him.' Verryn had unexpectedly returned to the Orlando West manse the previous day and spent several hours mediating a serious row between Falati and Thabiso Mono and Pelo Mekgwe. But he had left again to investigate a report from the Magaliesburg safe house that one of the youths there had been picked up by the police and had died in custody, allegedly by his own hand.

So Verryn was not there when the MUFC raiding party set out for the manse. Richardson, Katiza and the others wore greatcoats to hide the guns they were carrying. 'We didn't knock,' said Katiza. 'We burst in like police looking for notorious criminals. Richardson and the others grabbed the boys very roughly. There wasn't much they could say. People were scared of the Mandela United Football Club. I want to tell you, when Winnie's gang came you needed to ask yourself if it was the end.' Katiza's assertion of people's dread of the MUFC was only too true. 'At that time residents of Orlando West were frantic with fear of their sons being press-ganged by the Football Club,' wrote Nomavenda Mathiane. 'Members of the club were openly walking around Soweto with machine-guns over their shoulders, and people in Soweto were mystified as to why the police were laying off.'

Moeketsi, Kgase, Mekgwe and Mono were pushed into the kitchen. From there they were ordered out of the house and told to leave the property through a hole in the back fence. They walked for about two blocks to where John Morgan was waiting in the MUFC minibus to drive them to Winnie Mandela's Diepkloof residence.

Thabiso Mono, then aged nineteen, was bewildered by what was happening, but he was relieved when the minibus pulled up at Winnie's house and they were told to go inside. 'I had been supporting her wholeheartedly in the struggle, so I didn't have anything against her,' said Mono when he visited me at my Johannesburg home. 'When we arrived there I said to Pelo that nothing can happen to us because we are at the house of Winnie Mandela, the wife of our leader . . . only to find out I was wrong.'

CHAPTER FIVE

The Assault on Stompie

29–31 DECEMBER 1988

Katiza Cebekhulu helped hustle Stompie, Kenny, Pelo and Thabiso along the side passage of Mrs Mandela's house at 585 Diepkloof Extension into an outside room to the right of the jacuzzi in the back courtyard. Jerry Richardson brought them plates of food. Soon afterwards, Winnie Mandela entered. Katiza estimates the time was about 7pm. An assault began. Katiza gave me the following account of it.

'Winnie said: "You dogs, do you sleep with that white Reverend? Do you let him fuck you, you dogs?" They said no. Xoliswa said again that Stompie had been working with the police. Winnie asked him, "Do you work with the police?" and he said no. Xoliswa said Stompie was lying.

'Winnie turned to me and said: "Tell them what Paul did to you." I was afraid, so I told them Paul raped me and Winnie said to them: "Are you going to tell me this boy is lying?" She began to punch them. I can't remember who she started on, but she beat them all. She called for a sjambok. Xoliswa brought two sjamboks from the main house and I handed one to Winnie. It was the one she had used on Lolo Sono. She began whipping them on their backs.'

I interrupted to ask if she was whipping them very hard.

Katiza almost snarled with contempt as he replied: 'Obviously. How can you hit someone softly? Obviously, you can't play with someone when you are beating them. Obviously it is hard. She whipped them very hard.' Katiza said Winnie began punching the boys again, and went on: 'I joined in too. Everybody was punching. I can't say how many because when you are beating you don't have time to look.'

I asked Katiza whether he was happy as he beat Stompie and the others, whether he thought it was the right thing to do.

Again he replied with contempt: 'No. How can you say that it was the right thing to do to beat people?'

But at the time, I said, wasn't he loyal to Winnie?

'Even if I was loyal, I didn't like it.'

So he felt he had no choice?

'No choice.'

All the MUFC bodyguards participated as the beatings went on. 'They sang freedom songs so the neighbours could not hear the beatings,' said Katiza. 'Some of the Football Club beat the boys on their knees and feet with bottles. Richardson and Xoliswa were doing it to Stompie. Each time a boy fell to the floor he was kicked until he got up again. They tried to beg [for mercy]. But who was going to listen? They were crying. But who would help them? They were beaten until Stompie fainted. Someone poured water over him and Morgan told Winnie it had gone too far. But she began whipping Stompie again.'

When Mrs Mandela stopped whipping Stompie she picked the small boy up under his armpits and ordered Katiza to take hold of his legs. 'I lifted Stompie by his legs while Winnie held him by his arms: we lifted him high and threw him to the hard floor. I helped her do it once. Then she and Richardson did it several more times. Every time Stompie was dropped Winnie shouted, "Breakdown!" and we all began shouting it. It had something to do with a breakdown truck, but I don't know exactly what it meant.

'They all began confessing that they had slept with Paul. Stompie admitted he had worked with the police. When you got beaten that way by the Football Club, you had no choice. You had to accept.

'Winnie whipped Stompie again until the sjambok broke. Stompie's skull and face were swollen. The top of his skull was soft and blood was coming out from both nostrils and both ears. All the boys were bleeding. Stompie was bleeding the worst, but he was still alive.'

Katiza estimates the beatings on 29 December lasted almost fifty minutes and ended just before 8pm. Winnie then went into her house while Richardson told Stompie, Kenny, Thabiso and Pelo to wash and gave them blankets to make beds on the floor of the room.

When Katiza rose on the morning of Friday 30 December he sauntered into the back courtyard where Stompie and the others were sitting. 'Stompie's head was still swollen and bleeding. He was murmuring that he couldn't see. I brought him some water, but he couldn't lift the cup. Before I could help him Winnie came out of the house and shouted at me and said he and the others were to be given no food or drink.'

Katiza was then ordered by Winnie to get ready to go out with her in the late afternoon, this time for a visit to Dr Abu-Baker Asvat.

*

Abu-Baker Asvat was a radical, politically committed Indian with a medical practice in Soweto who first met Winnie

Mandela in the late 1970s through his friend and fellow doctor, Joe Veriava. Dr Veriava practised with Asvat at Coronation Hospital, serving coloured (mixed-race) ghettos on the south-western fringes of Johannesburg. Veriava was also Winnie's personal physician during her Brandfort years, making regular 400-mile round-trips to her place of internal exile to check her health and raise her spirits.

Dr Asvat, a leading member of Steve Biko's Black Consciousness Movement at the time of the 1976 black student uprising, was a fiery-tempered but gregarious son of a Moslem shopkeeper. Outside hospital hours he and his wife Zhora drove into squatter camps in the Johannesburg area towing a caravan packed with medical supplies. He treated the poor who had no other access to medical attention, charging no fees for his time or the drugs he administered. After a visit with Veriava to see Winnie in Brandfort, Asvat added the black township there to his list. His mobile clinic became so successful that he built a hut in Winnie's back yard to provide a waiting room and examination cubicle. On each trip he left behind medical supplies and grain from Operation Hunger, South Africa's own internal Oxfam, for Winnie to administer and distribute.

By the time Winnie returned to Soweto in 1985, Asvat had supplanted Veriava as her personal physician.

Asvat's radicalism had several roots. His father, a prosperous shopkeeper in Vrededorp, an Indian inner suburb of Johannesburg, urged his sons to do something more interesting with their lives than sell soap, sugar and self-raising flour. Get a profession, he urged them in the days when most vocations in South Africa other than the law, medicine and teaching were closed to non-whites. Abu-Baker's elder brother Ebrahim opted for medicine and left for Pakistan to pursue his studies.

His young brother followed: Abu-Baker entered the Department of Medical Studies at the University of Rajshahi in former East Pakistan, now Bangladesh, one of the most impoverished countries on earth, before transferring to Karachi University, whose medical degrees were recognized in South Africa – unlike Rajshahi's. He returned home deeply radicalized. His anger increased in 1973 when his parents were forcibly removed from their double-storey, colonial Victorian house with delicate ironwork and wide verandahs in Vrededorp to a new Indian location, Lenasia, twenty miles out of Johannesburg. 'We got peanuts for our property, and then the government broke it down,' said Ebrahim. It was at this time that Abu-Baker joined the Black People's Convention, one of the groups in Biko's Black Consciousness Movement.

Coronation Hospital and Natalspruit Hospital, in the Johannesburg township of Katlehong, where Abu-Baker first worked after his return from Pakistan, served coloured and black communities respectively. But the senior staff were all white. White salary structures were higher and their leave entitlements were better than those for Indians and coloureds, whose own salaries were better than those of blacks. The whites' tea and rest rooms were separate and the conditions were superior to those for non-white personnel. Abu-Baker fought constantly with the hospital authorities about these discriminatory practices. He was disciplined several times and eventually reported to the provincial authorities and dismissed.

Abu-Baker bought Ebrahim's private practice in Soweto. He hired as his surgery nurse and receptionist Mrs Albertina Sisulu, wife of Walter Sisulu, Nelson Mandela's lifelong friend and close ANC colleague. Albertina Sisulu was a courageous and disciplined woman. In contrast to Winnie Mandela, she was patient and unpretentious and truly motherly. Winnie was more glamorous and openly confrontational. But Albertina had a calmness and composure about her which attracted people to her for support and solace in tough and distressing times. Out of trust and respect, they affectionately called her 'Ma'.

Ma Sisulu had been imprisoned several times for defiance of apartheid laws. She had been tortured, held in solitary confinement, banned and put under house arrest for ten years. Her three children had also been detained at various times. On one occasion, in late 1958, she and Winnie Mandela were imprisoned together for defying the Pass Laws. It was the first time that Winnie, then only twenty-four years old and pregnant with her first child, Zenani, had been arrested. She started to bleed, but Ma Sisulu, a trained midwife, took charge and managed to avert the threatened miscarriage of the young wife of her husband's best friend.

The episode should have bonded two women who had so much in common, but thereafter they grew apart, and their mutual disapproval became outright hostility. During Winnie's internal exile in Brandfort the UDF was formed and Ma Sisulu was appointed co-President of the proxy ANC organization. The honour paid Albertina infuriated Winnie. She resolved to have nothing to do with the UDF and to act as a free agent without seeking a mandate from the community. It contributed also to her resolve to form the Mandela United Football Club. She believed these were her entitlements as the tragic consort of Nelson Mandela.

Abu-Baker and Ma Sisulu became very close. But, despite Ma's deep aversion to the younger woman, Abu-Baker maintained his professional and personal relationship with Winnie.

He and Ma visited squatter camps together, where he was addressed as 'father', although many of the youths nicknamed him 'Hurley', after Charlie Hurley, a footballer with the British professional club Sunderland, who had by some inexplicable means become a hero to aspiring township soccer players. Abu-Baker was himself a skilled sportsman, captaining Crescents, the most successful team in Johannesburg's Asian cricket league.

Albertina Sisulu helped distribute old clothing and food parcels collected by the Asvat family to the aged and destitute in the squatter camps. She admired the commitment of a man who at times provided shelter in his own Lenasia home for as many as twenty homeless people. 'My brother had real compassion for people,' said Ebrahim. 'He treated anyone, regardless of ideology. Once someone was referred to hospital he would visit them there regularly until they were discharged. If he was called out at midnight he would always go and come back as late as three or four in the morning. Sometimes the police would detain him, or he would close the practice for a week or two and go into hiding. The security police constantly hassled him, making threatening phone calls or searching his home for documents, usually in the early hours of the morning. He persuaded our family to raise money to put black people through college, including Frank Chikane.'

Much as Ma Sisulu loved Dr Asvat, she avoided the regular Friday-evening dinners Abu-Baker gave at his Lenasia home for Winnie, the Mandela daughters and members of the Football Club. Zhora Asvat too was uncomfortable with Winnie, especially since she sometimes arrived drunk, unheard of among women in traditional Moslem households. But, in the face of her husband's commitment to a woman who had been dubbed the Mother of the Nation, Zhora was powerless.

*

Winnie almost always left the Asvat household with the gift of half a freshly slaughtered lamb. So when on 30 December, according to Katiza's account, John Morgan drove him, Winnie and Xoliswa Falati to Abu-Baker's surgery Mrs Mandela was sure of a warm welcome. While Morgan stayed outside in the minibus and Falati waited in the reception area with Ma Sisulu, Winnie and Katiza entered the consulting room to be greeted by Asvat, who laughed and asked: 'What have I done to deserve a visit by big people like this?'

Katiza said Winnie replied: 'We've come with a big problem. This young boy has been sodomized by Paul Verryn.'

Abu-Baker Asvat's demeanour changed. He knew Verryn well and regarded him as a friend. He did not believe what Winnie was telling him, but she insisted that Abu-Baker examine Katiza and issue a signed medical report confirming he had been homosexually raped.

The doctor asked when the rape had occurred. Yesterday, replied Winnie, although several days had passed since Katiza reported it to her.

Katiza said: 'The doctor told me to come with him [to his examination cubicle] and he asked how Paul raped me. I told him that before I went to sleep Paul gave me some tablets and when I woke up I found sperms [semen] around my anus. He made a cotton swab [anal smear sample].' Asvat also took a blood sample, checked Katiza's heart and pulse, and measured his height and weight. 'He called Winnie and asked why she hadn't come the same day [as the rape],' said Katiza. 'I can't remember what she said, but Dr Asvat said he had taken a cotton swab that would not tell anything because I had been to the toilet and washed since Paul raped me.'

Asvat told Winnie to return in two to three weeks for the results of lab test on the samples he had taken. Katiza then left the consulting room and sat in reception with Ma Sisulu and Falati while Winnie and Asvat had a private conversation. Katiza estimated they were talking for about five minutes before Winnie came out and Morgan drove her party home.

The medical card filled in by Dr Asvat that day clearly shows the date of the visit as 30 December 1988. The date was to become of critical relevance and importance as the Katiza Cebekhulu/Winnie Mandela/Stompie Moeketsi saga developed. On the card Katiza's name is entered in Ma Sisulu's writing and his address is given as the Methodist church, Orlando West. Next to the stamped date there is writing, identified by Ebrahim Asvat as Abu-Baker's, which says: 'Mentally confused, Occ. [occasionally] cries. Occ. hyst. [hysteria?] Insomnia.' Dr Asvat prescribed sleeping pills called lethyl, plus paracetamol and multi-vitamin tablets.

*

When Winnie and Katiza returned from Abu-Baker's surgery Stompie Moeketsi was subjected to another savage beating in the back room of 585 Diepkloof Extension.

Stompie had spent the night of 29/30 December on the floor of the back room, silent except for the occasional groan in the presence of the terrified Thabiso Mono, Pelo Mekgwe and Kenny Kgase. On the morning of Friday 30 December Jerry Richardson lectured Stompie, Thabiso, Pelo and Kenny on the rules of the house: they were to address Winnie as 'Mummy', they were not to attempt to escape, they were to act obediently and, as a reward for good behaviour, they might be sent into exile to train as ANC 'comrades'. Richardson took the others aside from Stompie and told them the small boy had done something very bad and it was likely he would have to be 'dumped'. All four were ordered to clean the room in which they had slept and the courtyard, with specific instructions to get rid of their own bloodstains from the walls inside the room, on the outside paving and on the jacuzzi. Stompie was made to wash all the bloodstained clothing.

Some time after sunset a tall, muscular man entered the back room where Stompie lay wounded. Gybon Gabela, an MUFC member, asked Stompie why he had sold out people who were fighting for a just cause. When Stompie physically could not answer, Gabela began kicking him against the wall. While kicking Stompie, Gabela said: 'I'm not going to use my hands. If I use my hands, I can kill you.' The more frustrated Gabela became with Stompie's inability to answer the more angry he became and the more he kicked the boy.

The state would later prepare a case against Gabela for assault against Stompie. But a few weeks after the assault Gabela fled South Africa for East Africa and returned home only seven years later in strange circumstances.

Thabiso Mono told me he felt he was living through a nightmare as he watched Gabela attack Stompie. 'Gybon was a very big and tough guy. He kept saying Stompie was an informer and that he couldn't live with informers. He kept kicking Stompie against the wall. He kicked him very heavily. Stompie was in a terrible state afterwards. The whole of the following day [Saturday 31 December] he was vomiting and he couldn't eat.'

Winnie was deeply worried, according to Katiza, when on the Saturday morning she saw Stompie's condition. A huge lump had developed on the side of his head, he was still unable to speak and every time he tried to eat he threw up and was forced by the MUFC to clean up his own vomit. 'Stompie was very sick, so she telephoned Dr Asvat to come and check him,' Katiza told me. 'It was lunch time when he came, some time between twelve and one. He examined Stompie with a stethoscope in the back room the MUFC slept in. He examined Stompie's head, ears and chest. Winnie was in the room. I was there too.

'Dr Asvat checked all the other boys. They were not so bad, so he rubbed ointment in their wounds and gave Richardson ointment to use for Pelo, Kenny and Thabiso later. Turning to Winnie, he said: "The boy is seriously ill. He could die at any moment. I cannot save him. You must take him to hospital." Then the doctor asked Winnie: "Who beat the boy like this?" I can't remember whether he got any answer, but he quickly decided to leave.'

That night, Stompie was killed.

'I can only say it was at night,' Katiza said. He could not remember whether it was on New Year's Eve or in the early hours of the first day of 1989.

'At some time in the evening Jerry Richardson told Stompie "Pack your things, you are going home." Stompie could move a bit.'

Katiza had gone to bed in the outside room behind a row of plants to the left of the jacuzzi. Later he woke up and went outside to go to the toilet behind the room. As he walked back to the room he saw something through the foliage which made him crouch low and freeze in that position: 'Richardson was carrying Stompie.' Winnie was with them.

Richardson laid Stompie down flat next to the jacuzzi. 'I heard Stompie screaming.'

Winnie had something pointed in her hand. 'I can't say whether it was a knife or a pair of scissors. I saw her lift her hand and stab Stompie twice. I can't say exactly where she hit him, whether it was the neck or chest or somewhere else. Then they held him in the swimming pool [the jacuzzi]. I believe Stompie died at that moment. He was already so badly injured it wasn't possible for him to survive that kind of stabbing.'

Katiza stepped back into his room. 'They hadn't seen me. I was so afraid. I lay down and covered my head with my blanket. I was trembling and I felt my hair standing up. I didn't sleep. After they killed I heard the car start up and go. It was a red Toyota hired from Richard Maponya (a businessman friend of the Mandelas) and I think the body was taken away in that.'

Katiza heard the car return about an hour later. Richardson came into the back room, switched the lights on as though checking everyone was asleep and put them off again before going out. 'I was pretending to be asleep, but opened my eyes slightly and saw little spots of blood on Richardson's shoes. When I got up in the morning Richardson's clothes were in the toilet with blood on them. The swimming pool was empty, but there were small splashes of blood around it and it looked as though someone had tried to clear them up.'

Kenny Kgase testified in a subsequent trial that he, Thabiso and Pelo were confined to their room [opposite Katiza's] all evening and throughout the night of 31 December 1988 after Stompie was taken away. They were unable to sleep. 'We never left the room. There was a lot of movement outside, but we didn't know what was going on.'

On the morning of 1 January 1989 Katiza was dumbfounded

when John Morgan came to him and said Winnie was distraught because Stompie Seipei Moeketsi had 'run away'. Little did Katiza know that years later Morgan would reveal that he had refused to drive the red Toyota that night with Stompie's body in the boot after Winnie had instructed him to 'dump the dog'. In his confession Morgan told a newspaper reporter he knew Stompie was dead 'because he had already been stabbed and had blood on his neck'.

But a lot was to happen before Morgan confessed.

Katiza woke up on 1 January 1989 living a nightmare after witnessing three days of actions by the Mother of the Nation that the rest of the world would find impossible to believe. The nightmare was over for Stompie, but for Katiza, Winnie Mandela, Abu-Baker Asvat and Paul Verryn it was really only just beginning.

CHAPTER SIX

Andrew Ikaneng Survives

3–16 JANUARY 1989

Winnie Mandela, far from being racked by remorse for what she and her Football Club had done to Stompie Moeketsi and the other three boys, according to Katiza Cebekhulu quickly ordered her team to kill again.

As he had been with the Lolo Sono and Stompie killings, Katiza was a close observer of the raiding party which set out from Winnie's Diepkloof home to murder Andrew Lerotodi Ikaneng on 3 January 1989 – just three days after Stompie died.

Ikaneng had been a founding member of the Mandela United Football Club in 1986. He was then aged nineteen. Winnie had invited two rival groups of youngsters from the Soweto Youth Congress, a pro-ANC organization, to her small Orlando West home. She said they were all comrades in the struggle and they should stop fighting each other. A friend of Ikaneng's suggested they form a football club as a gesture of reconciliation. Winnie agreed to buy the kit, Ikaneng and some other boys moved into her house, and so the MUFC was born.

The Club got off to an unhappy start. On 27 January 1987 Ikaneng and all the MUFC members staying with Winnie were arrested in connection with two drunken killings carried out by Oupa Alex Seheri, an Umkhonto we Sizwe guerrilla who had been staying in Winnie's house. Ikaneng spent most of 1987 in detention, but was eventually released without charge (Seheri was tried and sentenced to death). In the course of the following year, however, he and his friend Tholi Dlamini had become so sickened by the Football Club's harsh rules and its growing arrogance and violence that they decided to quit.

Tholi was particularly distressed by what had happened to his twenty-three-year-old sister Phumlile, who was pregnant and in trouble with Winnie for having an affair with a man who, according to Phumlile, was also one of Mrs Mandela's sex partners. Winnie summoned Phumlile and beat her before handing her over to MUFC members, allegedly saying: 'Well, boys, see what you can do with her.' Phumlile told the *Sunday Times* of London: 'They punched me and kicked me and one said: "Sorry, lady, maybe you will make your delivery here. This is the hospital."'

Ikaneng and Tholi began breaking MUFC rules repeatedly, exposing themselves to serious accusations of being 'sell-outs' and 'informers'. They eventually defected after Winnie's Orlando West house was burned to the ground in July 1988 by the Daliwonga High School students. Both returned to live with their parents and Tholi began devoting himself enthusiastically to his old hobby of ballroom dancing.

'Winnie said we should look for Andrew,' Katiza Cebekhulu told me. 'So I went with some others and brought him to Winnie [at her Diepkloof house].' Ikaneng was confronted on arrival by a special disciplinary committee meeting attended by Winnie, Katiza, Zindzi Mandela, Jerry Richardson and about twenty other MUFC members, including Sizwe Sithole, Zindzi's boyfriend. Sithole had been appointed co-chairman with Richardson of the disciplinary committee.

Winnie demanded to know why Ikaneng had left and Zindzi accused him of being an informer. No immediate action was taken against him, but he was told that unless he returned he would be branded a police informer.

Ikaneng had no desire to go back. He defied Winnie's order and continued to stay with his parents.

Terrible revenge followed a few weeks later.

Tholi, after quitting the MUFC, had been detained by the police and had given evidence against a Football Club member. Free again, he and Ikaneng were on their way to an all-night funeral vigil in Soweto. Outside a shebeen Sizwe Sithole confronted them. Sithole was drunk and as he staggered around his coat flapped open, revealing an AK-47 strapped inside. He then removed the automatic rifle, fired a shot in the air and took aim at Ikaneng. Meanwhile, Tholi had fled. Sithole switched attention from Ikaneng and gave chase down an alley. Ikaneng heard two shots, ran in their direction and found Tholi lying shot dead in the road. According to one account, the top of Tholi's head had been blown off.

Ikaneng, distraught over the grisly murder of his friend, phoned Winnie the next day. She pre-empted him by asking whether it was true that Tholi had been shot dead. So she already knew, but Ikaneng confirmed it and said he and others wanted to talk to her about it.

Winnie sent a car to collect Ikaneng, Mrs Dudu Chili, a leading underground ANC women's activist, and another youth who had all been in the shebeen when Sizwe Sithole launched his attack. On their arrival at the Diepkloof house, Winnie called the MUFC together to hear Ikaneng demand an explanation of why Sithole had killed Tholi. There was no choice, replied Winnie, because Tholi had given evidence to the police while in detention. She then told Ikaneng he would have to go into hiding in a place arranged by the MUFC because it was possible the police would seek to question him about Tholi's murder. Ikaneng made no reply and was told by Winnie to go away and 'think better'.

Ikaneng did not sleep at home that night, but returned to his parents' house the following day to find the police had been seeking him for evidence concerning Tholi's death. He decided to go to Protea police station and make a full statement. Ten days or more passed before Ikaneng was approached – in October 1988, the southern African spring – at Orlando West swimming pool by Shoes, a Football Club member. Shoes said Winnie had sent him with an order for Ikaneng to report immediately at her nearby Community House office. On arrival he found himself facing Winnie, Katiza Cebekhulu, Zindzi Mandela, Jerry Richardson and other Football Club members.

Winnie told Ikaneng she had heard what he had told the police at Protea about Sizwe. She did not explain how it was possible she had heard it from the police, but she pulled Ikaneng from his chair by his shirt and began slapping and punching him. Katiza Cebekhulu described to me what followed. 'She shouted at Andrew and told the others to take him away,' said Katiza. 'Whenever she said "Take him away" it meant "Kill him."'

Shoes and another MUFC member took Ikaneng outside to a waiting vehicle. But Ikaneng, nicknamed 'Springbok' for his speedy running, slipped out of their grasp and escaped while they were opening the door of the motor. He ran home and while he was there a beige Mazda car pulled up outside containing Shoes and other MUFC members. Ikaneng left through the back door, jumped over the back fence and sprinted through the streets of Soweto to a railway station. He left for Sharpeville, fifty miles to the south, and returned home only three months later.

*

When Ikaneng returned to Soweto on 3 January 1989, three days after Stompie Moeketsi was murdered, Winnie's MUFC soon heard he was back in the township.

'Winnie told Richardson to find Andrew Ikaneng and "Take him away,"' said Katiza. 'There were many of us [in the attack party].' It included the three surviving boys kidnapped from Paul Verryn's manse – Kenny Kgase, Pelo Mekgwe and Thabiso Mono. The previous day the MUFC had begun talking to the terrified trio. 'They referred to us as comrades,' said Kenny Kgase. 'They told us that the past was forgotten . . . He [Jerry] said to us we are not supposed to hear anybody asking questions about what happened to Stompie.'

On 3 January Richardson came into the back room where Kgase, Mekgwe and Mono were being held under close guard and gave them training shoes. They were about to take part in a ritual murder as their initiation into the MUFC. Richardson told them they were going to do a 'duty' as soon as he had collected some money from Zindzi Mandela.

They found Ikaneng on his way home in the evening with a girlfriend. Richardson said he needed to talk to him and they all went into a shebeen together. After a short conversation Richardson took Ikaneng by the arm and hustled him outside. Ikaneng tried to run away but was caught and frog-marched by the MUFC through the Soweto suburb of Mzimlophe, across the Soweto–Johannesburg Highway on to some open veld, scarcely half a mile from where Stompie Moeketsi's then as yet undiscovered body lay rotting near New Canada Road.

Kenny Kgase later described, at a subsequent trial, an odd encounter with the police as the lynch mob moved towards the killing ground. 'The police came, the van of the policemen came, the curiosity was over us and the driver sort of, I don't know what kind of light, he made a flicker and then he continued with his journey, and Jerry said: "Look, the system has got nothing to do with us."'

As the mob moved on to the killing ground one of the MUFC minibuses drew up near by and a pair of garden shears was taken from it. Katiza told me: 'I stayed in the bus. I believe Winnie deliberately sent Kenny, Pelo and Thabiso [to take part] so they could not ever say they were kidnapped. It was always obvious that if they took someone in the bush he was going to be killed. Ikaneng was given what we called "total discipline". I thought he was dead.'

That was the intent.

Richardson ordered the three kidnapped boys to pin Ikaneng to the ground. A Football Club member called Slash wrenched apart the blades of the shears and handed one of them to Richardson who sliced across Ikaneng's throat. The MUFC coach took the second blade and stabbed Ikaneng several times as he moaned and gurgled. Richardson ordered the group to throw the apparently lifeless body into tall reeds lining a stream. Then everyone returned home to Winnie's house.

*

When Kenny Kgase, overcome by horror, returned to the back room at Winnie's, he told Pelo Mekgwe and Thabiso Mono: 'I'm a murderer from today.'

Andrew Ikaneng lay bloodied among the reeds after the barbarous assault upon him. There was a gaping wound on his throat, which had been slit from ear to ear. But he was not dead: the garden shears wielded by Richardson has somehow missed the jugular artery.

Ikaneng came round from brief unconsciousness and managed to stumble back across the Soweto Highway and bang on the front door of a house before collapsing outside. An ambulance was summoned and he was taken after midnight to Soweto's Baragwanath Hospital for emergency surgery on the massive wounds to his larynx. It would be almost a fortnight before the stitches were removed and Ikaneng ended an enforced silence.

At Winnie's on 4 January Richardson issued Kgase, Mekgwe and Mono with green and gold MUFC tracksuits. He said they would be attending a funeral that day with Winnie and other MUFC members. He warned them not to try to run away. If one should escape, he said, the consequences for those who remained would be grave. The funeral was for Sipho Mabuse, a musician whose son, 'Hot Stix', had become one of the country's leading pop artists.

Katiza Cebekhulu also attended the funeral. He told me the three kidnapped youths were instructed by Richardson to join other Football Club members forming a guard of honour with fists raised in the clenched ANC salute around the coffin as it was carried to the grave and lowered into the ground. Katiza said it was evident that Winnie wanted, in case it became necessary, to demonstrate to the public that Kgase, Mono and Mekgwe were willing participants in MUFC activities and that it was therefore impossible they could have been kidnapped. 'She wanted to give the impression that, if she had kidnapped them, then the boys would have found this as a chance to escape. But they hadn't, so they were obviously MUFC members by choice.'

Kenny Kgase was, however, planning to bolt. But too many MUFC eyes were watching him at the Mabuse funeral. A short, fat woman preparing food sympathized with the state of his eye, bruised six days earlier in the beatings after the kidnappings, and recommended he get it treated. 'She was behaving like a proper mother,' said Kgase. 'But she could never have guessed that the Mother of the Nation had done this.'

Kgase told Mono of his intention to run. Mono warned him he must be certain he could get away: if he was caught the MUFC would not give him a second chance. Kgase saw his opportunity to escape when he, Mekgwe and Mono were put on guard duty in the grounds of Winnie's house, patrolling at night in two-hour shifts with one other MUFC member. Just before dawn on Saturday 7 January 1989 Kgase walked around the back corner of the house and realized he was completely out of sight of his fellow guard. He removed his shoes, leaped over the wall and ran. He hailed a minibus taxi travelling towards central Johannesburg and at about 6.30 in the morning he knocked on the door of the Methodist Church headquarters. Kgase was let in by a pastor, David Ching, who contacted Paul Verryn, in Pretoria on the final day of his leave. Verryn arrived at the Methodist HQ by 10am to find Kgase there with a bruised eye and scarred back.

The first question Kgase asked Verryn was: 'Where is Stompie?' He had last seen Stompie before he was taken away by Richardson on New Year's Eve and, like Katiza, had seen Richardson's blood-flecked shoes the next day. Verryn, who had been told by a member of his congregation that Stompie was back in the community, repeated that story to Kgase, who said: 'There's no way that Stompie can be back in the community.' He said he was convinced Stompie was dead because of the terrible state he had been in, mumbling almost incoherently fragments of the ANC's Freedom Charter, before he disappeared from Winnie's house.

Kgase was hyper-alert and deeply agitated with fear. He kept repeating that he had learned to kill. Verryn, who did not at first understand what the youth was talking about, contacted friends who took him to see a doctor, Martin Connell, in the trendy liberal white suburb of Melville. Connell examined Kgase. His face, hip, left shoulder, chest, right arm and back were covered in scars and heavy bruises, one six inches long. The youth's emotional state reminded the doctor of South African soldiers he had counselled who had come under heavy mortar fire. Connell said Kgase was very frightened, especially about what might happen to Mono and Mekgwe. Connell hid Kgase at his home for several weeks. Explaining his role later in the attempted murder of Ikaneng, Kgase said: 'It was very scary. You couldn't resist.'

Meanwhile, on Friday 6 January 1989, a Soweto woman had stumbled across a small maggot-infested body in the veld near New Canada Road. It was taken to Diepkloof mortuary. No one claimed it, and since the police took no interest either it was deep frozen. Another six weeks would pass before the corpse was identified as that of Stompie Seipei Moeketsi.

Mrs Winnie Mandela was never questioned by police on her role in, or knowledge of, events leading to the attempted murder of Andrew Ikaneng. But Katiza insisted, in his conversations with me, that Richardson attacked only when ordered by Winnie.

*

The Methodist Church, whose head, Bishop Peter Storey, and other leaders were sympathetic to the democracy movement, was now in a difficult position. If Kenny Kgase was right – and the Church believed him totally – the wife of Nelson Mandela had kidnapped four youths from a Methodist refuge, participated in beating them and the youngest, Stompie, seemed to have died as a consequence of the assault.

Winnie was no longer a 'problem' but a full-blown crisis.

In a normal society Bishop Storey would have approached the police immediately. But South Africa was still an unreformed apartheid culture in the grip of a state of emergency imposed three years earlier by P. W. Botha, the melancholic and authoritarian State President.

The South African Police was heavily involved in enforcing the emergency with wide powers at its disposal, including detention without trial and assassination of government opponents by covert death squads. With the best will in the world, the police could rarely be trusted – especially with ruinous allegations against the wife of the world's most famous prisoner, Nelson Mandela, whose twenty-six years of incarceration meant it was impossible to separate the man from the myth. Winnie had become a moral and political surrogate for her husband. A huge, worldwide personality cult had grown around her, until she probably felt as invincible as Napoleon Bonaparte felt in 1807 just before leading his armies across the Niemen River into Russia – and ruination.

Storey sought therefore to work through the Mandela Crisis Committee and the multi-racial South African Council of Churches. The Crisis Committee had been established secretly, with the imprisoned Nelson Mandela's approval, within days of the burning down in July 1988 of Winnie's Orlando West home by the Daliwonga High School students. Ostensibly, the Committee's role was to help Winnie rebuild her house: its true agenda was to limit the damage Winnie and her Football Club were inflicting on the ANC and to try to guide her away from the ripening scandal surrounding her lifestyle.

The Crisis Committee comprised prominent individuals in the UDF/ANC liberation movement. It included the Reverend Frank Chikane, Secretary-General of the South African Council of Churches and a close friend of Winnie Mandela; Cyril Ramaphosa, the dynamic leader of the National Union of Mineworkers, a strong critic of Winnie seen by many as the eventual successor to Nelson Mandela at the head of the ANC; Sidney Mufamadi, the communist leader of the ANC-aligned Congress of South African Trade Unions; Sister Bernard Ncube, a Roman Catholic nun and ANC radical who was one of the leaders of the ANC-inspired Federation of South African Women; the Reverend Beyers Naude, a brave Afrikaner Dutch Reformed Church minister who, after condemning as religious heresy his people's embrace of apartheid, had joined the illegal ANC and been declared a banned person; and Aubrey Mokoena of the Release Mandela Committee, who had worked intimately with Winnie to raise funds to sustain the international campaign for Nelson's freedom.

Mokoena, in fact, had become so close to Winnie that rumours pervaded the township that he was one of her lovers. Several people involved in the campaign to release the captives suspected he was playing a double game – professing profound concern for the captives while reporting to Winnie what was going on elsewhere. Mistrust within the Crisis Committee caused vacillation and feebleness. Mokoena was the first Committee member to visit Winnie's home, as early as 4

January 1989, before Kenny Kgase escaped and began to tell his story. Mokoena reported back to the Committee then that Winnie denied any of the young men were in her home.

On Wednesday 11 January Chikane, Mokoena, Ncube and Mufamadi went to Winnie's house and asked to see Stompie Moeketsi, Thabiso Mono, Pelo Mekgwe and also Katiza Cebekhulu, who, at that time, they assumed had been kidnapped with the others from Verryn's manse. Winnie now admitted the youths were with her, but she declined to let the Committee talk to them.

Mokoena, Ncube, Mufamadi and Naude returned on 13 January to be greeted by Zindzi with the information that one boy, Stompie, had 'escaped'. Winnie then put out a statement appealing for Stompie to 'come forward'. This alarmed them, although they then had no way of knowing that Stompie's body had been lying frozen and unidentified in Diepkloof morgue for the past five days. Finally they were allowed to speak to Thabiso, Pelo and Katiza, who were led into Winnie's living room.

Katiza said he was there when the Crisis Committee filed in. He told me he was spoken to only by Ncube and an 'old white man', Naude. 'Richardson warned us not to tell about the beatings,' said Katiza. 'I told them I'd left Paul's because he raped me. So did Mono and Mekgwe. A newspaper later said I told Sister Bernard I had worked with the local branch of the security police in Hammarsdale. She never asked me about working with the police. The first I knew of it was when I read it in a paper much later.'

Thabiso and Pelo – whose injuries from their beatings a fortnight earlier were still obvious – and Katiza each told the Crisis Committee they were staying with Winnie of their own free will, having sought protection from Paul Verryn's sexual advances. But one of the three, never identified, broke down when momentarily alone with the Committee and admitted they were captives and had been instructed to lie about Verryn. 'I am going to die anyway, so I may as well tell the truth,' he said. It seems to me now that the individual was probably Katiza because, in a later report, the Committee named him as having told them Stompie was 'probably' dead: he was the only one of the trio in possession of such knowledge, and he would not have dared say that in front of Winnie or any members of the Football Club. The Committee left, keeping the admission to themselves and now realizing the gravity of the affair.

The moral feebleness of the Crisis Committee members reached a new low. They could have obtained a court interdict against Winnie forcing her to release the captives. They had seen the captives' wounds; they knew Kenny Kgase's story via the Methodist Church; they suspected Stompie was already dead; and another captive had told them he feared he would die. But not one of them was prepared to testify against Winnie. They were more concerned about how the 'Winnie problem' would look to the outside world than with the actual fate of the captives.

They decided to call a meeting of members of the Soweto community in an attempt to put pressure on Mrs Mandela, while a lawyer travelled to Lusaka to brief Oliver Tambo, the exiled President of the ANC, on developments in the Winnie saga. The ailing Tambo covered his face in his hands after the lawyer's briefing and groaned: 'What must I do? We can't control her. The ANC can't control her. We tried to control her, that's why we formed the Crisis Committee. You must tell the Crisis Committee they must do more.'

By Saturday 14 January 1989 Nelson's personal lawyer,

Ismail Ayob, who also acted for Winnie, regarded the situation as so serious that he flew 1,000 miles to the Cape for an emergency meeting with Mandela in Victor Verster Prison at Paarl. Ayob returned to Johannesburg late that night with instructions from Mandela to obtain the immediate release from Winnie's house of Stompie Moeketsi, Pelo Mekgwe, Thabiso Mono and Katiza Cebekhulu. Ayob asked the Methodist Church to prepare accommodation for the youths, but when he contacted Winnie she refused to let them go.

On Sunday 15 January Bishop Storey was informed by a source he trusted implicitly that Verryn's life was in extreme danger. He instructed the minister to move out of Soweto. Late that night Richardson and Xoliswa Falati finally emerged from Winnie's house with Katiza, Thabiso and Pelo. They took the trio to Ayob's office in central Johannesburg. Richardson said there were conditions for the release. The lawyer told them Nelson Mandela said it had to be unconditional. Richardson and Falati, following Winnie's instructions, declined to release the youths and took them back to their mistress's Diepkloof home.

Ismail Ayob, wearied and repulsed by Winnie's behaviour and its implications, resigned overnight as her lawyer – although he continued to act for Nelson. The final straw for Ayob had come when Winnie told him: 'I don't take my instructions from Mandela, I take them from Chris.' Chris Hani was the charismatic South African Communist Party chief of staff of Umkhonto we Sizwe with whom Winnie maintained a close friendship until Hani's assassination in April 1992 by white right-wingers. Krish Naidoo, a radical young Indian lawyer with ties to the ANC, replaced Ayob despite advice from the Crisis Committee not to sip from the poisoned chalice.

On the afternoon of Monday 16 January, after numerous submissions to Winnie, Richardson finally took Katiza, Thabiso and Pelo to Naidoo's offices for release and met Bishop Storey. Richardson said the trio wished to lay allegations of sexual abuse against Verryn. Storey agreed to listen, but said he also had questions he wanted to ask. The community meeting in Soweto to discuss the Winnie Mandela controversy was scheduled for that same evening. Storey asked to take the youths with him to the rendezvous. Mono and Mekgwe agreed to go with the Bishop, but asked to be taken to Verryn's manse first to collect some clean clothes.

*

Katiza declined to go to the Soweto meeting, which was cloaked in extraordinary secrecy. 'I was confused and afraid because I would be defending Winnie,' he told me. 'I knew they would ask a lot of questions and I was worried about answering them – because at that stage the police were still analysing the situation and no one had been arrested. I knew also that Paul was going to be there [although Verryn was now sleeping outside Soweto] and I would have to say he raped me. Krish Naidoo and I went back to Winnie's. I told her I didn't want to go to the meeting. But she made me go, although she said she was not coming.'

Some 150 people from every community organization in Soweto gathered at the Catholic church hall in Dobsonville, a suburb chosen for security reasons at the opposite end of the sprawling township from Winnie's Diepkloof home. After a prayer, Sello Dindwe, a youth living at Verryn's manse, began the meeting at about 6.30 by reading out a statement prepared by several fellow residents describing the raid by the Football

Club on 29 December and the forced abductions of Stompie, Kenny Kgase, Pelo Mekgwe and Thabiso Mono. Dindwe said the MUFC carried guns and he himself had been assaulted. There had been a debate among the raiders whether he should be kidnapped with the others, but he was eventually declared 'politically reliable' and allowed to remain at the manse.

Besides Verryn, others in the audience included Bishop Storey, Sister Bernard Ncube, the Reverend Beyers Naude and Frank Chikane. Mono and Mekgwe next told the meeting how they had been kidnapped by Football Club members, including Katiza, taken to Winnie's house and beaten there by her and her boys.

Then Katiza arrived with Krish Naidoo. 'Winnie sent six MUFC bodyguards carrying AK-47s with us,' said Katiza. 'People were angry with Naidoo for bringing the football team.' Not only were they angry – mainly as a result of what they had been hearing – they were terrified that more Mandela United heavies might be on the way to break up the meeting. People at that stage were unable to grasp fully what was going on, only that a nightmare was in the making.

When Katiza addressed the meeting he stuck to his story that Paul Verryn had sexually assaulted him. But he also described how Winnie had beaten Stompie – 'I said she used a sjambok and then people were asking how Stompie looked.' Katiza said the boy had been beaten to a point where he could not see and one side of his head was soft.

When someone asked outright whether Stompie was dead, Katiza replied: 'Yes.'

Looking back and reflecting on that simple statement, Katiza said: 'But why didn't they go deep and ask me who had killed him? That was what was important. Perhaps they were afraid of the truth?' I checked Katiza's statement about whether he had said Stompie was dead against Bishop Storey's unpublished Methodist Church report on the Stompie affair. It was as Katiza had described his answer to me. I asked the Bishop why no one had asked who killed Stompie. He replied enigmatically: 'Because I think everyone there knew.' I asked the same question of Paul Verryn, and he said: 'Katiza was brought there, as we understood it, by one of Mrs Mandela's people. To have asked him that question would have put him in the most invidious, not to say dangerous, position.' Today Katiza justifies his lie about Verryn raping him on the grounds that he was totally vulnerable, unprotected, frightened and mentally and emotionally confused by the sheer dreadfulness of the web in which Winnie Mandela had entangled him.

The meeting turned its attention to Paul Verryn. Katiza had stood by his false allegation against Verryn. The Crisis Committee announced that Thabiso Mono had made a similar allegation when they met him at Winnie's house. Mono was now asked if he upheld what he had said. He rose and said: 'I withdraw it unconditionally. I was forced to say it.' I later met Mono, who told me: 'You have to remember we had to say these things against Paul in order to survive. Winnie had told us we were not fit to be alive before she beat us.'

Storey addressed the meeting and invited anyone to speak who had fresh evidence against Verryn. The allegations were very serious and, if true, the Methodist Church was not prepared to have one of its ministers behaving in such a way. A youth who had lived at the manse for two years rose and said that because of overcrowding everyone there slept in close proximity, but Verryn had never abused them. Others followed, some affirming Verryn's honourable conduct and some protesting that the popular minister had ever been put in the invidious position of having to defend himself against such serious allegations.

Verryn himself spoke, saying beds were shared because of the overcrowding. But in the case of Stompie the reality was that he had never even slept in the same room as him.

Kenneth Kgase spoke and then towards midnight Andrew Ikaneng entered. His stitches had just been removed in hospital and the appalling scars across his throat were still raw and livid. Shudders of consternation went through the hall at the sight of him as he began telling his story.

The mass meeting resolved that Winnie Mandela was no longer worthy of her husband's name. She should be called by her maiden name, Winnie Madikizela. Likewise, the 'Mandela United Football Club' should be called the 'Winnie Football Club', distancing the Mandela name and the liberation movement from the team's activities. The meeting resolved to stage an immediate protest march on Winnie's Diepkloof house, but was dissuaded by the chairman.

It should all have been enough to inhibit Winnie Mandela and the Mandela United Football Club from further adventures. But ten days later she instructed Krish Naidoo to lay a formal charge with the police against Paul Verryn of homosexually raping Katiza Cebekhulu. She then asked her friend Dr Abu-Baker Asvat to verify the rape with a medical certificate – with ugly and infamous consequences.

CHAPTER SEVEN

Death at the Surgery

26–30 JANUARY 1989

It perhaps said something for the veneration in which Nelson Mandela was held that it took so long for the scandal and rumour enfolding his wife and her Football Club to surface in the public arena. It probably said more about the fear Winnie inspired.

In the weeks following the disappearance of Stompie Moeketsi and the other youths from Paul Verryn's manse their abduction was an open secret in Soweto, though Stompie's fate was unknown. By the time the community meeting took place on 16 January several Johannesburg newspapers knew fragments of the story, but did not publish them. It was not until 27 January – thirty days after the kidnappings, and twenty-eight days after the murder of Stompie – that the first tentative newspaper reports about the kidnappings appeared. The UDF/ANC's failure to find Stompie made it impossible for the liberation movement to suppress completely the story involving the leader's wife.

The story broke simultaneously in Johannesburg in the *Weekly Mail* and in London in the *Guardian*. 'Soweto anger at Winnie "team"', said the *Weekly Mail*'s front-page headline. The *Guardian* proclaimed, 'Row over "mother of the nation"

Winnie Mandela' above a story by its South Africa correspondent, David Beresford. Both accounts referred to the community meeting eleven days earlier; the abduction of youths from the Orlando West Methodist Church manse; the escape of one of the youths (Kenny Kgase); the release of two others (Pelo Mekgwe and Thabiso Mono); and explanations by Winnie and Zindzi Mandela and other members of the Football Club that Stompie Moeketsi had 'run away'.

With the great advantage of hindsight, the two newspaper accounts now look remarkably thin. The *Guardian*, for example, did not name Kgase, Mekgwe or Mono. Katiza's name did not feature either, though Beresford got much nearer to one of the central truths than any journalist would for many years to come. After relating an abduction of youths by the 'so-called Nelson Mandela Football Club . . . from a Methodist place of refuge in church grounds near Mrs Mandela's humble home in Orlando West', Beresford went on:

> According to Mrs Mandela, the boys were taken from the home after complaints had been received that a minister had been involved in sexual molestation of inmates. The allegations, which are believed to have come from a boy who has a record of making such claims, appear to be groundless. Boys in the home have been closely questioned about the allegations by community leaders and have denied them.

Beresford also said the unthinkable when he suggested that Winnie Mandela was less of a heroine than she had been portrayed over the years by the ANC and the international media. 'Her association with the Mandela Football Club has created particular exasperation among her advisers and in the ANC,' he wrote. 'The youths have developed a thuggish reputation.'

Meagre though the *Weekly Mail* and *Guardian* stories were, the courage of the journalists involved and the importance of their stories can hardly be overstated. These were papers and writers committed to the anti-apartheid cause who risked not only losing the ANC's goodwill but being sucked into a possible trap set by one of the South African state's many dirty-tricks departments in a bid to discredit the ANC.

The accounts meant the Stompie scandal had broken. They triggered a series of reactions.

*

David Beresford faxed a copy of his story to Winnie's lawyer, Krish Naidoo, on Thursday 26 January 1989 – the eve of publication – for comment. He received no response, but the impending publication of the story seems to have propelled Winnie into fresh action. Late that same evening she ordered Katiza to accompany Krish Naidoo to Orlando police station to make a statement alleging he had been raped by Paul Verryn. 'The duty police took it like a joke,' Katiza told me. 'They just laughed. They said: "Bring a letter and certificate from your doctor saying you've been raped. Then we can arrest the person who raped you."'

The police opened a docket and Katiza gave his address as Verryn's Orlando West Methodist Church before returning to Winnie's house with Naidoo to report what needed to be done if charges were to be laid against Verryn. The police may not have taken the complaint seriously, but at least they were now involved and Winnie Mandela had established on official record a bona-fide motive for taking Stompie and the other youths from Verryn's manse. It would eventually have a crucial impact as the Winnie Mandela–Stompie Moeketsi drama reached one of its many climaxes.

*

That same evening – Thursday 26 January 1989 – Abu-Baker Asvat was visited by a new patient at his Soweto surgery. Jerry Richardson, leader of the MUFC whom Katiza had seen pinning Stompie down next to Winnie's jacuzzi on New Year's Eve, complained that his anus was sore. Abu-Baker examined Richardson, but the medical card opened by the doctor for his new patient shows he was unable to find anything significantly wrong. In the diagnosis column he wrote, 'Peri-anal abscess' and put a question mark beside it. Above it he scribbled in contrasting red ink and big letters an unusual and medically irrelevant comment: 'Sent by Winnie.' It was almost as though he was leaving a clue in case something drastic happened to him.

Albertina Sisulu had already gone home. If she had been there she would have put a neat date stamp, as was her practice, on Richardson's card instead of the scrawled date inserted by her employer.

No one knows exactly what words were exchanged between Abu-Baker Asvat and Jerry Richardson at the surgery that evening. However, Abu-Baker Asvat's wife, Zhora, was struck by the terrified state in which he arrived home later that night.

After closing his surgery he drove into central Johannesburg for a Crescents Cricket Club meeting. When he arrived home at about 9.30pm he told Zhora he had driven seven miles with a puncture. When he realized his tyre was flat, he had stopped to examine it. He told Zhora he thought it was a set-up and was so frightened that something was going to happen to him on the road that he drove all the way on the flat tyre, and when he reached home both the tyre and the wheel rim were write-offs.

'I thought they were going to get me tonight,' he said. He did not tell Zhora who or what was unnerving him so much. One family member thought it was probably the security police. Zhora was less certain. Something had been troubling Abu-Baker for some time, but she could not persuade him to confide in her. He was unrelaxed and had lengthened his morning prayers, but was not saying them in the prescribed manner. Halfway through January Abu-Baker handed his wife a thick bundle of banknotes, something he had never done before in their many years of marriage: Zhora was to keep the notes in case 'something happened'. When she protested that she did not need the money, he insisted that she keep it – 'just in case'.

A member of the Mandela Crisis Committee was later to tell the Asvat family that Abu-Baker had contacted Frank Chikane and other members of the Committee shortly after his visit to Winnie's house on 31 December to tell them he had seen Stompie and that the boy was so badly wounded he would probably die. In mid-January the Crisis Committee paid a secret visit to Abu-Baker's surgery, probably after the 16 January meeting at which Katiza said Stompie was dead. The Asvat family learned later that Abu-Baker had told the Committee he was considering giving a statement to the police about what he had seen on 31 December.

Abu-Baker was still distraught the next morning, Friday 27 January, after his puncture scare. He received a call from Priscilla Jana, the lawyer who represented Stompie and had let him play in her house and office; she was a partner in Ismail Ayob's law firm, which had represented Winnie as late as 16 January and continued to represent Nelson. Furthermore, Abu-Baker was Jana's physician.

Abu-Baker left Jana's house in great distress. The Asvat

family assert that Jana later told them she would reveal many things Abu-Baker confided to her which would explain the terrible events which were about to follow. But Jana retreated – like so many who became entangled in Winnie's web – into the South African equivalent of the Italian family-solidarity code of *omertà* (silence). She later became an ANC MP.

But in June 1997 Priscilla's former husband, Reggie Jana, a successful businessman who had been a close friend of Abu-Baker since childhood, broke the *omertà* code. Reggie told me that on 30 December 1988 Abu-Baker had visited him at home. 'He looked very disturbed, a worried man. He asked for a drink,' said Reggie. Winnie Mandela had phoned him and he had agreed to let her send four youths from her Diepkloof house to his surgery for medical attention. He was shocked by the state of the four, who included Stompie Moeketsi. 'Abu-Baker said that, according to Stompie, Winnie wanted the four of them to make a statement to the effect that Father Verryn had sexually abused the four, and in fact nothing of that nature occurred.

'Abu-Baker could not [at first] understand how such third-degree body injuries could be inflicted on four young boys. [But then] Stompie said, "That fucking bitch and the henchmen, they beat me to this pulp." He [Abu-Baker] could not believe that Winnie had also had a hand in the assaults.'

Abu-Baker telephoned Winnie and told her the boys needed to be hospitalized. But the next day, 31 December, Winnie telephoned him to ask him to come to her house to conduct a fresh examination of Stompie and the other youths. He met Reggie Jana again afterwards and said he was shocked because their condition had deteriorated badly since the previous day. He had told Winnie they needed to be taken to hospital or 'Well, that's the last of them.'

Reggie remarked: 'Abu-Baker thereafter was not the same person I had known . . . He was never afraid of anyone, but after the events of Stompie he was a changed person. The man had fear in him.' Reggie said Abu-Baker came under increasing pressure from Winnie to say nothing about examining Stompie and the other boys. Reggie told me Abu-Baker said to him one evening: 'This effing bitch is giving me grief, causing problems and I fear for my life.'

From Priscilla Jana's home on the morning of 27 January, Abu-Baker Asvat went to the Lenasia office of his lawyer and close friend Yunus Mayet, who had been urging the doctor to make a will. Staff at Mayet's office said Abu-Baker was agitated and in obvious distress as he paced around waiting to see Mayet. Ebrahim Asvat said his brother met for about forty-five minutes with Mayet and gave the lawyer vital information which would explain later horrific events. Mayet promised to pass on the information to the Asvat family, but in due course he too retreated into silence.

Abu-Baker's movements during the next two hours cannot be precisely traced, but the Asvat family has been told he visited Winnie Mandela at her Diepkloof Extension home. What transpired there is unknown, but by the time he arrived home late for the family's weekly Friday Moslem prayers he was so distracted that he failed to follow the set rituals – for example, he stood instead of kneeling.

At 2.30pm he left for Soweto to conduct an afternoon surgery.

*

At lunchtime that same day Ebrahim Asvat sat in his Lenasia surgery reading the *Weekly Mail*'s front-page story about

Winnie's Football Club and the community meeting. 'It was the first time the story had gone public, so I read it twice,' he told me. 'Something about it worried me.'

With good reason. His brother, Abu-Baker, was only four hours away from death.

*

One of the first patients Abu-Baker saw after arriving at his surgery was Jerry Richardson, who had returned for a penicillin injection to treat his dubious anal ulcer. Immediately after seeing Richardson, at about 3pm, Abu-Baker telephoned Winnie, according to evidence given by Xoliswa Falati as a witness in a trial the following year.

It is not known what was discussed on the phone by Abu-Baker and Winnie, but soon afterwards she left her house with Katiza Cebekhulu and drove to the doctor's surgery. According to Katiza, Winnie took him with her to secure from Asvat the doctor's certificate the police needed to lay charges of homosexual rape against Paul Verryn. Katiza sat in the reception area with Ma Sisulu while Winnie was admitted to Abu-Baker's consulting room. There was a volcanic row. 'I heard Winnie shout, "If you don't co-operate I'll deal with you!"' Katiza told me. 'She definitely threatened the doctor, but I couldn't hear everything because I was in reception.'

Katiza and Winnie left Abu-Baker's surgery without the medical certificate for the police.

*

According to Katiza, in extended conversations with me more than six years after the events of January 1989, Winnie had asked him that same month to show two unemployed Zulu

96

youths where Dr Abu-Baker Asvat worked. After such a long period of time most people's memory would fail them on details. But Katiza gave me two versions which differed in important respects.

The first, early in our conversations, had the two youths arriving in a car at Winnie's house late in the afternoon on the day Abu-Baker died. 'Winnie told me to take them to show them Dr Asvat's house,' said Katiza. 'I showed them the house and I remained in the car until they came back. We returned home [to Winnie's], but they didn't come in. Winnie received a call around 7pm and she told everyone in the house Dr Asvat was dead. So many people [in Winnie's house] were crying.'

But in our later discussions Katiza said he had thought about the events of January 1989 and he believed his memory was wrong when he gave me his first version of the visit by the Zulu youths. He now said the youths had driven up to Winnie's house a few days before 27 January. 'They were already in the house when I came in,' he said. 'Winnie turned to me and asked me if I was doing anything. I said, "No." And she said: "Please show these men Asvat's surgery."

'I showed them. We spoke in Zulu. They came back [from a foot survey of the surgery to the car in which they had all travelled] and dropped me at the house. About one week later Zindzi received a telephone call when we were watching TV in Winnie's house. She handed the phone to Winnie, who said Asvat was dead. I believe they [the youths] were the men who killed the doctor.'

I pointed out to Katiza the discrepancy between his two versions of the story. He insisted the second story was correct. He said he had never asked the youths their names or been told them.

*

Whichever of Katiza's accounts is correct – and as this story unfolds the grave importance of pinning down the correct version will be apparent – it is a fact that Abu-Baker Asvat was shot dead in his surgery just after 4pm on 27 January 1989 by two unemployed Zulu youths. It is a fact that among his last visitors before his death were Katiza Cebekhulu and Winnie Mandela in search of a medical certificate which would have made possible the laying of false charges of homosexual rape against the Reverend Paul Verryn.

Zakhele Cyril Mbatha, then twenty-one, who gave the false name of Mandla Ekwanyana, and Thulani Nicholas Dlamini, then aged twenty, had entered Asvat's waiting room, where Ma Sisulu filled out medical cards for them as new patients.

When Mbatha and Dlamini were admitted to the consulting room Ma Sisulu heard the security door between it and reception click. Next she heard a gunshot, followed by a scream from Abu-Baker Asvat. She shouted to him through the hatch connecting their rooms, but there was no response. Gripped by fear, she screamed and ran into the street to seek help. As she ran she saw Mbatha and Dlamini running from the surgery: it occurred to her later that they could have left the consulting room only by opening the security door, controlled by Asvat with a special button, and they would need to have been told about it by someone who had previously visited the surgery and seen how the doctor operated the release.

Ma Sisulu returned to the surgery, unlocked the security door from the outside with her own key and found Dr Asvat lying wounded in a pool of blood. She was joined by Thandi

Tshabalala, who had heard the shots from across the road and run from her house into the surgery.

Dr Asvat was still alive when Miss Tshabalala reached him. 'I tried to talk to him,' she said. 'His lips were moving and he was showing me with his hands that the telephone was on the wall.' But Abu-Baker had died by the time the police arrived, taking with him his knowledge about the final day of Stompie Moeketsi's life; the secrets of his conversations with Winnie Mandela, Jerry Richardson, Priscilla and Reggie Jana and members of the Mandela Crisis Committee; and his reasons for declining to issue a certificate verifying the homosexual rape of Katiza Cebekhulu.

*

Ma Sisulu telephoned Ebrahim Asvat, who raced by car from Carletonville to Abu-Baker's Soweto surgery. 'When I arrived my brother's body was still lying there on the floor of the consulting room,' Ebrahim told me. 'Ma Sisulu burst into tears.'

Ebrahim picked up his brother's medical cards and the log-book, vital evidence about who had visited the surgery and when. The logbook was part of a meticulous double-entry system maintained by Ma Sisulu. Details from individual medical cards were duplicated in the daily, comprehensive logbook. Ebrahim checked, for example, the 30 December 1988 date of Winnie's visit, with Katiza, to his brother on the medical card against the logbook entry: the dates were the same. Winnie would claim at her later trial that she was in Brandfort, 200 miles from Soweto, on that date. The police later took the cards and logbook away from Ebrahim, but only after he had photocopied all the cards. He did not photocopy the logbook and has not seen it since; the police never presented it in any subsequent trials. Its fate is a mystery.

Ebrahim returned to comfort Zhora. 'Winnie phoned me at ten that night,' Ebrahim told me. 'She said: "Who could have done this? Whoever did it must pay for it." She didn't sound genuine. And then she pitched up around midnight with Zindzi, Richardson and Krish Naidoo to see my sister-in-law.'

Ebrahim said he thought at the time Winnie's behaviour was odd. She was not crying, despite the death of her close friend Abu-Baker. 'She didn't look into my sister-in-law's eyes,' said Ebrahim. She just sat at Zhora's feet, rocking on her heels and staring at the floor without speaking. 'Jerry Richardson didn't say one word, even to say he had seen my brother twice, as I knew, in the twenty-four hours before he died.'

Winnie Mandela attended Abu-Baker's funeral, uninvited, with twenty members of her MUFC the following day – Saturday 28 January 1989.

Late that night Ebrahim sat at his home reading the first edition of the following day's *Sunday Times* of Johannesburg. 'I was suddenly overcome by fear,' said Ebrahim. 'It was then that we all began to become frightened. Mrs Mandela told the *Sunday Times* she knew why my brother had been killed. It was because he was the only one who could have proved sexual misconduct against Paul Verryn.' More precisely, the *Sunday Times* had quoted Winnie as saying: 'Dr Asvat was the only professional witness to back my story that the boys, alleged to have been kept against their will in my house, were in fact victims of abuse.' It was 'uncanny', she said, that an important witness who may have been able to help one of his own patients was dead.

If Katiza Cebekhulu's version of events is accurate, Winnie Mandela knew as she spoke to the *Sunday Times* that Asvat had categorically refused to falsify evidence backing her story of rape by Paul Verryn. She knew as she spoke to the newspaper that the dead Abu-Baker would not have supported her story. The biggest question of all is whether she also knew he was preparing to tell the police about his examination of Stompie, whose body still lay unidentified and deep-frozen in Diepkloof mortuary as Abu-Baker died.

Emma Gilbey, in *The Lady*, her biography of Winnie, made the point: 'Implying that the Methodist Church had in some way caused the death of Asvat, it was Winnie who first drew public attention to a possible connection between the kidnapping from the Methodist manse and the murder of Abu-Baker Asvat.'

*

'Before I read the *Sunday Times* article I assumed my brother's murder was a security police job [because of Abu-Baker's activities in the Black Consciousness Movement]. But after reading it I thought: something is not right. Something is happening that is unthinkable. I wasn't aware at the time that Abu-Baker had examined Stompie, but still a ghastly situation was developing before our eyes.'

Ebrahim's growing perturbation was fed by the visit of Major Henk Heslinga, a white police officer assigned to investigate the murder, who said he had already concluded that the motive was robbery. Ebrahim was stunned that such an inference had been drawn so quickly. It did not anyway make sense to him. 'Those boys took only Rand 135. They left Rand 300 behind. My brother was not the sort of person to put up a fight. He would just have given them the money.'

Katiza, who believes the men he accompanied from Winnie's

house to identify Abu-Baker's surgery were the doctor's murderers, independently shared Ebrahim's scepticism. He told me: 'You have to ask: why didn't they take all the money if they were thieves? Why did they take so little?'

Winnie during this period gave only one, lengthy interview to a reporter, Robin Lloyd of the National Broadcasting Corporation of America. She pursued her vendetta against Paul Verryn, telling American TV viewers: 'I don't understand how a man of his standing continues to sodomize black children. There is clear evidence that he has fallen victim to a medical problem which should be addressed quietly with his doctors. He brutalizes these youths who are with him because one youth [Katiza] would not give in to his sexual advances. This is how it arose.'

She went on: 'The youths in my premises did not abduct any children. It came about when a woman who was staying with Paul Verryn told me about this child [Katiza] and he was later fetched. There is a gigantic cover-up by the Church. Xoliswa brought the boys – especially the traumatized child – because she panicked when he [Katiza] said the only way to deal with the white man is to kill him.

'The focus should have been on Paul Verryn and the SACC [South African Council of Churches]. The SACC are worried about their image because when people discover that Paul Verryn is not very well their overseas funding may be affected ... We thought we were assisting the Church in a problem and their only interest is in covering their image.'

The police in due course found Cyril Mbatha and Nicholas Dlamini, arrested them and charged them with the murder of Abu-Baker Asvat. They both gave statements to an Afrikaner police officer, Lieutenant Gert Petrus Zeelie, who translated from Zulu and typed the manuscripts in Afrikaans for signing by the two youths. Dlamini in his statement said Mbatha had told him: 'Look, I've been bought by Winnie Mandela and I must go and shoot Dr Asvat dead . . . I must go and fetch the money on Friday.' Dlamini added: 'The money was Rand 20,000.' Extraordinarily, and for reasons that have never been satisfactorily explained, Dlamini's statement implicating Winnie was not produced in court when his and Mbatha's trial for the murder of Abu-Baker began in October 1989. Only Mbatha's statement was presented: it made no mention of Winnie Mandela. It said the motive was robbery, although Mbatha testified in court that the statement had been tortured out of him. It did, however, say that a man, identified only by the pseudonym 'Johannes', had shown him the location of the doctor's surgery two days before the shooting occurred.

Neither Winnie Mandela, nor any of her daughters, nor any members of her Football Club were questioned or called to make statements prior to the Abu-Baker Asvat murder trial or give evidence during it. Dlamini and Mbatha were both found guilty and sentenced to death. They both remain in prison. Dlamini's sentence was reduced on appeal to life imprisonment. Mbatha was saved from hanging by a Presidential moratorium suspending state executions.

The Asvat family has never accepted robbery as the motive for Abu-Baker's murder. 'We know the killers, but we do not know the motive,' Ebrahim once told me. 'We will never stop seeking the truth. We want justice to be done. My personal feeling is that these boys were hired assassins.'

CHAPTER EIGHT

A Decision to Kill

FEBRUARY 1989

Ordinary mortals might have thought it probable that Winnie Mandela would order her Football Club to exercise maximum restraint following the death of Abu-Baker Asvat and the emergence into the public arena of the controversy linking her to Stompie Moeketsi. Instead, Katiza Cebekhulu told me, she ordered the killings of Andrew Ikaneng and Ikaneng's friend, Sibusiso Chili. The decision was taken in Community House on Saturday 11 February 1989, with Winnie and Zindzi Mandela co-chairing the meeting. Katiza heard Winnie pronounce that Ikaneng and Chili had become 'too problematic' and were to be 'eliminated'. Ikaneng, who had already had one death sentence passed on him by the MUFC and had survived Jerry Richardson's 3 January attempt to kill him, was a marked man again because of the evidence he had given to the Soweto community meeting on 16 January.

One of the organizers of that meeting was Mrs Dudu Chili, full-time co-ordinator of the UDF/ANC's Federation of Transvaal Women (Fedtraw), mother of Sibusiso Chili and close colleague of Albertina Sisulu. Dudu Chili and Albertina Sisulu had concluded long before Stompie's abduction from Paul Verryn's manse that Winnie Mandela was out of control, that power had gone to the head of the Mother of the Nation. They teamed up to set up an underground escape route for Soweto youths who wanted to break free of the clutches of the MUFC. Paradoxically, while Winnie Mandela ferried boys clandestinely across the border to Botswana and beyond to train as ANC guerrillas, Ma Sisulu and Chili were sending youths through their own secret network to the same countries to escape the MUFC.

Dudu Chili was active at both community and political levels, a mediator to whom township residents took their many problems. Unusually for a township resident in the 1980s, she had a car and a telephone, for her work with Fedtraw, and so spent a lot of time ferrying people to hospital who were shot by police during that turbulent decade. 'When Winnie formed this [Football] Club, children started disappearing from their homes,' Mrs Chili told me at my home in Johannesburg. 'Sometimes parents would ask me for help to demand their children [back from Mrs Mandela], but she has always been such a lion that we couldn't do anything. Children started running away from Winnie and would tell us what horrible things were happening there. How people were assaulted. They would even say of some that they didn't know whether they were dead or alive.' Rumours circulated of youths being hacked to death inside the Mandela household.

'The community was very much affected by the Football Club,' said Dudu. 'People were crippled, people lost their homes, people lost their children at the hands of the Football Club, which of course took their orders from Winnie as the head. At the beginning we all regarded her as the Mother of the Nation because she was Nelson Mandela's wife, not realizing that we were building a monster with the help of the rest of the world. We built her into this character by popularizing her for the sake of Mandela, not knowing we were destroying ourselves.'

Absconders from the MUFC often phoned Albertina Sisulu to ask for help. Because she was under a restriction order until 1988, which limited her movements, Albertina would then send messages to Dudu Chili to ask her to organize escapes to Botswana. 'Ma Sisulu would say: "You've got the car. Let's hide these children and get them out." But one boy came back and gave the game away to Winnie. Ma Sisulu phoned me and said, "Dudu, we are in trouble." Shortly afterwards Ma Sisulu's house was petrol-bombed, but no one was hurt.'

Winnie had also begun putting pressure on Dudu Chili's eldest son, Sibusiso, and his two younger brothers to join the Football Club soon after it was formed in 1986. When Sibusiso resisted, Winnie branded him as the leader of an alleged anti-MUFC faction. 'I think Winnie wanted me to be her boyfriend,' Sibusiso used to joke. But Mrs Chili said: 'They began to hunt him like an animal, and I went to see Winnie Mandela to find out why. She just said that if my children didn't join the Football Club, then they were sell-outs.' Mrs Chili nevertheless instructed her sons not to join the MUFC. 'I knew there was something wrong. Winnie was using the boys to do her dirty work. I did not understand why when we had so much else to do, such as supporting political prisoners, she had to be in charge of the Football Club.'

Dudu believes her sons' refusal of Football Club advances fuelled the resentment Winnie already felt against her as a rival for the community's loyalty. She recalled a visit from Mrs Mandela soon after Winnie's 1985 return to Soweto from exile in Brandfort. At that time youths loyal to the banned ANC gathered regularly at Dudu's house to resolve fights, thefts and other conflicts without resort to the white-controlled courts. 'On one occasion she came to ask if we could help recover one of her relative's cars which had been stolen,' Dudu told me. 'We found it and returned it entirely as a result of negotiation. Winnie said to me: "I don't know how you do it." That's when, I'm convinced, she must have sat down and thought: "I've got to use these boys for my own interest." She wooed them by forming the Football Club, with uniforms, balls and boots. Boys love that kind of thing. But the only things her Football Club kicked were people.'

The betrayal by the MUFC defector to Winnie of the Sisulu–Chili escape route made retribution almost inevitable. It became certain when Winnie learned that Sibusiso Chili and Andrew Ikaneng had taken two MUFC members to Dudu's house, where they were urged to sever their contacts with Winnie.

On the day – 11 February 1989 – Katiza heard Winnie issue the death sentences on Sibusiso Chili and Andrew Ikaneng (according to what he told me), a Football Club member named Dodo turned up at Dudu's house to warn her of the decision. 'Dodo liked Sibusiso,' said Dudu. 'He had been working with him in the Orlando West youth branch of the UDF. "I'm telling you this, but I fear for my life and I'm going far away," he said. I haven't seen Dodo since.'

Dudu was not altogether surprised by Dodo's stark news. After the 16 January community meeting her neighbours noticed that her house was being watched by MUFC members. She asked Sibusiso to go into hiding then, but says he replied: 'If I start running from Winnie Mandela now, when will I stop?' From 11 February the youths lurking around her house began wearing scarves to disguise themselves and also appeared carrying heavy bags which neighbours suspected contained weapons. When Dudu went outside they turned so she could see only their backs.

It was only a matter of time before the attack came.

*

It happened on Monday 13 February. Katiza said he walked from Silelekele High School at lunchtime to Winnie's office at Community House with fellow MUFC member Maxwell Madondo, who was in another class. 'Winnie told us to find Sibusiso Chili and bring him to her,' said Katiza. 'She said Sibusiso was a sell-out. We were joined by Killer [an MUFC member known only by that name].'

Katiza, Madondo and Killer, who had a gun, knew they might be able to intercept Sibusiso somewhere near his mother's house in Orlando West. But eyes in Soweto are always watching and word spreads quickly. A local girl ran into Dudu Chili's house screaming, 'Mama, they've caught up with Sibusiso.' Sibusiso had left Dudu's house on an errand to the local shops. Dudu immediately called Sibusiso's two younger brothers, Mbuso and Phika, who gathered friends and ran towards a bridge across a road where Katiza and the rest of the MUFC hunting party had been sighted.

The MUFC and Sibusiso met just before the reinforcements sent by Dudu Chili arrived. Madondo and Sibusiso began to argue after the MUFC ordered the Chili boy to report to Winnie Mandela. But when the helpers arrived the three Football Club members were overwhelmed. At some point Andrew Ikaneng also arrived on the scene: he was working in a local shebeen, but was alerted quickly on the bush telegraph to what was happening.

'They grabbed us,' Katiza told me. 'But Killer and I broke free when we saw Sibusiso's brother coming towards us swinging a pickaxe handle. Killer and I ran back to Winnie's office to get help. But by the time the others came Maxwell was dead with a hole in his forehead. Killer just disappeared after that: we never saw him again.' Left alone after the first blow with the pickaxe handle, Madondo was further beaten before being carried across the street into some long grass where stones and rocks were hurled on to his body until it was lifeless.

Dudu Chili flew out of South Africa soon after the clash which left Madondo dead. She was a guest speaker, as a representative of the Soweto Civic Association, at an Anti-Apartheid Movement conference in Sheffield, England. She arrived back in Johannesburg on 21 February and was immediately arrested and detained in cells at Kliptown police station to be questioned about the murder of Maxwell Madondo. Her sons had gone into hiding, but were arrested later.

A day earlier, on 20 February, police had raided Winnie Mandela's Diepkloof house and found a handwritten hit-list in one of her rooms. There were eleven names on it, including Dudu Chili's three sons, Andrew Ikaneng and two nephews of Albertina Sisulu. The hit-list featured prominently in the defence in the subsequent Maxwell Madondo murder trial, but strangely it was never used against Winnie Mandela.

Some time between 13 and 16 February – Katiza does not remember the precise date – Winnie called a meeting at which she ordered an attack on the Chili family to avenge Maxwell Madondo's death. She also condemned the entire Chili family as 'sell-outs' because they had resisted her demands and those of the MUFC. 'She was very angry,' said Katiza. 'I was there for the meeting at which she announced the attack. Then she met us [those assigned to the attack group] one by one to tell what she wanted. Gybon Gabela and Charles Zwane were among the leaders.'

The plan was to destroy Dudu Chili's house.

Gabela was the man who had kicked Stompie Moeketsi around the room at the back of Winnie's house on 30 December 1988. Zwane had been a party to the Seheri killings of 24 January 1987. Zwane's one-year suspended sentence from that case was still hanging over him as he accepted the order to take revenge for Madondo's death.

The attack party, bearing guns, grenades and petrol bombs, set out from Winnie's on the evening of Wednesday 22 February 1989 for Dudu Chili's house. Although Dudu was in the police cells at Kliptown in connection with Madondo's murder, the house was not empty. Dudu's nieces, thirteen-year-old Finkie Msomi and twelve-year-old Judith Msomi, were there with their aunt Barbara, Dudu's sister.

Barbara heard metallic scraping and her dog whimpering outside the house. She opened the front door and stood on the small porch. In the shadows she saw a tall man, his face covered by a balaclava. He was holding a gun which pointed towards her. At the moment she saw him the gunman fired, but missed. Barbara fled back into the house and hustled her nieces towards Dudu's bedroom. She frantically telephoned a friend for help, but even as she shouted down the line a window shattered, the room was raked by AK-47 automatic rifle fire and a petrol bomb was thrown.

Finkie, who had been standing next to the window, was hurled across the bedroom like a rag doll. Barbara, her clothes ablaze, tried to drag Finkie's limp body into the passage. 'She had a big hole in her left-hand side, then here she was all burned, all open here, like when a sausage has been put into the fire,' said Barbara. Finkie was already dead. A bullet had entered her head. Judith, who had been standing in the passage, avoided the worst of the blast. She ran into the room with water to put out the flames on Barbara's clothes. Judith took over the task of trying to drag Finkie to safety, but she didn't have the strength.

Soon the whole house was an inferno. Another petrol bomb had been thrown and Charles Zwane had poured petrol under all the outer doors. It took only a few minutes for Dudu Chili's house to be reduced to ashes in a spectacular conflagration. Barbara and Judith, nearly overcome by the flames, ran out at the back of the house and hid from Winnie's men in a chicken coop. When they thought it was safe they escaped over a fence and were taken to hospital by Barbara's husband for treatment to their burns. Finkie's body was burned to a cinder, but a pathologist who did the post-mortem found an AK-47 bullet lodged in what remained of her skull.

Dudu Chili described to me how the police took her the following day, 23 February, to view the remains of her house after being charged with the murder of Maxwell Madondo and then released on bail. 'On the way to the house I could see newspaper billboards saying a thirteen-year-old girl had died in a bombing and shooting,' said Dudu. 'Then I saw my house like a skeleton. When neighbours saw me arrive with the police they started coming out to greet me. I told them, "Winnie's supposed to have been in the cells, not me." It was either my sons' lives or those of the assassins sent by Winnie that were on the line. Then they began telling me that Winnie's minibus was sitting across the street from my house during the attack. Finkie's mother cried to the people in the minibus to help her save the children in the burning house, but they refused.'

Dudu Chili remains to this day an implacable foe of Winnie Mandela, striving to reopen police investigations into her role in the murder of Finkie and other unsolved killings and 'disappearances' in Soweto. 'We need to know who is behind her protection,' said Dudu. 'Why if there is law in this country can it not take its course? Finkie died for me. That little girl was too young to die. To think that Winnie, the wife of our leader all those years, is the one responsible for her death – how does one condone that?'

Dudu expressed particular anger against Archbishop Trevor Huddleston, a leading British anti-apartheid activist who defended Winnie Mandela on the ground that she was a victim of apartheid. 'We are all victims of apartheid,' said Dudu. 'Winnie is not a special exception. Apartheid was a fact, but we still live, we are still human beings, we are still proud of our humanity. Her actions were not human.'

*

During Dudu and Sibusiso Chili's brief detention, police questioned Katiza Cebekhulu about the planning of the MUFC attack on Dudu's house. Katiza said in a statement that Winnie Mandela had chaired a meeting, at which he was present, and had ordered the killings of Sibusiso Chili and Andrew Ikaneng.

The trial of Sibusiso for the murder of Maxwell Madondo began more than a year later. Sibusiso Chili went into the dock with his mother, Dudu Chili, and with Andrew Ikaneng and four other youths.

The state prosecutor decided not to call Katiza into the witness box, for reasons that have never been properly explained. However, the prosecution allowed the defence to place in the court record Katiza's police statement incriminating Winnie

Mandela in planning the attempted murders of Sibusiso Chili and Andrew Ikaneng. In the course of the trial all charges were dropped against Dudu Chili and two of the youths. The defence advocate subsequently said in open court: 'The admission the State will make is that the deceased, Maxwell Madondo, was a member of the Mandela Football Club and that a decision was made by Mrs Winnie Mandela and the Football Club to kill accused number one [Sibusiso] Chili and accused number six [Andrew] Ikaneng. That the witness, my lord, whose name I shall not mention now [that is, Katiza], together with Killer and the deceased [Madondo], all were instructed and went to carry out the decision to kill accused number one and six.'

The presiding judge in the Madondo murder trial, Mr Justice A. J. Solomon, took Katiza's damning evidence against Winnie into account when reaching his verdicts and deciding sentences on Sibusiso Chili, Andrew Ikaneng and two other co-accused. Isaac Mazibuko and Sandilo Blanket. Ikaneng was found not guilty. Mazibuko and Blanket were found guilty of assault and given short suspended jail sentences.

Judge Solomon found Sibusiso Chili guilty of murdering Maxwell Madondo, but, in a verdict and sentence his Old Testament ancestor might have admired, he observed: 'I must stress that we cannot and do not overlook the effect upon him [Sibusiso] of the actions and threats to him of the Mandela Football Club which have been described to us. Those actions and threats, although they do not relieve the accused of responsibility for the death of the deceased, in our view provide a powerful ground for this Court to find that there are strong extenuating circumstances.'

Judge Solomon said it was clear that Maxwell Madondo, Killer and Katiza had set out to kill Sibusiso and had taken the trouble to investigate his movements and lie in wait for him. 'The State had admitted that the deceased was a member of this so-called "football club" and indeed was one of a "hit squad" which was organized to take your life,' the judge told Sibusiso. 'You have been subjected to tremendous pressure by the threats of this gang.'

Judge Solomon found Sibusiso Chili guilty of murder and sentenced him to six years' imprisonment, but suspended four of the years in view of the extenuating circumstances. In the event, Sibusiso served less than two years in prison.

Despite acceptance by the state and by Judge Solomon of the veracity of Katiza's statement indicting Winnie Mandela, and despite the discovery by the police of the handwritten hit-list at Winnie's home, Mrs Mandela was never charged nor even questioned in connection with the murder of Finkie Msomi, the burning down of Dudu Chili's house or the plot to kill Sibusiso Chili and Andrew Ikaneng.

CHAPTER NINE

Arrest

FEBRUARY–NOVEMBER 1989

Katiza, who was at the meeting at which Winnie Mandela ordered revenge on the Chili family, said he would probably have taken part in the 22 February attack which took the life of Finkie Msomi – but by then he was sitting in a jail cell in central Johannesburg. A series of dramatic events had run in parallel with the Maxwell Madondo–Finkie Msomi murder sagas which distracted press attention from them and from the significant central role Winnie had played in their planning.

On Wednesday 15 February the body of Stompie Moeketsi had finally been identified – almost seven weeks after he was murdered and just two days after Maxwell Madondo died.

Two forensic scientists at Johannesburg Police HQ, in John Vorster Square, had sat over morning coffee on 14 February discussing speculative newspaper articles about the missing boy. The Johannesburg *Sunday Star*, for example, surmised that Dr Abu-Baker Asvat had visited Winnie's home on 31 December 1988, found Stompie near death and secretly reported the situation to the Mandela Crisis Committee. The junior scientist, Dr J. C. W. Cook, who had only recently joined the department, told his superior, Dr Patricia Klepp, that he had performed an autopsy a few weeks earlier on a decomposing youth, identified only as corpse number DK 48/49: he wondered if it was possible the body was Stompie's.

Klepp phoned the Diepkloof mortuary, confirmed that DK 48/49 was still there and drove with Cook to Soweto to begin a fresh examination. DK 48/49 was deep frozen, so they returned twenty-four hours later after it had defrosted.

Klepp's report, based on the work she now undertook and on Cook's earlier autopsy, said DK 48/49 was infested with maggots when found on 6 January. She estimated the body, that of a boy only four and a half feet tall, had been rotting for at least five days before it was discovered. The brain had turned to liquid and all organs were decomposing. Blood had poured from two penetrating wounds on the right side of the neck behind the ear and a third across the bottom of the neck on the left side. Blood had poured over his collar and across a sunset-over-the-sea scene printed on the front of his red and blue shirt.

The boy had been beaten heavily on most parts of his body, causing extensive internal bruising. Dr Klepp identified the skull, lower back, both buttocks and the left and right calves as areas where he had been particularly severely battered. The left collarbone was fractured. The stab wounds to the throat were so deep that they had penetrated the boy's chest cavity, causing both lungs to collapse. There was blood in his stomach which he had swallowed.

Klepp said the injuries to his skull alone could have caused his death, even before the stabbings. Because the brain had liquefied by the time of the post-mortem it had been impossible to determine brain damage. But there was extensive bleeding and bruising of the tissues beneath the skin. 'This alone can kill,' reported Klepp. 'I mean had I not found the penetrating incised wounds of the neck, the subcutaneous contusion alone could have killed him.' This means that one can literally bleed to death, not externally but into the tissues, muscle and fat immediately beneath the skin. There had certainly been substantial internal bleeding in this case, said Klepp. 'In my experience what I have seen here is sufficient to kill,' she went on. 'You can die days later of a beating.'

Klepp and Cook removed samples from the fingers for fingerprint identification. They matched those on Stompie's ID card records. Stompie's mother was then brought in to identify her son. Joyce Seipei recognized him mainly from a birthmark on the sole of his left foot and by the fact that the foot turned outwards at a slight angle.

Stompie Seipei Moeketsi had been found.

*

Events moved fast after Major-General Jaap Joubert of the South African Police announced on 15 February that forensic tests had identified a decomposing body as that of Stompie Moeketsi. General Joubert said Stompie had last been seen alive on New Year's Eve at Winnie Mandela's Diepkloof house. He did not say how Stompie had died or who had last seen him, but some newspaper and radio reports said it was believed he had been stabbed in the back.

General Joubert's announcement was made as Winnie flew into Cape Town to visit Nelson at Victor Verster Prison in nearby Paarl. There were frenzied scenes as she flew back into Johannesburg's Jan Smuts Airport later that day. 'Reporters formed something of a scrum around her and bombarded her with questions relating to the death of Stompie and public undertakings she has given that, in the event of his body being found, she and members of her football team would immediately present themselves to police to help with their inquiries,' wrote David Beresford of the *Guardian*.

Winnie weaved her way through the reporters, ignoring their questions, to find her minibus and her daughter Zindzi waiting at the airport entrance. She was driven off towards Soweto, but half a mile or so down the highway police cars intercepted the vehicle. Winnie and Zindzi were ordered out and left standing by the side of the road as a white police officer drove the minibus away while her driver was put in the back of a police car and driven off.

Winnie and Zindzi hitched a lift home to Soweto and her driver was dropped off at Winnie's house by police late that night. A police statement said the minibus had been impounded 'for examination purposes' in connection with the death of Stompie.

The next day, Thursday 16 February, reporters from *City Press*, South Africa's biggest-circulation newspaper among black readers, interviewed Jerry Richardson and Winnie at her Diepkloof house. Richardson began by denying any assault on Stompie, Pelo Mekgwe, Thabiso Mono and Kenny Kgase. But Winnie interrupted him and said: 'You are not protecting me by denying you assaulted the boys. Tell the truth.'

Prompted by his boss, Winnie's chief coach then admitted he had beaten the boys, but only to make them 'tell the truth' about committing indecent acts with Paul Verryn. *City Press* also reported Richardson as saying Stompie had admitted responsibility for the murders of four 'comrades'. A few hours later Winnie told a BBC Television team that Richardson had only klapped, or cuffed, Stompie and the others.

While *City Press* was interviewing Winnie and Richardson

the UDF – now rechristened the Mass Democratic Movement (MDM) but still the internal front for the banned ANC – called a press conference and publicly distanced itself from Winnie and the Mandela United Football Club.

Murphy Morobe, the MDM/ANC's publicity secretary, read out a statement directly linking Winnie to Stompie's death. 'We are outraged at Mrs Mandela's complicity in the recent abductions and assault of Stompie,' said the statement. 'Had Stompie and his three colleagues not been abducted by Mrs Mandela's "Football Team", he would have been alive today.'

The MDM/ANC statement gave routine fulsome praise to Nelson Mandela, but pursued its attack on his wife in language which propelled the story around the world. 'We are outraged by the reign of terror that the [football] team has been associated with,' read Morobe. 'Not only is Mrs Mandela associated with the team, in fact, the team is her own creation. We are of the view that Mrs Mandela has abused the trust and confidence she has enjoyed over the years . . . Her practices have violated the spirit and ethos of the Democratic Movement [that is, the ANC]. The Democratic Movement has uncompromisingly fought against violations of human rights from whatever quarters. We are not prepared to remain silent where those who are violating human rights claim to be doing so in the name of the struggle against apartheid.'

When asked whether the political ostracism by the MDM/ANC would affect Winnie's relationship with Nelson, Morobe replied: 'Comrade Nelson, in consultation with all the parties, will have to make a decision.'

Oliver Tambo, the ANC President, and the rest of the movement's exiled leadership responded four days later by issuing their own denunciation from Lusaka. Referring to the 'unbecoming activities' of the MUFC, Tambo and the ANC Executive said in a statement: 'It is with a feeling of terrible sadness that we consider it necessary to express our reservations about Winnie Mandela's judgement.' It rejected Winnie's depictions of Stompie as a police informer, offered condolences to his mother and described him as a 'committed young lion who had made an immense contribution in the mobilization of our youth'. Tambo's men said it was necessary to help Winnie re-integrate into the structures and discipline of the MDM/ANC.

But Winnie Mandela had ideas of her own. Her reaction to the ANC's statement from Lusaka was to dispute Joyce Seipei's identification of the Diepkloof corpse as that of Stompie and to say she believed the boy was still alive. 'I am convinced Stompie has not been killed,' she told Dutch Television on 19 February. 'That poor mother is being forced into admitting that is the corpse of her son.' Winnie appealed to Stompie to 'come forward', asserting that he had escaped from her house on New Year's Eve.

Joyce Seipei rejected Winnie's claim the next day, telling reporters: 'Stompie is dead. I have seen the evidence. I have seen his body. I have seen his clothes. He is dead.' Any claims to the contrary, she said, were lies.

*

Winnie, meanwhile, sent Katiza Cebekhulu off to Honeydew, north-west of Johannesburg, within forty-eight hours of her return from Cape Town on 15 February.

Miranda Harris, a white South African friend of Winnie's who worked as a journalist for an international TV agency, World Television News (WTN), lived with her husband Roger on a Honeydew smallholding. Winnie frequently sent members of the Football Club to the Harris home for R and R. Her motives for sending Katiza to Harris at this time are not clear, but, according to Katiza, Winnie told him Harris wanted to interview him. Harris did not welcome his arrival. Katiza seemed to be extremely disturbed and kept asking her to film him and broadcast to the world a story she did not find credible but which nonetheless frightened her.

To appease Katiza she gave him her tape-recorder and he sat under a mango tree with the machine and spoke his story into it in Zulu. 'I made tapes with Miranda describing how Winnie killed Stompie,' Katiza told me.

I had sought out Harris, who had quit international journalism and opened a boarding house in the Eastern Cape, as part of the process of validating as much of Katiza's story as possible. Harris told me she had never listened to the tapes. They were too hot and she wanted rid of them. Instead she drove to Melville, a chic and hilly Johannesburg suburb, on Saturday 18 February to give the tapes and the recorder to one of the country's leading human rights lawyers, Fink Haysom, who coincidentally happened to be Paul Verryn's lawyer. Haysom listened as Harris told him she was not prepared to keep the tapes because they endangered her life. Haysom told friends that Harris was highly agitated: she said Cebekhulu was asking to be sent back to Paul Verryn's house because he feared for his life and the minister was the only person he could trust. Haysom accepted the tapes but they were never broadcast; the lawyer kept them and has never made them public. In 1994 Haysom was appointed legal adviser in the office of the newly elected State President of South Africa, Nelson Mandela.

Harris returned to the farm in Honeydew and, she said, telephoned Frank Chikane to plead with him to take Katiza off her hands. The SACC Secretary-General drove Katiza to Hillbrow Hospital in central Johannesburg and had the youth admitted on 19 February, telling doctors he seemed to be having a nervous breakdown. Katiza confirmed to me that it had been Chikane who urged him to go to Hillbrow. 'But Chikane tricked me,' said Katiza. 'I was under guard there by two police with rifles.' Katiza repeated to psychiatrists his story of the events in Winnie Mandela's home of 29–31 December, culminating in the stabbing of Stompie. 'I was examined by doctors, who said there was nothing wrong with me. Then the police took me away to Protea police station.'

Katiza arrived at Protea on 21 February. His was one of a series of arrests being made in connection with the death of Stompie. Jerry Richardson and another MUFC member, Jabu Sithole, were already there. John Morgan, Xoliswa Falati, Nompumelelo Falati and two other MUFC members, Mpho Mabelane and Brian Mabusa, followed within a few days. All were detained for long periods and questioned about their roles in the abduction and beating of Stompie Moeketsi. All were required to make statements.

Winnie Mandela was neither detained nor required to make a statement.

*

Katiza made two statements – one to a lawyer, Kathy Satchwell, who took on his case, and the other to an Afrikaner police officer, Captain Fred Dempsey of the Soweto Robbery and Murder Squad, who had a liaison role with the National Intelligence Service, the state's top security organization.

In his statement to Satchwell, never made public, Katiza repeated yet again his story that Stompie had had serious head wounds and that he had seen Winnie Mandela stab the boy in the throat. Friends of Satchwell say two events convinced her of the essential truth of Katiza's statement. First, it was consistent with the evidence he had given to the Soweto community meeting on 16 January. Second, when Dr Patricia Klepp eventually made public her report on the nature of the wounds inflicted on Stompie it gelled with Katiza's statement: at the time Katiza made his statement to Satchwell, neither he nor the lawyer had any knowledge of the contents of the report being drawn up by the pathologist.

In the statement taken by Captain Dempsey, assigned by the state to investigate Stompie's disappearance only after the boy had been missing for six weeks, Katiza described how Abu-Baker Asvat has been summoned to Winnie's home after Stompie's beating to attend the badly injured boy. 'Dr Asvat came to Winnie's house and investigated Stompie,' declared Katiza's statement as written out by the officer. 'While Dr Asvat examined Stompie, I saw that he shook his head. He spoke to Winnie in English.'

Katiza said he did not hear clearly all that was being said but at one point 'I heard Dr Asvat say the word "hospital".'

According to the account drawn up by Dempsey, Katiza said Winnie and Jerry Richardson and two other MUFC members 'put paper in Stompie's mouth. They put a rag around his mouth and tied it behind his head. They tied his hands and feet with a rag as well. Stompie could do nothing.' They put Stompie in the boot of a red car – 'Stompie was still alive. They drove away . . .' Jerry Richardson returned later with two MUFC men, and one told her: 'It is finished with Stompie.'

Katiza described to me, more than six years after his interrogation by Dempsey, the circumstances in which it had taken place. Katiza said he was terrified at the time because he had seen so many dreadful things and because he had played a pivotal role in Winnie's plot to traduce Paul Verryn. 'I knew this thing had spread like fire from the moment I had been sent to Paul,' he said. 'Otherwise all these other things might not have happened. I never told the police Winnie sent me to Paul. I was scared. I didn't think they would believe me and I didn't know what might happen to me.'

When Dempsey interrogated him it was through an interpreter, Dempsey asking questions in Afrikaans and Katiza, who neither speaks nor reads Afrikaans, replying in Zulu. 'Dempsey wrote it down in Afrikaans,' said Katiza. 'When we had finished he said "Sign it." I refused at first. The statement was in Dempsey's handwriting in Afrikaans. I didn't understand what he had written.' (I later obtained a copy of Katiza's statement to Dempsey. It was, as Katiza had suggested, handwritten and in Afrikaans.)

Katiza claimed he eventually signed the statement under duress. 'You don't understand about these things,' he told me. 'If you are a black man in those days and a white policeman tells you to sign, you sign. You could die otherwise. Dempsey said he was charging me for murder, kidnap and assault. I told him I didn't kill or assault. Dempsey said I was the cause of it all.'

Katiza said he never saw a translation into either Zulu or English of the statement Dempsey ordered him to sign until I showed him a shortened version of it in English in July 1995. 'I deny Dempsey's statement that I saw Winnie tie and gag Stompie and put him in the boot,' Katiza responded. 'And why, in my statement, is my evidence [to Dempsey] that I saw Winnie killing Stompie missing?'

Katiza's complaint against Dempsey is therefore that the

police officer prepared a statement in a language he did not understand; forced him to sign it under duress; omitted crucial testimony; and manufactured additional facts.

*

Shortly after the arrest of Katiza, Richardson and the others, Stompie Moeketsi was buried in his home township of Tumahole on 25 February 1989. Bishop Peter Storey, giving the funeral address, described Stompie's 'terrible and violent' death as an 'unspeakable crime', and went on: 'These past few weeks . . . have probed below the surface of South Africa's shame and exposed the deeper, hidden wounds these years have carved into a people's soul – the erosion of conscience, the devaluing of human life, the evasion of truth and the reckless resort to violence.'

Winnie Mandela was absent from Stompie's funeral. It would, of course, have been almost impossible for her to have attended and retain any credibility, having asserted just three days earlier that Stompie was still alive. The graffiti on walls along the funeral route – 'Winnie is a killer' – might also have upset her equilibrium.

Paul Verryn was there. Over Stompie's small white coffin in the township's Catholic church, he said: 'I come to express to the people of Tumahole my own sadness and loss at his death.'

*

It was difficult for outsiders to understand the enormity of what was going on. For example, within days of Stompie's remains being consigned to the grave, British film director Sir Richard Attenborough reminisced about his research for the film *Cry Freedom*, the story of Steve Biko, and wrote gushingly of meeting Winnie Mandela in the course of it – 'Winnie lived in two rooms, each about ten foot square.'

A letter published in the *Star* speculated whether Sir Richard would return to make a film called *Stompie*.

*

Katiza Cebekhulu spent more than seven months in prison after his arrest on 21 February 1989 in connection with the murder of Stompie Moeketsi. In the remand section of Soweto's Diepkloof Prison he was held with other detainees suspected of involvement with the kidnap and assault on Stompie. 'We called it Sun City,' he said, after the luxurious gambling resort carved into the Pilanesberg Mountains to the north of Johannesburg by South Africa's billionaire hotel and casino king Sol Kerzner. 'We had bedsheets, things most of us had never had before, and we played snooker, tennis and volleyball.' But there were also police interrogations. 'I used to get annoyed when the police didn't believe me that Winnie Mandela killed.'

There were also visits by Dali Mpofu, Winnie's young lawyer lover, to Katiza, Jerry Richardson, Xoliswa Falati, John Morgan, Nompumelelo Falati, Jabu Sithole, Mpho Mabelane and Brian Mabusa. Dali's calls disturbed Katiza. The photograph he had stolen of Winnie and Dali making love was still hidden beneath the dog kennel behind Mrs Mandela's house. And Katiza had not felt enough confidence in anyone to be able to share the burden of this secret about the Mother of the Nation. He felt confused and trapped by the tangled web of events into which he had been drawn since meeting Winnie Mandela and signing up with the Football Club. Dali's visits confused and trapped him further.

All those arrested had given initial statements to the police saying Winnie was present in her Diepkloof house throughout the events of 29 to 31 December 1988 prior to the death of Stompie. Now, Katiza told me, Dali brought clothes, money and food for the detainees and instructed them to embrace a new reality in order to 'save' Winnie. 'Dali used to say all the statements we made to the police we should deny. He said we should say Mrs Mandela was in Brandfort. I said yes, OK. There was no choice because I was in prison.'

*

The police sent a docket on Jerry Richardson and the death of Stompie in July 1989 to Klaus von Lieres, the Attorney-General of the Transvaal province of which Johannesburg was the main city. On 4 November 1989 Von Lieres formally charged Richardson alone with the murder of Stompie and the attempted murder of Andrew Lerotodi Ikaneng. Richardson was also charged with kidnap and assault. Von Lieres scheduled the trial to begin in February 1990.

Katiza, John Morgan, Xoliswa and Nompumelelo Falati, Jabu Sithole, Mpho Mabelane and Brian Mabusa were re-manded on four counts of kidnap and four of assault with intent to cause grievous bodily harm. Winnie paid Rand 500 for each to be released on bail: one of the bail conditions required them to report to their local police station every day.

No charges were laid against Winnie Mandela in connection with the kidnap, assault and murder of Stompie Moeketsi.

*

On 16 November 1989 the murderers of Dr Abu-Baker Asvat were found guilty in the Rand Supreme Court and sentenced to death. Despite Dlamini's statement implicating Winnie, the police investigating officer, Major Henk Heslinga, continued to insist there were no links between the murder of Stompie Moeketsi and Cyril Mbatha's and Nicholas Dlamini's murder of Abu-Baker.

Ebrahim Asvat said publicly that justice had been cheated. The Asvat family was bitter and angry about the slack police inquiries into their relative's murder. Several things did not add up. 'We know the perpetrators of the crime but the truth we do not know,' said Ebrahim.

Albertina Sisulu, wife of Nelson Mandela's best friend, active enemy of the Mandela United Football Club and the nursing sister of Abu-Baker Asvat, was griefstricken after giving evidence at Mbatha's and Dlamini's trial. Recalling finding Abu-Baker in a pool of blood, she said: 'Dr Asvat was my child. Losing him was like losing my own child. But then he was also a father to me. He was also the person I went to when I was in trouble.'

Abu-Baker Asvat had, of course, also been the person Winnie Mandela went to when she was in trouble – and the consequences had been tragic.

CHAPTER TEN

'Nelson Mandela Is Free!'

JULY 1989–FEBRUARY 1990

Katiza Cebekhulu, languishing in prison through 1989, attracted scant public attention, despite being held on suspicion of involvement in the death of Stompie Moeketsi. The domestic and international media in South Africa were by now fully obsessed with the fate of another prisoner – Winnie Mandela's husband, Nelson.

On 5 July 1989 Nelson Mandela was taken from his prison bungalow at Victor Verster Prison to Tuynhuys, the official Cape Town residence of his arch-foe, State President P. W. Botha. The two men – both elderly but towering political figures – chatted for forty-five minutes over tea and cucumber sandwiches. No cameras were present to record the brief foray into the outside world of a man who had been hidden from public view for almost three decades. So clandestine was the meeting that most members of Botha's government knew nothing about it until it was over.

Few details emerged of the discussion between Botha and Mandela. However, it signalled clearly the inevitability of Mandela's release and the coming of a great reversal in the tide of South African history. The Johannesburg *Sunday Times* described the tête-à-tête as 'the most important political development in South Africa for decades'. Botha's spokesman, in an interview with Canadian television, said the jailed ANC leader was 'a key figure in any future negotiation about South Africa's constitutional future'.

The encounter was dramatic and historic – but it was important only for its symbolism, not for its substance. P. W. Botha was known as the Groot Krokodil (Great Crocodile) for the belligerency of his Presidential style and his hostility to black opposition movements. He had a legendary reputation as a table-thumping, finger-wagging tough whose corrosive temper had reduced his own Cabinet ministers to tears. He had begun his rise to power in the mid-1930s as a National Party organizer championing Afrikaners who had been denied education because of impoverishment, following their defeat by the British in the 1899–1902 Boer War, and because their language, unrecognized by the British, bestowed upon them an inferior social position. The politics of the Afrikaner poor were raw before the National Party finally won power in 1948: 'PW' was a street fighter in an era when a clean political fight was defined as one in which the bicycle chains were coated with nickel. He had introduced some tentative reforms of apartheid, but could not make the imaginative leap necessary to achieve significant negotiations with the ANC. Major developments came only with the accession to power of Frederik Willem de Klerk, who in August 1989 forced Botha's resignation in a Cabinet *coup d'état.*

State President de Klerk went to the country on 6 September to secure a reform mandate in what proved to be the last South African general election from which the black majority was excluded. De Klerk's style was a far cry from P. W. Botha's. Well educated, well mannered and approachable, he was a pragmatic conservative who had reluctantly come to believe that 'grand apartheid' had failed the practical test. 'We shall develop a new dispensation in which all can participate without domination,' he said in a television address to the nation immediately after toppling Botha. 'This we shall achieve through talks and nego- tiations . . . We shall break loose from the evil circle of stagna- tion, distrust, division, tension and conflict. We shall make a breakthrough to a totally new South Africa.'

Five weeks later De Klerk released Walter Sisulu from prison together with six other long-term ANC prisoners who had been jailed for life with Mandela back in the early 1960s for sabotage and plotting to overthrow the state. The prisoner release fol- lowed De Klerk's decision to legitimize public protest marches at which illegal ANC and Communist Party flags were being flown in defiance of a host of prohibitory laws. The new President also desegregated South Africa's racially separate beaches and halved the period of compulsory national military service for whites as part of his bid to create a fitting atmosphere for Mandela's release and the opening of negotiations.

De Klerk had deliberately stepped off a cliff, hoping for a soft landing. From prison, Mandela meanwhile sent the President a long document setting out his thoughts on how to do more to pave the way for negotiations on a new constitution between all South Africa's interest groups.

De Klerk moved quickly after Walter Sisulu's release and after receiving the Mandela document. Mandela, then aged seventy-one, had already been visited many times during 1989 in his prison bungalow – where the ANC leader had his own kitchen, cook, TV, fax machine and swimming pool – by Justice Minister Kobie Coetsee and Constitutional Development Minister Gerrit Viljoen as part of what had become an almost continuous dialogue with the government's Public Enemy Number One. Nelson Mandela's personal diary records forty-seven meetings, while he was still a prisoner, with Coetsee. On 13 December 1989 Mandela was driven to Tuynhuys for talks with De Klerk lasting several hours about conditions for his release. The two men agreed that their moments of destiny, inextricably linked, were fast approaching.

On 2 February 1990 De Klerk, opening a new session of Parliament in Cape Town, announced the unconditional release of Mandela and the lifting of the thirty-year-old ban on the ANC, the South African Communist Party and the Pan Africanist Congress.

And on Sunday 11 February Nelson Mandela ceased to be prisoner number 0221141011 and made his sweet walk to freedom from Victor Verster Prison, an event watched by hundreds of millions of television viewers around the globe. At that moment Nelson Mandela was the most famous man in the world and perhaps the most revered. At his side as he walked through the prison gates was his wife Winnie. They held hands as they smiled and acknowledged the cheers and tears of the vast crowds in a crowning moment of what appeared to be a great love story.

Winnie said she was 'ecstatic' and the exiled South African poet and ANC member Breyten Breytenbach wrote from Paris: 'Nelson Mandela is free! The word rustles like a breeze through the townships, whispered in awe, shouted in triumph from mouth to mouth, from shack to boxhouse. Did you hear? We have liberated Mandela! Grown fighters sob. Professionals plot new allegiances. Ancient companions review their splattered lives. "Now the problems start." His wife is working out which dress to wear for what occasion.'

Makaziwe Phuma Mandela, Nelson's eldest daughter by his former wife Evelyn, was less ecstatic. She was studying for a doctorate in anthropology at the University of Massachusetts. When Makaziwe had written to her father in prison for help to study in the United States, he had replied: 'Go to Mama Winnie.' Makaziwe was refused assistance from Winnie and raised money elsewhere. Just before her father's release she told the *Washington Post* that too much was being expected of him. 'He has earned this image of being more-than-hero, this fairy godfather who has a magic wand in his hand – when he comes out everything is going to turn out to be rosy. No single man can achieve that.'

*

Katiza Cebekhulu also was less than ecstatic as Nelson Mandela walked to freedom. In fact, he was very frightened. Sizwe Sithole had just died in horrible circumstances, and Katiza and the wife of the world's most famous man had together plotted the events which led to his demise.

*

In the weeks before Nelson Mandela's walk to freedom Katiza Cebekhulu grew more and more troubled by his own unique store of knowledge about Winnie Mandela – the attempted blackmail of Paul Verryn; the way Stompie Moeketsi had died; Abu-Baker Asvat's visit to the battered boy; the circumstances of Dr Asvat's murder; the unknown fate of the tape he had given to Miranda Harris; Dali Mpofu's prison briefings on the stories that all Winnie's cohorts were to tell if they came to trial; David Themba's strange death ...

He still possessed Themba's photograph of Dali Mpofu

making love to Winnie. It was at a time when South African newspapers, almost oblivious to the discovery of Stompie's body just a year earlier, were writing about Winnie Mandela's painstaking reconciliation with the people. 'Now the old cries of "Viva Mother of the Nation! Viva!" are ringing out again at political rallies,' wrote a correspondent for the Johannesburg *Star*. Newspapers spawned articles about the fairytale marriage between Nelson and Winnie, even publishing his love letters to her from prison. 'Your beautiful photo still stands about two feet above my shoulder as I write this note,' said one sent from Robben Island on 15 April 1976. 'I dust it carefully every morning, for to do so gives me the pleasant feeling that I am caressing you as in the old days. I even touch your nose with mine to recapture the electric current that used to flush through my blood whenever I did so.'

Katiza, still living behind Winnie's Diepkloof Extension house, felt barely able to hold on to his sanity as the excitement mounted prior to Nelson Mandela's release. He felt he must confide in someone about the photo. He retrieved it from under the dog kennel behind Winnie's house and showed it to Sizwe Sithole, whom Katiza regarded as one of his best friends.

Sithole, an Umkhonto we Sizwe soldier, was joint head of the MUFC disciplinary committee. He was also the current boy-friend of Zindzi Mandela and the father of her most recent child, a boy called Bambi. Sithole lived part of the time with Zindzi at Winnie's house and part in a rented room in the neighbouring Soweto suburb of Molofo. He was the man who had shot dead Andrew Ikaneng's friend, Tholi Dlamini, back in 1988. Hard man though Sizwe Sithole was, Katiza told me he was shocked when he saw the photo of Winnie and Dali Mpofu in the throes of passion. 'I suppose he was shocked because of the kind of picture it was. He asked me where I got it, so I told him.'

A short time later Winnie ordered Katiza to put some AK-47 rifles, ammunition and grenades from her weapons store into a bag and give it to Sizwe Sithole to hide at his Molofo house in preparation for an attack on a police station. Winnie told Sithole to wait at his house for orders.

'One evening, some days after Sizwe left, Winnie told me to ring the police and tell them there was someone with guns and ammunition planning to attack Orlando East police station,' said Katiza. 'I was to tell the police his address [in Molofo]. I rang from a public phone booth and came back and told Winnie I had rung the police. The next day Winnie told us that Sizwe was arrested. Zindzi was worried, but Winnie didn't seem upset.'

Sithole was arrested in Molofo at 11.45am on Friday 26 January 1990. Nelson Mandela's freedom was two weeks and two days away. However, Sizwe Sithole of the Umkhonto guerrilla army founded by Mandela in 1961 would not live to see his leader achieve liberty.

*

The police took an AK-47 rifle, two AK-47 magazines, a .38 Special pistol and twenty-seven cartridges from Sithole's house. The house-owner said Sithole had admitted to the police that he owned the weapons and that he had obtained them from a youth, Philemon Menzima, who lived across the street. The house-owner and the alleged arms-dealer were also arrested.

Sithole was interrogated several times that day and confessed to three crimes, including the killing of Tholi Dlamini. In the evening he was locked in cell number 231 at John Vorster

Square police station in central Johannesburg. The police officer who admitted him to John Vorster Square subsequently testified that Sithole was searched on arrival and was found to have neither shoelaces nor trouser belt.

On Saturday 31 January Sithole spent nine further hours under interrogation by police officers. He was taken back to his room at Molofo, where the police seized more guns and ammunition. On Sunday he took two policemen to the scenes of the three crimes he had admitted committing.

On the morning of Tuesday 3 February – the day after President De Klerk announced Nelson Mandela's impending unconditional release from life imprisonment – Sithole was again taken back into Soweto. In Protea police station at 9.46am he made a further confession and told his interrogators that Winnie and Zindzi Mandela were guilty of serious crimes. For nearly five hours that Tuesday Sithole gave details to police of Winnie and Zindzi Mandela's alleged criminal conduct. The session ended just after 2pm. Sithole was told he would be questioned again the next day.

But at 5pm he was found hanging by shoelaces and a belt from a water pipe of shower room 5 in John Vorster Square. The shoelaces had constricted his neck so tightly that two officers were unable to unknot them, according to evidence at the subsequent inquest.

*

Katiza told me he immediately doubted the official version of events when the news broke that Sithole had committed suicide. 'Was it really the photo that led to Sizwe's death?' he asked me rhetorically. 'I think Sizwe must have told Zindzi about the photo, and Zindzi told her mother. I believe the police hanged

Sizwe and the next morning they reported that he hanged him-self.'

Katiza said that by this time he was convinced that Winnie Mandela was working hand in hand with the South African Police. 'It was obvious,' he said. Why else had Winnie asked him to tip off the police about an impending attack by Sithole that she herself had planned? Who seriously believed it was physically possible for someone to hang themselves by their own shoelaces? And anyway what were the shoelaces and belt doing in the shower room when the police themselves testified that Sithole had arrived at John Vorster Square with neither laces nor belt?

Many deaths by hanging in South Africa's prisons in the apartheid years had been found to have occurred when asphyx-iation torture used in interrogation was pushed too far. South Africa's top pathologist, Dr Jonathan Gluckman, played a prominent role in exposing this corruption of the justice system and abuse of human rights. Dr Gluckman had gained inter-national renown in 1977 when he performed a post-mortem on the body of Black Consciousness leader Steve Biko at the request of the dead man's family and stated that it was not star-vation (as claimed by the authorities) but head wounds that caused Biko's death.

Gluckman acted as a private pathologist, performing post-mortems at the request of victims' families on those who died in state custody. He tried hard throughout his career to remain detached from the implications of his findings. 'I am an objec-tive scientist,' he said in one interview. 'I report to lawyers – they are the officers of the court.' But before his death from cancer in 1994 Dr Gluckman opened his files to reporters in a despairing attempt to stop the killings of prisoners in South

African Police custody. 'I can't stand it any longer,' he said. 'I get speechless. I get sick at heart about the whole affair. It goes on and on. I don't know how to stop it.' In his offices in central Johannesburg Gluckman had 200 files on post-mortems he had performed on people who had died in police custody. 'This is the fruit, or detritus, of a lifetime,' he said. 'Ninety per cent of the people in these files, I am convinced, were killed by the police. I have constant evidence of police handling people in a vicious manner. My impression is that they are totally out of control. They do what they like.'

Gluckman received a series of death threats following his public allegations. He removed all his documents from his office for safekeeping, recalling: 'I had all my files in the Biko case stolen and I don't want to lose any more.'

*

The inquest into Sizwe Sithole's death was perhaps even more bizarre than that into the death of Steve Biko. The government elevated it into a Commission of Inquiry, headed by Judge Richard Goldstone, later to be appointed to the International Court of Justice at The Hague. Judge Goldstone opened the inquest in Johannesburg City Hall on 2 February 1990, closed it on the 7th and gave his verdict on the 20th – nine days after Nelson Mandela walked free.

Sithole's allegations, on the day he died, about Winnie and Zindzi Mandela were made to Sergeant Jan Augustyn, who took copious notes. These have never been made public and at the inquest Augustyn told Goldstone he had not discussed Sithole's accusations with senior officers because he 'did not think it necessary'.

Chris Loxton, the lawyer who represented the Sithole family, was perplexed by Augustyn's evidence. Accusations made by Sithole against Winnie and Zindzi Mandela in the hours before his death were bound to be pertinent. Loxton applied for Sithole's police docket so that he could conduct a cross-examination based on the dead man's claims as made to Augustyn. The police protested, saying the document contained information about police investigations into anonymous 'others'.

To Loxton's astonishment, Goldstone upheld the police objections. The judge ordered the police to hand him the docket and he ruled that he personally would decide which of its contents were relevant to the inquest and would release only those documents to Loxton. He decided that the lawyer could have access to Sergeant Augustyn's notes, but added: 'I do not consider that it is relevant or in the interests of fairness and justice for the details of these untested allegations to be made public.' All the lawyers involved in the inquest swore to keep secret Augustyn's notes, and therefore also Sithole's crucial testimony. As a consequence, noted Emma Gilbey, author of The Lady, 'Sithole's accusations made against Winnie and Zindzi Mandela in the final hours of his life would not be read aloud. The notes were never released.'

The youth who Sithole said had provided his weapons, Philemon Menzima, testified he had seen Sithole briefly as he was returned to his cell at John Vorster Square on the afternoon of his death. Sithole quickly told Menzima he had been falsely accused by 'certain people'. Earlier Sithole had told Menzima that 'the people of Orlando West' (where Winnie Mandela had two of her three houses) had given false information about him.

Menzima, aged twenty, further testified that several policemen had hit and kicked him during his own interrogation.

Menzima, subsequently released, said that at one stage the police pulled an inner-tube over his face, covering his nose and mouth so that he could hardly breathe. A policeman warned him they were able to kill him without leaving any wounds.

Goldstone, in his verdict, said Sithole had killed himself. He explored three theories in reaching his conclusion. First was Sithole's anger that 'certain people from Orlando West had provided the police with fake information against him'. Sithole, said Goldstone, may well have believed he had been set up as a scapegoat 'for some reason' by people close to him. Goldstone said Sithole felt he had been totally abandoned by the Mandelas after his arrest. This was the Goldstone theory, which gelled most closely with Katiza's account.

The second theory was that Sithole feared being detained, perhaps indefinitely, under South Africa's powerful Internal Security Act, which historically had banned any organized black political opposition. Imprisonment under the Act required no proof to be offered nor charges to be laid. It required only an arbitrary declaration by the Minister of Justice, with no appeal permitted.

The third theory left swarms of questions buzzing in the air, which could not be tested because of the suppression of evidence by the judge. Goldstone said Sithole perhaps committed suicide because of 'his having implicated people very close to him in criminal conduct, i.e. Winnie and Zindzi Mandela'.

Goldstone's extraordinary behaviour has never been explained. Chris Loxton, according to his friends at the Johannesburg bar, could not understand why the state was attempting to conceal evidence against Mrs Mandela. His friends said that among the confidential evidence released to the lawyers by Goldstone in chambers was a decision the police

had made to charge Sizwe Sithole with the murder of a policeman. Mere suspicion of such an act would have guaranteed
Sithole extremely rough treatment at the hands of what was still
a police force forged by the culture of apartheid.

But Goldstone also disclosed evidence in secret to the lawyers
which included photographs of a car to which Sithole, following one bout of interrogation, had directed police. The police
had taken a bag containing guns from the boot. The car
belonged to Winnie Mandela. At the public hearing Loxton
asked the police to produce the investigation diary of the
Sithole case. They declined to do so. When asked what had been
pointed out by Sithole in the boot of a car he had taken them to
(its owner not identified in public session), the police declined
to answer.

Loxton, dismayed by the conduct of the inquiry, withdrew
from criminal work and subsequently built a career in commercial law. Winnie Mandela was never prosecuted in connection
with the guns found in her car boot as a result of information
given by Sithole in his confessions. She does not even appear to
have been questioned about the discovery: such a find connected with any other black person at that time in South Africa's
history would have resulted in immediate detention.

*

Sizwe Sithole's body was collected from the police mortuary by
his family. His cousin, Khumbuzile Ramogase, whom he had
regarded as a sister because her mother had brought him up
since he was just seven months old, arranged his funeral.

On the day the family was to bury Sizwe they waited and
waited for the body to be delivered in its coffin from Kupane
Undertakers in Soweto. 'We were all waiting for the funeral

ceremonies to begin, but the body didn't turn up,' said Khumbuzile. Eventually she went to the undertakers. Neither the body nor the proprietor was there. One of the workers said that Winnie Mandela had arrived and taken Sizwe Sithole's body.

Khumbuzile, consumed by anger, phoned Winnie's house. 'Zindzi picked up the phone,' said Khumbuzile. 'When I demanded to know where our brother was, Zindzi said, "Sizwe does not belong to you. He belongs to us."

'I went to Orlando police station to lay a charge against the undertakers and the Mandelas. The duty policeman said, "You must be very careful. Winnie Mandela is going to hurt you." So I withdrew the charge and walked to the Sisulu house to get advice from Albertina [Sisulu]. She was kind, but said, "Let go of this or you will get hurt."'

*

On Friday 9 February 1990 – two days before Nelson Mandela was released from imprisonment – Winnie and Zindzi Mandela and hundreds of youthful ANC supporters attended the Mandela-arranged funeral of Sizwe Sithole. Winnie wore a khaki guerrilla uniform trimmed in the gold, green and black colours of the ANC, unbanned just seven days earlier by President de Klerk. Unprecedentedly for a political funeral in Soweto, no police were present.

Neither were any members of Sizwe Sithole's family. They boycotted the ceremonies. 'Winnie stole him from us,' said Khumbuzile. 'Up to this day I'm waiting to bury my brother's body.'

CHAPTER ELEVEN

The Trial of the Chief Coach

FEBRUARY–SEPTEMBER 1990

Jerry Richardson's trial for the murder of Stompie Moeketsi had been scheduled to begin in February 1990. But it was postponed. The date would inevitably have caused political embarrassment to both the government and the ANC, coinciding as it did with Nelson Mandela's release and the lifting of the thirty-year ban on the ANC. Publicly the Transvaal Attorney-General justified the delay until 2 May 1990 on the ground that the proceedings were to be transferred from a regional court to the Rand Supreme Court – but no one doubted that the considerations were political.

Richardson was also charged with the attempted murder of Andrew Lerotodi Ikaneng and with the kidnap and assault of Stompie, Kenny Kgase, Thabiso Mono and Pelo Mekgwe.

The kidnap and assault charges stood also against Katiza Cebekhulu, Xoliswa and Nompumelelo Falati, John Morgan, Jabu Sithole, Mpho Mabelane and Brian Mabusa with a view to a later trial. No charges had been made against Winnie Mandela.

Katiza and the others had been briefed by Dali Mpofu on Winnie's assertion that she was in Brandfort, 200 miles away from Soweto, at the time of the assaults on Stompie in late

December 1988. Prior to the Richardson trial, Katiza said, Mpofu was making unexplained visits to Brandfort. The reason for Mpofu's fixation on Brandfort became evident during the Richardson trial, which focused at times so heavily on Winnie that Judge Brian O'Donovan felt it necessary to issue a public warning to prosecution and defence lawyers: 'This trial is not about Mrs Mandela.'

Kgase, Mekgwe and Mono all gave evidence of being assaulted by Winnie on the evening of 29 December 1988 after their kidnap from Paul Verryn's manse. Kgase and Mono had asked to give their evidence *in camera*. 'I fear for my life,' said Kgase. 'I believe that no one cares, no one cares . . . I want to tell the whole truth, but one doesn't have anything left in terms of security.' Mono said: 'What I am going to say, which is the truth, will put my life in danger because of the present situation in our country.' Judge O'Donovan refused their request and ordered them to testify in open court.

With hindsight – as later chapters will attempt to explain – Pelo Mekgwe's evidence in Richardson's trial was particularly significant. He said ten or more people had taken part in beating him, Stompie, Mono and Kgase. The assailants included Winnie, Katiza, Richardson and three MUFC members he knew as 'Scar', 'Slash' and 'Black Sunday'. Mekgwe said Winnie began insulting them – 'I remember the words she said. She said we are not fit to be alive . . . We were assaulted with open hands, fists, with sjamboks. We were also hit with a bottle on the knees.'

Mekgwe said Winnie accused him and the others of sleeping with Paul Verryn. 'I denied such allegations,' Mekgwe told the court. 'I said I never slept with Paul.'

Asked if he could say who assaulted Stompie, Mekgwe

replied: 'Yes. Winnie was the first, Jerry was next, Slash, Xoliswa, Nompumelelo, Scar, Jabu, Desmond.' Asked how the assault stopped, Mekgwe said: 'I was taken outside together with Kenny, Thabiso. The three of us were taken out and they were busy assaulting Stompie. He was continuously assaulted.' Mekgwe was then asked to describe how Stompie looked after these assaults. 'What I remember is that his face was swollen,' he said. 'And his eyes were almost closed. His head was also swollen.'

Richardson's counsel, Advocate Henti Joubert, challenged Mekgwe: 'The accused says Mrs Mandela was not there that night [of 29 December 1988].' Mekgwe replied: 'That is what he is saying, but I know that she was present.'

Joubert made similar challenges to Kgase and Mono. To Kgase, Joubert said: 'The accused told me that this evidence of yours that Mrs Mandela arrived on the scene and that you were assaulted for a period of two hours is a lie?' Kgase replied: 'I say it is the truth.' Joubert then asked rhetorically: 'As far as he [Richardson] can remember, Mrs Mandela went away the morning of 29 December, and as far as he can remember she only returned the next Monday, which was 2 January.' Kgase responded: 'I saw Mrs Mandela and all the things she did.'

To Mono, Joubert issued the challenge: 'He [Richardson] will also testify that Mrs Mandela was not at her home that night of 29 December 1988.' Mono replied: 'That is not the truth because she is the first person to assault us.'

*

Katiza Cebekhulu and the other co-accused were not called as witnesses in the Richardson trial: it would have prejudiced their own trials. Winnie Mandela, who had not been charged with any offences, could however have been called as a material witness. Early on Kathy Satchwell, Richardson's solicitor instructing Advocate Joubert, attempted to get Winnie into the witness box to testify on behalf of Mrs Mandela's MUFC chief coach. 'It is absolutely essential for preparing and presenting the defence of Mr Richardson that we have the opportunity to consult with Mrs Mandela timeously with regard to various of these allegations,' Satchwell wrote to Ismail Ayob, who on Nelson Mandela's instructions had resumed his role as Winnie's solicitor.

Ayob replied that he had advised Winnie not to give evidence and she had accepted the opinion.

Satchwell herself took the stand on the third day of the trial and said Winnie was aware of the evidence that had been laid in court on the opening days. 'She [Winnie] indicated to my clerk a witness whom we could contact and possibly bring to court as a defence witness,' said Satchwell. The clerk was Dali Mpofu, Winnie's lover, who, Katiza told me, had been busy in the previous months constructing a 'Brandfort alibi' and instructing Richardson, Katiza and others on the details of the alibi.

At Winnie's suggestion, said Satchwell, Mpofu had visited Brandfort and met the witness for the defence, Mrs Nora Moahloli, a primary schoolteacher who befriended Winnie during her eight years of internal exile. Moahloli lived four houses away from Winnie in Phathakahle, Brandfort's tiny township which in the mid-1970s was home to about 5,000 black people. Although it was illegal in the early days to speak to Nelson Mandela's exiled wife, Moahloli began sending her young son Monwabisi with gifts of pumpkins and vegetables as a gesture of solidarity. A friendship grew and Winnie eventually helped Moahloli to set up a crèche for pre-school children.

Appearing at Richardson's trial, Moahloli testified that Winnie had arrived in Brandfort from Soweto on the evening of Thursday 29 December 1988 – the time when Kgase, Mono and Mekgwe testified Mrs Mandela was participating in the first beating of Stompie Moeketsi, accounts confirmed by Katiza in his conversations with me. Winnie stayed for two days, returning to Soweto on New Year's Eve, said Moahloli. While in Brandfort Winnie had discussed with her how to rebuild social-work projects which had collapsed since 1985. Winnie had also attended township meetings and visited old folk. Moahloli's testimony had nothing at all to do with Jerry Richardson, Emma Gilbey observed in *The Lady*: 'It mapped a strategy for a future Mandela defence. For the first time in the seventeen months since the abduction, an alibi had been mentioned.'

But confusion reigned in court over the Brandfort alibi. Richardson contradicted Moahloli, saying Winnie was in Brandfort for four days, not two. He had her leaving Soweto early on 29 December and not returning until Monday 2 January 1989, some thirty-six hours or more after Stompie Moeketsi's 'disappearance'. Under intense questioning, Richardson stuck to his story, saying at one point: 'Mrs Mandela was absent the day when I went to fetch them [the youths in Verryn's manse], the 29th.'

Xoliswa Falati contradicted Richardson. Falati said she and Winnie had visited Dr Abu-Baker Asvat in the late afternoon of 29 December with Katiza so that evidence of the youth's alleged homosexual rape could be medically authenticated.

The state prosecutor, Advocate Chris van Vuuren, contested Nora Moahloli's status as an independent witness. 'I submit that she has very much an interest in the matter which is obviously to protect Mrs Mandela, to try and clear her name.' Van

Vuuren asked Moahloli about other dates, to which she gave ambiguous answers. He submitted that she therefore could also have been confused about the exact date of Mrs Mandela's visit to Brandfort.

Van Vuuren confronted Falati with the evidence of the medical card from Dr Asvat's surgery showing that she, Winnie and Katiza had visited the doctor on Friday 30 December, not 29 December. That was not possible, said Falati, because Winnie was in Brandfort on 30 and 31 December. She insisted that the date on the medical card must have been changed. (Falati would later admit to journalists that she had perjured herself on Dali Mpofu's instructions and assert that Winnie had not travelled to Brandfort, but had remained in Soweto throughout the period 29–31 December 1988.)

Van Vuuren also pointed out that none of the allegations of rape against Katiza had been entered on his medical card by Asvat. Van Vuuren said Asvat's only written remarks about Katiza read: 'Mentally confused, occasionally cries, occasional headaches and insomnia.' Falati responded by saying that someone had obviously killed Asvat because he was the only person who could prove that Katiza Cebekhulu had been homosexually raped. Her precise words were: 'That was the reason then why Dr Asvat was killed, because he was the only professional man who could prove these that I am saying. That is the reason why they killed him . . . so that there should be nobody to give evidence in this case.'

Richardson admitted stabbing Andrew Ikaneng and assaulting Stompie, Kgase, Mono and Mekgwe. But he categorically denied murdering Stompie Moeketsi. He said he knew nothing about Stompie's death and had no idea who might have murdered him. He denied evidence given by Kgase, Mekgwe and

Mono that he had taken Stompie away from Winnie's house on New Year's Eve. He said he had discovered only on 1 January 1989 that Stompie was missing. 'We were amazed for the whole day, because we did not know where Stompie was.' He and other MUFC members had looked for him everywhere 'thinking that he might be in the toilet or another room, but we could not spot him.'

By the time Henti Joubert came to make his closing speech for Richardson he had decided the best defence was to argue that his client had been lying throughout to protect Winnie Mandela. 'He is protecting others because if he mentions their names his life won't be worth much,' said Joubert. 'He is protecting himself, protecting others and protecting himself from others.' There was no doubt, said Joubert, that Mrs Mandela had not only been involved in the assaults but had started the whole process.

Concluding the prosecution's case, van Vuuren said Kgase, Mekgwe and Mono had had no reasons to lie about Winnie Mandela's assault on them or about her presence in Soweto when Richardson, Falati and Moahloli asserted she was 200 miles away in Brandfort: 'They testified in court that they feared for their lives, so why would they lie about Mrs Mandela's involvement and by doing so enhance the danger to themselves?'

On Friday 25 May, Judge O'Donovan summed up and gave his verdict. He said there had been some inconsistencies in evidence given by Kgase, Mono and Mekgwe. The defence had tried to exploit these, but he added: 'It would be surprising if there were not such inconsistencies, having regard to the lapse of time, the scene which was constantly changing, and the fact that different witnesses may observe different facets of a situation or that their powers of recollection or memory may vary.' Their evidence was credible and had 'a ring of truth'. Judge O'Donovan went on: 'No reason was suggested why the State eyewitnesses, who had every reason to remember 29 December, should be untruthful on that point.'

Commenting on evidence that Winnie was present during the beatings of Stompie and the state witnesses, O'Donovan said: 'Mrs Mandela herself, acting on legal advice, declined to testify. This is a matter which was canvassed extensively by both the State and the defence and on which both asked the court to make a finding as to whether Mrs Mandela was present at any time during the assaults. The court finding on this issue is that Mrs Mandela was present on 29 December for at least part of the time.'

This last part of the summing-up caused an absolute sensation, overshadowing the subsequent verdict on Richardson. Winnie's alibi had been rejected by one of the most senior judges in the land, meaning there would now be pressure to indict Winnie on charges related to the kidnap, assault and murder of Stompie Moeketsi.

Dudu Chili, who sat in the public gallery throughout the Richardson trial, had no doubt about what should be done. She told reporters something 'very fishy' was going on, for she knew, from her knowledge of the MUFC attacks on her own house and the statements given by Lolo Sono's parents, that the police had accumulated what she described as such 'a thick pile of evidence' against Winnie that she should have been charged long ago.

Judge O'Donovan said no evidence had been produced to substantiate the rumours concerning Paul Verryn. The evidence against Richardson was solely circumstantial, but the

accused's testimony had contained 'manifest absurdities'.
O'Donovan convicted Richardson of murdering Stompie
Moeketsi, of attempting to murder Andrew Ikaneng, and of
kidnapping and assaulting Stompie, Kenny Kgase, Thabiso
Mono and Pelo Mekgwe. He said the court would reconvene on
6 August for sentencing.

*

Winnie Mandela appeared unfazed by O'Donovan's remarks.
Her husband, the centre of world attention following his release
from prison, visited Nigeria and openly defended her. 'Even
now as I am talking to you she is still being persecuted in South
Africa,' he declared as Kgase, Mekgwe and Mono gave evidence
of her assault on Stompie.

Nelson at that time was clearly intent on rehabilitating
Winnie. Within a month of O'Donovan's verdict he took her
on a ten-day triumphal visit to eight United States cities. On 19
June Winnie addressed an ecstatic crowd of 200,000, mostly
black Americans, in Harlem. 'We want to count on you if things
go wrong on that negotiation table,' she said. 'We will know
you will be there with us when we go back to the bush to fight
the white man.' It was a speech which caused immense embarrassment to senior ANC officials, who were trying to project a
moderate image to George Bush's White House administration. As the tour continued Americans were bombarded with
images of Nelson and Winnie riding together in a flashy
'Mandela-mobile'. One newspaper described Winnie as 'looking like a latter-day Boadicea in a Xhosa caftan'.

Asked on television about her husband's capacity to with-
stand the tough pace of their travels, Winnie replied:
'Physically, he is in perfect health, and I should know best,'

giving the studio audience a coy, coquettish and knowing smile. In fact – as Nelson would publicly acknowledge years later – they had not made love since he left prison and would never do so again.

Winnie was on such a high that her exuberance enchanted her New York hosts, Mayor David Dinkins and his wife Joyce. When Winnie went with Mrs Dinkins on an hour-long shopping spree on 7th Avenue she entered a boutique, chose three expensive outfits and emerged from the changing room wearing one of them, a purple silk ballgown, and whooped and danced in response to the applause of her entourage. An ANC aide asked the boutique owner if there was 'any consideration' he could give Mrs Mandela. With a rictus smile, the owner said: 'How about if I just donate the dresses to her?' The offer was accepted with alacrity.

Julia Belafonte, wife of the singer Harry Belafonte, who helped organize the Mandela visit, described as 'irrelevant' the allegations against Winnie back in South Africa, and went on: 'She's a wonderful role-model for women.'

Emma Gilbey noted that Winnie's speeches were framed as though from South Africa's Mother of the Nation, heavily sprinkled with references to family and children. 'In New York,' said Gilbey, 'she specifically gave thanks that the Americans had not forgotten South African children.'

*

By the time Winnie returned with Nelson from America two months had passed since Judge O'Donovan had found Jerry Richardson guilty of murdering Stompie. One of the state witnesses, Kenny Kgase, was becoming agitated because it seemed the authorities still planned no move against Mrs Mandela.

Patrick Laurence, one of South Africa's most respected liberal commentators, noted the inertia of the authorities and wrote: 'If Mrs Mandela is not charged there will be allegations of a political deal between President F. W. de Klerk and Mr Nelson Mandela, struck in the interests of a Government–ANC settlement.'

Kgase made a move which, in the long run, would cost him dearly.

I was away in Namibia, researching a story about Bushmen, when Kgase walked into the Johannesburg offices of the London *Daily Telegraph* and *Sunday Telegraph* and offered his own written story to my colleague, Peter Taylor. His tale was an expanded version of the evidence he had given in court. It seemed safe to publish it in a newspaper: the verdict in the Richardson trial had been given, although the trial was technically unfinished pending the sentencing. Kgase felt passionately that the time had come for more publicity to force the issue of Winnie's involvement with Stompie.

Peter Taylor polished and edited Kgase's fractured prose, which eventually appeared as a two-page spread in the *Sunday Telegraph* of 22 July 1990. Describing his arrival with Stompie at Winnie's home after their kidnapping from Verryn's manse, Kgase wrote: 'Mrs Mandela came into the crowded room. Her movements were slow and weary, but she seemed to tower over everyone. She had the confidence which comes from power, and she eyed us one by one. "For 26 years uMthetheli [a reference to Nelson Mandela] has been inside for your benefit, yet you are continuing your nonsense," she said. "You are not fit to be alive."'

Kgase described Mrs Mandela calling for sjamboks to be brought as part of her subsequent assault on Stompie, Kgase,

Mono and Mekgwe. 'I could hardly believe that Winnie Mandela, a Mother of the Nation, could assault people in this way,' read Kgase's text as edited by Peter Taylor. 'I had admired and respected Nelson Mandela all my adult life. But she obviously thought that no one could ever challenge her behaviour. I don't think that she even realized she was doing wrong. She had been harassed, and that gave her the right to harass other people. Thanks to the media, she thought of herself as an international figure. She was spoiled.'

The beatings continued, said Kgase. By the time Stompie's severe lambasting on the second day had finished there was a big lump on the side of his head and he was 'wriggling in agony, utterly destroyed'.

By the third day, New Year's Eve, there was a terrible sense of foreboding. 'Stompie could not eat,' wrote Kgase.

He threw up every time he tried to force something down his throat, and the sick little boy was made to clean up his vomit.

Later, Jerry asked him to write down his address, which he did with difficulty, and gather his belongings. Stompie managed to get to his feet, grabbed anything that looked like his, and was gone after Jerry without even saying goodbye. We could not sleep that night. None of us wanted to believe that Stompie was going to be killed and the thought of his death terrified me.

In the morning people were quiet and kept their distance, as though something terrible had happened. I saw Jerry's light boots standing against a wall, and they had spots of blood. Truly, Stompie was not living. Stompie's death was a way for them to demonstrate their power over us. They could take life and no law could prevent them.

*

Kgase's apprehension seemed justified when, three months later, there had still been no move to prosecute Winnie and Nelson appointed her head of the ANC's Social Welfare Department, which had as one of its responsibilities child-care policy. The appointment attracted widespread protests from within the ANC. More than 100 ANC branches within the Johannesburg area sent letters lamenting Winnie's promotion. And when one branch failed to get a reply to its objection, one of its members wrote a letter to the *Weekly Mail* protesting: 'Just where are we heading? What culture are we building within the movement? Is this the beginning of going like the rest of Africa, like Imelda Marcos?'

At the time of Winnie's appointment she was not a member of the powerful and active Black Social Workers' Association: she had never been involved in the extensive network of health and welfare agencies and organizations that had emerged through the grass-roots democratic culture of the 1980s. South African journalist Mark Gevisser, writing in the *New York Times*, quoted a 'health professional and leading ANC member' – believed to be Albertina Sisulu – as saying: 'It's a travesty that she got the post. There's a whole theory of post-apartheid welfare that's developing and Winnie has never shown the slightest interest in it.'

Their apprehension was compounded when Winnie appointed a deputy with absolutely no social work experience. His name was Dali Mpofu.

*

By the time the men, and women, of the law reassembled at the Rand Supreme Court on 6 August for the sentencing of Jerry Richardson for the murder of Stompie Moeketsi, Advocate

Henti Joubert had decided how to frame his final plea for leniency. He would cite evidence, given at the trial, of Winnie Mandela's heavy involvement in the events and use that to argue in mitigation of sentence.

Joubert called a clinical psychologist, Midge Doepel, who testified that Richardson appeared to idolize Mrs Mandela. 'He fears and admires Winnie Mandela so much that he feels the need to protect her, even to the point of dying for his struggle,' said Ms Doepel. 'His regressive tendency needs are explicit in calling her "Mummy".' Richardson was of low intelligence (an IQ of only 63) from a poor and emotionally deprived background which left him with a sense of inadequacy. He regarded Winnie's acceptance of him and his residence at her home as status symbols. His repeated lying in the face of damning evidence could have emanated from his need to protect Mrs Mandela as the source of his self-worth.

When Joubert rose, he said Winnie had started the whole saga and had been involved in the assaults until the walls of the room in her house were spattered with blood. His client had been unable to leave the room where Stompie was beaten for fear of falling from Winnie's favour. He said the MUFC, Mrs Mandela and the struggle had given Richardson's life meaning: as a consequence, Richardson's admittedly 'terrible qualities' were 'easily exploited by people involved in the struggle, people like Mrs Mandela'.

Judge O'Donovan was not persuaded. He sentenced Richardson to death for the murder of Stompie, plus eighteen years' imprisonment for the attempted murder of Ikaneng and the kidnapping of Stompie, Kgase, Mono and Mekgwe and the assaults upon them. Richardson was saved from the gallows only on appeal, when his sentence was changed to life imprisonment.

Henti Joubert told me he was both amazed and distressed by how philosophically Richardson took his fate. Joubert said: 'Jerry believes Winnie will come riding on a white charger to release him from Pretoria Central Prison.'

*

Meanwhile, another trial began that August in the Rand Supreme Court. Charles Zwane was charged with murdering thirteen-year-old Finkie Msomi when the MUFC fire-bombed Dudu Chili's house on 22 February 1989. Zwane faced eight other counts of murder, eight of attempted murder, one count of arson and one of illegal possession of firearms. Gybon Gabela, who was also alleged to have taken part in the attack and to have kicked Stompie Moeketsi brutally on 30 December 1988, was meant to face the same charges. Gabela, however, was absent: he had fled the country and sought safety in an ANC camp in distant Tanzania.

Zwane's counsel, Advocate S. Jacobs, attempted to bring Jerry Richardson from prison to testify about Winnie's Football Club and the powerful effect it would have had on his client's actions. Jacobs contacted Kathy Satchwell, who referred him to her articled clerk responsible for Richardson. Dali Mpofu said he had visited Richardson and his client did not want to testify. Jacobs argued in court, nevertheless, that Zwane had been influenced by Winnie Mandela's powerful personality. But no effort was made to summon Winnie to give evidence.

Zwane was found guilty on all charges and sentenced to death, commuted to life imprisonment under an amnesty declared by President F. W. de Klerk as part of his attempt to create a constructive atmosphere for negotiations with Nelson Mandela and the ANC.

*

The day after Zwane was sentenced, 17 September 1990, and nearly twenty months after Stompie Moeketsi had died, the Attorney-General announced that an eighth name would be added to that of Katiza Cebekhulu and six others already indicted for kidnapping and assaulting Stompie Moeketsi, Kenny Kgase, Pelo Mekgwe and Thabiso Mono.

The new defendant would be the ANC's Director of Social Welfare, Nomzamo Winifred Zanyiwe Madikizela Mandela.

CHAPTER TWELVE

Time to Run

SEPTEMBER 1990–FEBRUARY 1991

Who ultimately decided that Winnie Mandela had to be prosecuted may not be known for a long time. She was a source of
embarrassment all round. By September 1990 the South
African peace process had reached an extremely delicate stage.
The government had desegregated hospitals as another signal of
its good intent and on 7 August the ANC had suspended its
thirty-year armed struggle – probably as important a conces-
sion as De Klerk's 2 February decision to unban the ANC and
release Nelson Mandela from prison.

To prosecute Winnie, who was being rehabilitated by the
ANC, taking her place alongside her husband at township
rallies and glittering banquets abroad, would be to risk squand-
ering the goodwill built up with Nelson. Speaking of De Klerk
in one interview in September 1990, Nelson Mandela said: 'I
still regard him as a man of integrity, and I think he feels the
same way about me. We have developed enormous respect for
each other. I can call him at any time, I can get him out of bed
or out of Cabinet meetings.'

A tremendous amount rested on the Mandela–De Klerk relationship. The two men were meeting frequently to discuss how
to clear the way for full-scale constitutional negotiations in

1991. On 1 September De Klerk said 1,300 political prisoners would be released; a month later he announced that 22,000 exiled South Africans, most of them ANC loyalists, would be allowed to return home.

The dignity and moral seriousness of Nelson, even in his most hardline speeches, had earned him grudging respect from whites. His conciliatory policies were not universally popular among his followers. When he announced the suspension of armed struggle there were angry mutterings among ANC Young Turks, Winnie's favoured constituency, that the movement had discarded one of its best bargaining tools too soon, leaving the white-controlled army and police as masters of the game.

Diplomats reported that several members of the government wanted Transvaal Attorney-General Klaus von Lieres to forget about charging Winnie in the interests of the greater historical cause, a peaceful solution to South Africa's agonizing political problems. These ministers, including Justice Minister Kobie Coetsee, feared that the strain on Nelson of a Winnie trial and possible jail sentence would be too great. Also, might not a jailed Winnie become a martyr figure able to set the country ablaze from her prison cell and destroy the last chances of a settlement? And what would be the consequences of a flawed justice system, forged under apartheid, pitting itself against the romance of what the media had projected as one of world history's greatest love stories?

But the government had also to consider the consequence of failing to prosecute and openly demonstrating that a suspected accessory to murder might be above the law simply because she was the wife of a great leader. This might be especially dangerous as South Africa inched towards equality before the law for all citizens. The allegation would have arisen that there was one law for the lofty and another for the lowly, that a precedent was being set for a 'new South Africa' modelled on the most reprehensible of black states north of the Limpopo River.

Paradoxically, some of the strongest resentment about the government's tardiness in prosecuting Winnie came from within the ANC. 'It is an open secret in ANC circles that some of Mr Mandela's oldest and closest friends in the movement cannot bear the sight of his wife,' wrote John Carlin, the South African correspondent of the *Independent*, in a seminal and courageous article on 21 September 1990. Carlin, who investigated sixteen murders in which Winnie's Mandela United Football Club had been involved, wrote that many people with impeccable ANC credentials worried about Winnie getting off and had felt compelled to assist him in exposing her. But most who spoke to Carlin in the course of his investigation – carried out also for a BBC radio programme *File on Four* – begged for their names not to be made public. 'I'll be dead meat if you do,' one lawyer well informed about the MUFC told him. Another lawyer locked his door on Carlin, saying: 'She's mad, evil and very, very dangerous.'

Carlin said Nelson Mandela was vulnerable because he believed Winnie had been unswervingly loyal to him throughout his twenty-seven years in prison. 'He even hinted once to feeling a degree of guilt for having failed to be around when his family needed him,' wrote the *Independent*'s correspondent. 'It is the one regret he has expressed publicly over his long years of imprisonment. No one inside the ANC has had the courage to confront him with the unpleasant truth that lies behind the face she presents to him. It is a truth that Mr Mandela himself has consistently refused to contemplate.'

Whatever the pressures on Attorney-General von Lieres –
and there were surely many – Judge O'Donovan's conduct of
the Richardson case made a decision to prosecute Winnie virtually inevitable. The defence strategy had deeply implicated
Winnie in the events leading to Stompie Moeketsi's death. Nora
Moahloli, who was totally ignorant of the facts in the
Richardson case, had been produced solely to exonerate
Winnie – and the strategy failed when O'Donovan rejected the
alibi that Winnie had been far away from Soweto by the evening
of 29 December 1988.

The decision was made. The stage was being set for a great
real-life drama, a trial that might become more famous than the
one that led to Nelson Mandela's life sentence in 1964.

*

I was in court on 24 September 1990 with scores of reporters to
watch Winnie Mandela charged formally with kidnapping and
assaulting Stompie Moeketsi. She was charged also with the
same offences in relation to Pelo Mekgwe, Kenny Kgase and
Thabiso Mono.

Some 200 members of ANC Women's League groups from
outside Johannesburg had been bussed in to give Winnie moral
support. They sang liberation songs and danced around Winnie
and Nelson as they walked from their car to Courtroom 8 at
Soweto's Protea Regional Court. The women carried a variety
of banners. One said: 'We Love Our Winnie', and another
'Mama we Sizwe [Mother of the Nation] we admire your
courage'. Yet another proclaimed: 'Veterans condemn homosexuality.' We didn't understand that one at the time, but with
hindsight it was a clear reference to the allegations Winnie had
made, and would continue to make, against Paul Verryn.

There were about eighty heavily armed policemen on duty. Nelson Mandela held his wife's hand as they pressed through the crowds towards the courtroom. He refused to make any comment on the proceedings, but joked with reporters and television teams hemming him in: 'Let me past. I've already been in prison too long.' Winnie, dressed in a chic navy-blue suit with a frilled white silk blouse, looked radiant while by Nelson's side. But once she entered the narrow plywood dock, next to the seven other defendants, including Katiza, she seemed apprehensive and nervous and occasionally rested her head on her clenched hand.

Nelson sat upright on the wooden public benches behind the dock with a severe look on his face throughout the hour-long proceedings. The magistrate, T. F. Veldman, ordered that the case be transferred to the Rand Supreme Court on 4 February 1991. He did not ask the defendants to plead and he dismissed demands by a state prosecutor for the trial to begin on 30 October. Veldman said the trial would not be a simple matter and was likely to last more than four weeks. The Attorney-General had decided only seven days earlier to prosecute Mrs Mandela, so she was entitled to plenty of time to prepare her defence.

Veldman released Winnie, Katiza and the six other accused on Rand 500 bail each – bail for all of them was paid by Winnie. Bail conditions required them to turn up at the Rand Supreme Court on 4 February, report to their local police station twice a week until then and inform the court of any change of address. Veldman said Winnie would be allowed to leave the country in October to accompany Nelson on visits to the Soviet Union, Japan, India, Singapore and Australia.

I remember Katiza only vaguely from that day, a short,

sullen-looking, somewhat dishevelled youth. If I had known his full story I would have shown more interest. If I had known what was about to happen to him every nerve-ending would have been fully alert. None of us on the press benches realized the importance of this small man, a fugitive from Mpumalanga who was about to become a fugitive all over again.

*

Katiza returned from the Protea court appearance to his room at the back of Winnie Mandela's Diepkloof Extension house – just beyond the jacuzzi beside which he said he saw Stompie being stabbed – where he had lived and kept a low profile in the months following Nelson Mandela's release from prison.

He wondered what would happen next. Winnie's situation had changed. She was in serious trouble and he knew a lot, perhaps too much, about her – the sting on Paul Verryn; how he had joined her in beating Stompie; Stompie's ordeal by the jacuzzi; Winnie's orders which had led to the deaths of Lolo Sono and Finkie Msomi and the attempted murder of Andrew Ikaneng; the sting on Sizwe Sithole; how the Brandfort alibi was constructed. He was also sure that Sizwe Sithole had told Winnie, through Zindzi, about the photo in which she was entwined with Dali Mpofu.

Katiza did not wait long for an answer to the thoughts racing through his mind. A few evenings after the court hearing one of his co-accused, Winnie's driver, John Morgan, entered his room. Morgan was extremely disgruntled after his court appearance. He had complained about the unfairness to a foreign journalist who gave him a lift back from Protea into Johannesburg: he could not understand why he had been charged at all; he was only a witness to events; he had been arrested for what he had seen, not for what he had done.

Now Morgan woke Katiza and told him to run quickly. 'Morgan said Winnie and the others were planning to kill me,' Katiza told me.

Katiza Cebekhulu had seen the consequences of MUFC death sentences many times and needed no second urging. He dressed frantically and slipped on his trainers. He had no time to collect any of his meagre possessions before he hurdled the fence at the back of the Diepkloof house and ran and ran.

*

'So I ran, sleeping all over the place in and around Soweto, in drainage pipes, in toilets at the back of houses,' Katiza told me. 'I was so afraid. One woman I knew found me in the toilet of her house. It was raining heavily, so she asked me why I didn't knock. I said Winnie Mandela wanted to kill me and she should report it to the police. So she sent her child to the police station, and he came back and said the police said it was a trick [hoax]. So they didn't come.'

Katiza was now alarmed at the length of the delay Magistrate Veldman had decreed before the trial of Winnie, himself and others should begin. Believing his life was in danger unless Winnie was brought quickly to court, he decided to try to seek access to the judge scheduled to preside at her trial. One day in early November 1989 he called at the Rand Supreme Court in central Johannesburg and managed to meet Advocate Chris van Vuuren, who had prosecuted Jerry Richardson and had been appointed assistant state prosecutor for Winnie's coming trial. 'I complained [to van Vuuren] that my life was in danger,' Katiza told me. 'I said I was being harassed by Winnie and I wasn't safe, and I said there shouldn't be any delay in trying her. He said Winnie couldn't do anything to me.'

Katiza said he left in a state of depression after van Vuuren told him he could not see either the trial judge or any senior officers in the Soweto Murder and Robbery Squad.

I sought out Advocate van Vuuren in September 1995 to check whether he remembered the meeting six years earlier with Katiza. He confirmed that he did: 'He [Katiza] arrived one day at my chambers, and I told him that as a state prosecutor in the coming trial [at which Katiza would be a defendant] I couldn't speak to him.' It would have been a breach of legal ethics.

Van Vuuren phoned Advocate Henti Joubert, who was being instructed to present Katiza's defence when he came to trial. 'Henti told me he was coming from his chambers to speak to Cebekhulu. But by the time he arrived Cebekhulu had scuttled.'

Back on the run, Katiza moved constantly for weeks between five black townships around Johannesburg, breaking his bail conditions by failing to report twice a week to the police. During the previous months he had removed the photo of Winnie and Dali making love from its hiding place under the kennel behind Winnie's house and reburied it in its plastic cover near Orlando swimming pool. Now he crept back one night, dug it up and burned it.

Sometimes he slept with the hundreds of poverty-stricken down-and-outs and alcoholics at Park Station, in central Johannesburg, where both he and the fictional Absalom Kumalo had first arrived from Natal. 'I was looking for food in dustbins. Sometimes I slept on local trains for twenty-four hours, just moving backwards and forwards. One night I stayed in Soweto with my friend Churi Mdanis, who worked at the swimming pool. Winnie had cars out looking for me, and Jabu

Sithole [of the MUFC, and one of Winnie's and Katiza's co-accused] turned up outside Churi's house. Jabu came to the door carrying a gun and told Churi he believed I was inside and that Winnie had accused me of working with the police – if you left Winnie's house they always said you worked with the police. When Churi saw Jabu approaching he told me that if I went out they would kill me. He protected me and managed to persuade Jabu I was not there.'

One night watching a television set through the window of a fish-and-chip shop Katiza saw a police photo of himself on *Police File*, a TV programme which appealed for the public's help in tracking wanted criminal suspects.

While on the run Katiza had plenty of time to consider why John Morgan had warned him of the plan to kill him. He assumed it was because Morgan was the only MUFC member he had confided in about seeing Winnie stab Stompie by the jacuzzi. He had told Morgan about it when he was arrested on 21 February 1989 and taken to Protea police station, where Morgan was also detained.

In the three months Katiza was a fugitive within South Africa, events moved on in the drama of a fast-changing South Africa. Though his photograph had been shown on *Police File*, Katiza's flight did not otherwise make news: no one attached any significance to yet another disappearance of yet another impoverished Zulu from Natal into the maw of the townships where people died violently and anonymously every day. In December 1990, as Katiza continued to hide, army and police reinforcements were sent in to the Johannesburg township of Tokoza, where sixty-five people were shot or hacked to death in one day of fighting between ANC and Inkatha supporters. On 13 December, seventy-three-year-old Oliver Tambo, the ANC's

President, returned home after thirty years of exile to a tumul-
tuous welcome by thousands of people at Johannesburg's Jan
Smuts Airport. Mandela, although the *de facto* leader of the
movement, was at that time the ANC's Vice-President.

*

Katiza's three months as a fugitive came to an end on 21
January 1991. He had returned briefly to Soweto and in the late
afternoon was helping an acquaintance sell newspapers on a
street corner. A police car drew up and two armed white officers
arrested him and drove him to Protea police station.

Katiza said he was ushered into the office of Captain Fred
Dempsey, the Soweto Murder and Robbery Squad officer in
charge of investigating alleged MUFC offences and the Abu-
Baker Asvat murder. Katiza was warned in English about the
seriousness of his offence in jumping bail. The opening of the
trial of Winnie, Katiza and their six co-accused was only a fortnight away. Dempsey, said Katiza, began a discussion with the
two other officers in Afrikaans and Katiza was then ordered
back into the police car.

Katiza assumed he was going to be handed over to the
Attorney-General's office and detained until 4 February, the
first day of the Rand Supreme Court trial. But, in a bizarre and
dramatic development, the police took him elsewhere.

'They drove me to Winnie's [Diepkloof] house. I thought
they were going to arrest her too. But they spoke to her in
Afrikaans and then handed me over to her. I couldn't believe it.
I refused to get out of the car, but they grabbed me and pulled
me out. Jabu Sithole [one of the co-accused] tied my hands
behind my back and took me to the same back room in which
Stompie lay after Winnie had beaten him.

'I was lying there on the floor when Winnie appeared in the doorway. She leaned on one side of the entrance with a hand on her hip and said: "You. Give me the picture."'

As Katiza's words tumbled out, I tried to picture the image he painted of this forceful, famous woman towering over him and issuing her demand.

'I said I didn't have it. She said: "Do you want to become my enemy?" I said again that I didn't have it. She asked me where I got the photo from in the first place. I told her I got it in Themba's room. She said: "You *will* give me the picture."'

'Then Winnie, Jabu, Brian Mabusa, Mpho Mabelane and others started to kick me all over. I couldn't do anything because my hands were tied. I was in the middle of a circle of them. My teeth began to be loose and some fell out. They beat me until I can't even feel the pain: I couldn't feel anything. [Mabusa and Mabelane were also co-accused in the impending trial.]

'It was then, because the police had handed me over to Winnie and because Jabu, Brian and Mpho were there with her, that for the first time I realize Winnie is working with the police. As I began thinking about all these things, I told myself it was entirely possible also that the police had killed Dr Asvat.'

Katiza paused, lowered and slowed his voice and said to me: 'You know what she did then?'

I shook my head.

'They came with boiling water like this . . .'

'In a kettle?' I asked.

'Yes. They pour me like this [demonstrating water being poured over his head] from the hair. If you can see here . . .' Katiza showed me the faint scars of the burned skin remaining beneath the mat of his hair, and he ran my fingers over them.

'They poured the water like this to me. So all the water came out here [demonstrates it running down the side of his face, shoulder and arm]. I was burned down my arm. My skin all here it was burned . . . I was so frustrated and dizzy, but I heard Winnie say: "Take him."

'When I got my senses again I was in the boot of a car. My hands had come free, but at first I couldn't open the boot. I kicked and kicked and then we went over some bumps and at last the boot came open. I rolled out and ran and the next thing I remember is being in Baragwanath Hospital. But I can't remember how I find myself in the hospital.'

Katiza estimates he was a patient in Baragwanath from the night of 21 January 1991 to 1 or 2 February. His head, arms and leg burns were treated and all his back teeth, broken and loosened in the beating, were removed. He recalled burned skin being removed with a razor and his arm being plunged in warm water.

On being discharged from hospital, Katiza went to John Morgan's house and asked for a place to sleep. (His friend Churi Mdanis had disappeared from Soweto after rumours went around that he had killed a girl.) He described to Morgan what had happened since Winnie's driver warned him to go on the run. Morgan promised to hide him.

*

John Morgan appeared at the Rand Supreme Court with Winnie Mandela, Xoliswa Falati and Nompumelelo Falati on Monday 4 February 1991 at the opening of the Stompie kidnap and assault trial.

The four other co-accused were missing. Katiza, identified perceptively by John Carlin of the *Independent* as being 'expected to deliver damning testimony against "the Mother of the Nation"', was hiding in Morgan's home after his stay in Baragwanath. And on Thursday 31 January the Soweto Murder and Robbery Squad had announced that three other co-accused – Jabu Sithole, Brian Mabusa and Mpho Mabelane – had skipped bail and had not been traced. The police announcement came just ten days after Sithole, Mabusa and Mabelane joined Winnie in beating up Katiza – according to Cebekhulu's allegations – after officers of the Soweto Murder and Robbery Squad had delivered him to the MUFC.

Commentators had scant knowledge then of Katiza's story, but they were critical of the apparent police laxity. 'What was surprising was that none of the accused or key witnesses were kept in custody as permitted under South African law,' wrote the veteran liberal South African journalist Stanley Uys. 'Nor were the police their normal vigorous selves in enforcing the bail requirements of accused persons to report regularly to police stations.'

John Carlin wrote:

> What was puzzling several lawyers was the laxity of the police in their supervision of the four missing accused . . . When a first postponement of the trial was agreed in court last September, the prosecution made a deliberate point of asking the magistrate to ensure that the police kept a close watch on the accused, who had been granted bail.
>
> The fact that they did not, and that the police failed to take action immediately, is almost without precedent, lawyers said.
>
> When Mr Von Lieres announced last September that the eight would stand trial, he emphasized the need for the police to ensure that neither they nor any of the witnesses be exposed to threats or intimidation.

Reports would subsequently appear, two weeks after the trial began, that Sithole, Mabusa and Mabelane had been spotted at an ANC transit camp at Dukwe in Botswana, near that country's border with Zimbabwe. A faxed request for extradition of the three men was sent to Botswana by the South African government. But, despite the fact that the two countries had had an extradition agreement since 1969, the trio were not produced before the end of a trial which continued for almost four months.

*

Winnie arrived with Nelson at the Rand Supreme Court in her husband's armour-plated red Mercedes. A thousand or more ANC supporters chanted: 'We love Winnie, we love Nelson', 'Kill the Boers' and 'Viva Winnie and Saddam Hussein' – the Gulf War, launched against Iraq by the West and its Arab allies, had just begun. Winnie was dressed in an elegant dark-blue and yellow tartan jacket, dark-blue blouse with matching kerchief, a dark-blue pencil skirt and matching tights and shoes. In her lapel was an ANC badge and she wore heavy amber earrings with a necklace of big amber and blue beads. When asked by the crush of reporters where she had bought her outfit, she snapped: 'At a time when the country is going up in flames, how can people be concerned about clothes?'

Her irritation was exacerbated when reporters instead began directing their questions at Nelson. This time she snapped at one journalist: 'My husband is not on trial, sir.'

Otherwise, Winnie looked surprisingly relaxed, considering the gravity of the charges she faced. Nelson kissed her on the lips before she took her place in the dock of the small, wood-panelled Courtroom 4E.

Dali Mpofu sat two rows in front of Winnie. He was part of the defence team comprising solicitor Kathy Satchwell, Advocate Henti Joubert and Advocate Hendrik Kruger for Morgan and the Falatis. But halfway through the trial it emerged dramatically that Mpofu was also working on behalf of Winnie, who officially was represented by Advocate George Bizos, instructed by the Mandelas' lawyer Ismail Ayob. Mpofu's employment with Satchwell came to a quick end.

Nelson sat on the public benches surrounded by leading ANC personalities, including Chris Hani, chief of staff of Umkhonto we Sizwe, ANC Secretary-General Alfred Nzo, South African Communist Party leader Joe Slovo, firebrand ANC Youth League leader Peter Mokaba, a particularly close friend of Winnie's, and Mrs Fatima Meer, Nelson's official biographer. By now the ANC was firmly resolved to depict Winnie's trial as an example of continued apartheid oppression. Just before proceedings began the ANC's National Executive Committee issued a statement depicting it as part of a 'pattern of harassment and persecution to which Comrade Winnie has been subjected for the last 30 years . . . an orchestrated campaign through the media to pre-judge the facts'. It was a political trial 'in breach of the spirit of the agreements entered into between the government and the ANC'.

Four days after the release of the ANC statement, the government was also reviled by the white right-wing Conservative Party, which branded President de Klerk a traitor. De Klerk announced in Parliament on 1 February the impending scrapping of all South Africa's remaining racial apartheid laws. All forty-four opposition Conservative MPs walked out after one of their members described De Klerk as the 'hangman of the Afrikaner'. The State President said that the Land Acts, which

reserved 87 per cent of the country's land for the white minority, and the Group Areas Act, which dictated where people
should live according to their racial classification, would be
repealed within weeks. Also the Population Registration Act,
which effectively underpinned the whole apartheid system by
requiring people to be classified at birth in one of four racial
categories, would be allowed to lapse the following month.

*

Advocate Bizos, leading Winnie Mandela's defence, was born in
Greece to a socialist father who in 1941 fled his homeland to
South Africa to escape Nazi occupation. Twenty-eight years
earlier, the young Bizos had been a member of the defence team
under Bram Fischer which saved Nelson Mandela from the gallows at the Rivonia Treason Trial.

Bizos began with an immediate application for all the charges
against Winnie to be quashed on the ground that they had been
phrased too vaguely by the state for his client to be able to plead.
Judge Michael Stegmann rejected the application, but
adjourned the trial until Monday 11 February to give the state
time to provide more details of the charges and to give the
defence more time to prepare its case.

Stegmann also issued warrants for the arrests of the missing
Katiza Cebekhulu, Jabu Sithole, Brian Mabusa and Mpho
Mabelane. Had Stegmann but known it, he could have had
Katiza arrested there and then. Katiza had travelled from
Morgan's home to join the public throng on the steps of the
Rand Supreme Court. 'I stood among everybody,' Katiza told
me. 'There were police all around me. I was confused at that
time, I didn't know what to do. I suppose I wanted to hear the
trial, to see what was going on. I remember wondering what

would happen if I just walked into the court and said Mrs Mandela had attacked me. A *Sunday Times* reporter recognized me and took my photo. Then I saw Zingiswa Mkhuma, a newspaper reporter I knew. I told her what had happened.'

The photograph of Katiza on the steps of the Supreme Court did not appear in the Johannesburg *Sunday Times* for another six days – as a 'scoop' on 10 February. The big front-page colour photo provoked a furious statement from the South African Police, who had failed to account to the court for the non-appearance of Cebekhulu, Sithole, Mabusa and Mabelane. A police spokesman complained that the *Sunday Times* had made 'a joke of the call to responsible newspapers to assist police to maintain law and order'. He added that although the police had been gathered in force around Cebekhulu on the Supreme Court steps they could not be expected to be familiar with the face of every missing suspect.

The report by Mkhuma, a Soweto-based reporter for the Johannesburg *Star*, was held up by the editor for unexplained reasons for another fortnight, by which time it was much too late to influence the course of events. Mkhuma's story on 18 February stated that Sithole, Mabusa and Mabelane had beaten up Cebekhulu because Katiza had *wanted* to stand trial and give evidence. Zingiswa described sores on Cebekhulu's head and arm, consistent with the claim made to the reporter that boiling water had been poured over him and that he had been treated in Baragwanath while giving a false identity. The reporter wrote that Cebekhulu was on the run, and no one knew where he now was.

*

Katiza had returned from the Supreme Court steps to Morgan's house in Soweto and stayed there until Friday 8

February. That afternoon Morgan suggested that Katiza drive with him into central Johannesburg, where he said he wanted to get a camera serviced and cleaned. Morgan drove to Shell House, the ANC's new skyscraper national headquarters given to the movement by the Royal Dutch Shell Oil Company. 'It was the first time I had been there,' Katiza told me. 'Morgan pressed the lift button and we went up many floors, I think it was to twenty-two, where you can see the cars below are so small.

'Morgan took me into an office. So when I enter with Morgan, believe me, Winnie was sitting on the sofa with her back to me. When Winnie turned I wanted to run. My tears came out. Morgan had disappeared.'

Katiza went on: 'You know what Winnie said to me?'

I shook my head.

'"Did you tell the police that I boil you with hot water?" I said: "No." She said: "Why?" I said I was afraid. Winnie said: "Now you must choose. If you decide to go to Swaziland I'll give you money, a car, a house and education. If you don't accept I'll deal with you right now." I knew what that meant: there was no need to ask. So I accepted to go to Swaziland because it was near South Africa and I thought I would be able to come back any time. I was taken away by two men. I didn't know them.'

And so Katiza Cebekhulu's journey into long exile began. There would be no money, no car, no house and no education at the end of the African rainbow, only fresh horrors. The only possessions he left with were the shoes, khaki trousers and tracksuit top he wore as he stood before Winnie Mandela.

*

That same day as Winnie sent Katiza into the unknown, 8 February 1991, her husband publicly proclaimed her innocent of all the charges laid against her. In the same Shell House from where Katiza had been despatched towards Swaziland Nelson called a press conference to mark the coming first anniversary of his release from imprisonment. Nelson told the crowded meeting: 'We have no hesitation whatsoever in asserting her innocence.' He denied that Winnie's appointment as head of the ANC's Social Welfare Department had been strongly opposed within the ANC and chided a journalist who suggested Winnie should not have accepted the post – 'For you, for anybody, to say that Mrs Mandela should stand down until the case is resolved is to find her guilty before her trial.'

The previous day Winnie had reassumed her role as Mother of the Nation, addressing a rally in Bekkersdal, a black township thirty miles south-west of Johannesburg torn by violence between three black political factions, the ANC, Inkatha and AZAPO (successor to Black Consciousness).

At a time when the ANC was making sincere, albeit feeble, efforts to dampen communal passions, Winnie delivered the kind of speech which made her the darling of the radicals and a headache for ANC moderates. A dozen people had been killed and scores made homeless over the previous few days in the clashes between Bekkersdal's political cabals. Winnie was sure where the blame lay – 'Any white person who comes here to interfere with us or who comes to preach peace, that person must not leave Bekkersdal alive. Their wives and mothers will have to fetch them as corpses.'

It was the most vitriolic speech Winnie had delivered since her notorious call in Soweto three years earlier to black radicals to liberate the country with 'our matches and necklaces'.

Winnie, alternating between English and Xhosa, blamed the Bekkersdal violence on 'the Boers and the apartheid government'. She went on: 'Your spears should be pointed in the direction of Pretoria. Our enemy is in Pretoria. We have never had enemies within ourselves. We are all here because of our fight for freedom. The enemy come here to exploit our differences. We are normal human beings. We all have our differences and it is healthy to debate among ourselves. But we are not going to allow the brute boys to come and exploit us.'

CHAPTER 13

Winnie on Trial

FEBRUARY–NOVEMBER 1991

As Katiza was being hustled into exile, Winnie Mandela's trial resumed on Monday 11 February 1991 at the Rand Supreme Court. However, not only were Katiza, Sithole, Mabusa and Mabelane absent, but now one of the key state witnesses, Pelo Mekgwe, had gone missing as well.

The state prosecutor, Deputy Attorney-General Jan Swanepoel, dropped the bombshell in mid-morning. He said Mekgwe had been kidnapped and it would affect the willingness of Kenny Kgase and Thabiso Mono, the state's other witnesses, to testify. Swanepoel sought a postponement until May to allow Mekgwe to be found and said he had asked Captain Fred Dempsey to investigate the disappearance. The police never would produce Mekgwe.

Swanepoel said that Mekgwe, returning from his home in Potchefstroom, had stopped at Paul Verryn's manse in Soweto on the Sunday evening before the resumption of the trial. Verryn was absent. Some men had turned up and Mekgwe had been driven away in a Mercedes, according to Swanepoel's informant.

More details of the kidnapping were provided by Patrick Laurence, the respected liberal commentator, writing in the

Johannesburg *Star* and the London *Guardian*: 'According to an impeccable source, Mekgwe left the Methodist Church manse in Soweto last Sunday in the company of three ANC men. One holds a senior position in the ANC. Another is said to have developed specialist skills [a euphemism for guerrilla training] when the ANC was a banned organization.' The ANC issued a statement denying that it was 'organizationally responsible' for the disappearance, inviting conjecture that individual members of the ANC certainly were. (A year later, however, Tokyo Sexwale, head of a secret ANC guerrilla organization, the Special Projects Unit, admitted to a South African newspaper that his team had been used to smuggle Pelo Mekgwe out of the country. Sexwale said one of the unit's officials, Mangaliso Simelane, had arranged the operation. Sexwale denied personal involvement.)

In a bizarre development the police arrested Laurence after demanding he reveal his 'impeccable source'. He declined to do so, citing his commitment to a code of journalistic ethics requiring him to protect sources of information. The police prosecuted and Laurence was sentenced to ten days' imprisonment. In the wake of international protests he was released on the night of his first day in prison.

Kenny Kgase and Thabiso Mono, who had spent more than two years in limbo following the death of Stompie, waiting to give evidence in both the Richardson and Mandela trials, now also found themselves sentenced to imprisonment. They had told Judge Stegmann that, following the kidnapping of Mekgwe, they would not testify: the dangers had become too great. Before explaining why he was no longer willing to give evidence, Kgase first looked up at Nelson Mandela sitting in the front row of the public gallery. Then he told the judge: 'I've got to make a decision between my obligation [to testify] and my life. I really want my life. I like my life. If people can remove someone who has been subpoenaed [Mekgwe] when the case is going on, then there is more to all this than meets the eye. I think my life is at stake. I am very, very scared.' To reach the witness box Kgase had had to pass within three feet of the dock where Winnie Mandela sat, wearing a long, green African-style print dress and a stunning emerald headscarf.

Thabiso Mono said: 'I fear for my life. I would rather go to jail than testify.' Paul Kennedy, the advocate for Kgase and Mono, told Judge Stegmann: 'Their fear that they could suffer death or bodily harm, even years after the trial is over, is well founded.'

The judge ruled, however, that Kgase and Mono would go to jail immediately for refusing to give evidence. Stegmann said the initial sentence could be for up to five years, and he went on: 'That five-year sentence can be renewed indefinitely if his [the witness's] recalcitrance is without a just excuse. Unless he relents he could spend the rest of his life in prison.' Stegmann added that he would postpone the trial until 6 March and delay sending Kgase and Mono to prison until that date to allow them to think things over.

*

Two days before the trial began again – on Wednesday 6 March – Kenny Kgase and Thabiso Mono, having contemplated Judge Stegmann's threat of potential imprisonment for life, agreed reluctantly to give evidence.

Kgase was first into the witness box. Five days of gruelling and brutal cross-examination by Advocate Bizos followed. Broadly, Kgase repeated the story he had told in the Richardson trial and in his *Sunday Telegraph* article. In its essential details it matched the evidence Mono and the now-missing Mekgwe had given in the Richardson trial. When eventually I first met Katiza Cebekhulu – four years after the end of Winnie Mandela's trial – his account corroborated the pillars of Kgase's testimony.

'Mrs Mandela was humming a tune then and dancing to the rhythm,' said Kgase early in his evidence. 'She kept punching him [Stompie]. He was feeling the pain. He was pleading with her ... And, all of a sudden, I saw her waving a sjambok. Before she said anything she struck several blows.'

Bizos, in a determined bid to undermine Kgase as a witness, constantly asked him about Verryn's alleged homosexuality and confronted him with every detail of the various accounts he had given of the events of 29–31 December 1988 and after. In the Richardson trial, said Bizos, Kgase had stated that Winnie punched him in the right eye; now he was saying it was the left eye. In the current trial Kgase had claimed that Winnie 'suddenly' had a sjambok in her hand; in his *Sunday Telegraph* article he had said she called for sjamboks to be brought.

Bizos mocked Kgase cruelly about his article. Seeking to disprove Kgase's assertion that the article was not ghostwritten, the lawyer made him read out in court extracts from his own attempts at writing a novel. Like a spiteful schoolmaster, Bizos let Kgase finish and said: 'Although your English has improved, would you agree you are incapable of writing intelligible literary English?' Judge Stegmann intervened to quash the question, observing: 'But, Mr Bizos, if this was James Joyce there would have been people who would have regarded his work as unintelligible also.'

Bizos' forensic dissection of the detail, but not the framework, was relentless. What would tell most against Kgase was his denial of having been paid for his article in the *Sunday Telegraph*. Since Kgase did not *seek* payment for the article, it is entirely possible he misunderstood the question – not least because Bizos himself had pointed out that Kgase's English was less than perfect. But denying payment – which Peter Taylor, subpoenaed to give evidence, confirmed had been routinely made – exposed him to withering attack from Bizos, who argued: 'If he is prepared to perjure himself for his own, sometimes obscure, purposes why should he not be held to have falsely implicated Mrs Mandela?'

On Tuesday 12 March Bizos completed his five-day cross-examination of Kgase, calling him a dangerously unreliable person who had lied in order to incriminate Winnie. But the central thrust of Kgase's evidence was corroborated by Winnie's co-accused, John Morgan, in the statement he had made to the police when he was arrested on 21 February 1989. Morgan said Winnie took part in the assault on Stompie and the others on the evening of 29 December 1988 and that she questioned the youths extensively about homosexual behaviour at Paul Verryn's manse. Before the group beating began, Morgan said he saw Winnie slap Stompie and ask him: 'Such a little person, do you also sleep with Paul Verryn and let him fuck you up your arse?' Morgan's statement also quoted Winnie as saying 'This thing speaks shit' when Stompie denied having had sex with Paul Verryn. Morgan said in his statement he left the room at the back of Winnie's house because he could no longer stand watching the assault.

Morgan now alleged, through his advocate, Hendrik Kruger, that his statement was false because it had been tortured out of him through electric shocks administered by policemen. And while forcing him to sign, the police had failed to tell him that he too was a suspect. Kruger argued that in these circumstances Morgan's police statement was false and therefore inadmissible. The truth was, Morgan now said, through Kruger, that Mrs Mandela was not at home on the evening of 29 December 1988; she was in Brandfort.

Jabu Sithole, Mpho Mabelane and Brian Mabusa had also made police statements placing Winnie at the scene of the beatings on the evening of 29 December 1988. But following their disappearances none of their statements was admissible in the trial.

Many months later Morgan would admit that he had lied in court at Winnie Mandela's insistence and that the true statement was the one he gave the police. By then it was too late to change the course of 'justice'.

*

The state finished presenting its case on 28 March 1991. No evidence had been presented against eighteen-year-old Nompumelelo Falati. She had worn her school uniform throughout the trial, but had missed two years of schooling since the events of 29–31 December 1988. Judge Stegmann dismissed the charges against her and said she could go free. Only three – Winnie Mandela, Xoliswa Falati and John Morgan – of the original eight charged with Stompie's kidnapping and assault were in the dock when the court reconvened after a ten-day adjournment on 7 April 1991.

Winnie Mandela finally took the stand on Tuesday 16 April, more than two months after the trial had begun. In December 1988, she said, a friend, Xoliswa Falati, had reported to her that a boy had been raped by Paul Verryn. They took the boy on 29 December 1988 to 'a doctor', who examined him and said he was disturbed and should see a psychiatrist; Winnie said she left immediately afterwards between 6.30 and 7.00pm for Brandfort, arriving there some time after ten, and returning to Soweto only on 31 January. On return she was met by Falati. Winnie testified: 'She [Falati] said she was sorry, she had brought some children there [to the house] and she hoped I didn't mind.' Winnie said Falati had added 'something to the effect' that the children were 'similar victims of Paul Verryn'. Mrs Mandela said she was unwell at the time and did not take the matter any further.

In the second week of January, however, said Winnie, members of the Mandela Crisis Committee came and said that 'there were serious allegations against me, that there were certain children in the house and that they had been kidnapped'. Bizos asked his client how she had reacted. 'I was outraged,' she said. 'I was furious. I told them I knew nothing about the allegations.'

Winnie presented her alibi and Nora Moahloli testified that Winnie arrived on the evening of 29 December 1988 in Brandfort and left two days later. But, said Swanepoel, hadn't Moahloli's police statement said Winnie arrived on 28 December? Moahloli said she was ill at the time and had obviously made a mistake.

Exploring the Brandfort alibi, Swanepoel said Winnie claimed to have driven to Brandfort in her own minibus in the late afternoon of 29 December 1988. But, said Swanepoel, Morgan said in his police statement that he drove the same minibus, that same evening, taking Stompie and the other youths from Verryn's manse to Winnie's Diepkloof house. Later that evening he had driven Falati and her daughter from Diepkloof to another house in Soweto. The following morning – 30 December, when Winnie said she was in Brandfort – he said he washed the minibus and used it to ferry Falati and Mrs Mandela from Diepkloof to Community House.

When asked by Swanepoel whether she could explain the contradiction of how the minibus could have been in two separate places 200 miles apart at the same time, Winnie replied: 'I have no idea how he [Morgan] drove her [Falati]. I was in my combi [minibus].'

Swanepoel suggested that Jerry Richardson had allowed himself to become a scapegoat for Winnie Mandela's crimes, motivated by his devotion to the Mother of the Nation. 'I put it to you,' the state prosecutor said to Winnie, 'that you wanted Richardson to take the blame, no matter what the consequences to himself would be, in order to protect you.'

The suggestion was absurd, replied Winnie. Richardson was simply a man of honour wishing to tell the truth. He was also anxious to protect the Mandela family name from further false charges. Winnie said she had little or no contact with the rooms at the back of her house and that she had no knowledge of what happened in them – 'I respected their [MUFC members'] privacy.'

She also had no knowledge of bloodstains found by police on walls, or of sjamboks, a club and a knife discovered in the back rooms. But Mrs Mandela did make one extraordinary admission when Swanepoel asked: 'It actually suited you that Jerry Richardson implicated himself?' 'Yes,' she replied.

*

Judge Michael Stegmann gave his verdicts on Monday 13 May 1991. Unlike Judge Brian O'Donovan, who in Jerry Richardson's trial had rejected Winnie's Brandfort alibi and said she had been present for at least part of the time during the 29

December 1988 beating of Stompie, Stegmann accepted the alibi. He said the state had failed to disprove that Mrs Mandela was in Brandfort that evening; he had to accept that it was 'reasonably possibly true' that she left her house by 7pm and therefore was not at home when the assaults took place.

O'Donovan had accepted the evidence of Kgase, Mono and Mekgwe as credible and having 'a ring of truth'. Stegmann dismissed Kgase's and Mono's evidence as unreliable and unacceptable without corroboration. Mekgwe, who could have provided corroboration, was now missing, having been kidnapped by the Special Projects Unit.

So earlier 'truths' under O'Donovan's administration of justice had been tipped on their heads to become 'falsehoods' under justice as dispensed by Stegmann.

However, said Stegmann, although Winnie Mandela may not have known of the assaults during her 'reasonably possibly true' absence in Brandfort, she certainly knew about them after her return and she continued thereafter to conceal them. She deliberately forbade inquiries into the assaults and refused to allow two of the victims – Mono and Mekgwe – to be freed for at least two weeks after they had been kidnapped from Paul Verryn's manse. 'Mrs Mandela showed herself on a number of occasions to be a calm, composed, unblushing liar,' said Stegmann. She was 'vague, evasive and lacking in candour' and had 'played fast and loose with the liberty of others'. She had deliberately 'fudged' replies to prevent the prosecution from proving her answers false.

Stegmann said Winnie had authorized the kidnappings and found her guilty on four charges of kidnap in relation to Stompie Moeketsi, Pelo Mekgwe, Thabiso Mono and Kenny Kgase. Since she was in Brandfort when the assaults upon the youths took place, said the judge, he was clearing Mrs Mandela of the assault charges. But by continuing to hold the four captive and to shelter those who had committed the assaults she had associated herself with the crime. She was therefore an accessory after the fact. 'To imagine that all this took place without Mandela as one of the moving spirits would be like imagining *Hamlet* without the prince,' said Stegmann.

Nelson Mandela swept to his wife's side as soon as Stegmann adjourned the court. He embraced and kissed her and asked: 'My darling, how are you?' The second person to step forward and embrace her was Dali Mpofu; he also kissed her.

The following day, Tuesday 14 May 1991, Judge Stegmann sentenced Winnie Mandela to six years' imprisonment – five years on four charges of kidnap plus one year for being an accessory to four assaults.

Xoliswa Falati was also jailed for six years. John Morgan was found guilty of kidnap and acquitted of assault; he was sentenced to one year's imprisonment suspended for five years.

George Bizos gave immediate notice that he would appeal the sentence and Winnie was released on Rand 200 (£40) bail. The money was lodged by Dali Mpofu.

Nelson was 1,000 miles away from Johannesburg – at Stellenbosch University in the Cape, addressing Afrikaans-speaking students – when his wife was sentenced. He said he expected Winnie to win her appeal: 'We trust that soon her name will be cleared completely. The last word on the matter has not been spoken . . . My faith in her has been fully vindicated. I also believe she did not know there was anyone at the back of the house.'

Winnie emerged from the Rand Supreme Court building, gave a clenched-fist salute and said: 'We were found guilty by the media.' Then she shouted: '*Amandla! Amandla!* [Power! Power!] The struggle goes on.'

Within days she was again attacking Paul Verryn, who had had all allegations against him dismissed by both Stegmann and O'Donovan. Winnie still presented Verryn as the guilty party, a man of the cloth whose reality 'stinks of such filth'. She told *Tribute*, a glossy magazine directed at black professionals: 'I could not believe that a minister of religion entrusted with children's lives would abuse them. What kind of beast is this who wears a collar on Sunday and goes to preach to parents of these children, and preaches the word of God even to some of these children? At night he becomes something else.' (Verryn maintained silence on the Stompie affair when the trial ended. He continued to live in his Soweto manse, running five Methodist churches with congregations of more than 3,000.) Winnie told *Tribute* that she would continue to provide a refuge for children who came to her who 'truly have nowhere to go'.

The *Tribute* interviewer did not flinch from asking her whether she ever thought about Stompie. 'I had nothing to do with Stompie's death,' she said. 'Unfortunately I do not even know the child. In retrospect I would have loved to speak to the child. I would have loved to give him the warmth he seemed never to have had.' This was a strange statement, for it reversed her arguments that Stompie had 'escaped' from her Diepkloof house and her belief that he was probably still alive.

*

Winnie Mandela's conviction was not the end of her troubles. On 27 April 1991, a fortnight before the end of the trial, she had flown 300 miles to Kimberley for the first congress of the ANC's Women's League held in three decades. Winnie confidently expected to be elected League President and reinforce her political comeback following her appointment as the ANC's Director of Social Welfare.

Winnie was one of three candidates for the post. Her opponents were Albertina Sisulu, Dr Abu-Baker Asvat's nurse/receptionist and long-time adversary of Mrs Mandela, and Gertrude Shope, an occupational therapist who led the ANC's women's section in exile. Albertina Sisulu, with the organizational backing of her old colleague Dudu Chili, withdrew her candidacy at the last moment and publicly asked her supporters to back Mrs Shope. Winnie lost the election, gaining only 196 votes to Mrs Shope's 633. Winnie sat weeping in the hall after the conference rejected her.

Another setback came after the trial ended. In June 1991 speculation about a romance between Winnie and Dali Mpofu appeared in the press for the first time. Mpofu dismissed as 'false' the rumours in the black Sunday newspaper *City Press*, which said that the information was being disseminated by an anti-Winnie faction inside the ANC.

A week after the *City Press* report, a London newspaper also reported rumours of Winnie's affair with Mpofu and of discord in the marriage between Winnie and Nelson. Teresa Oakley-Smith, Mpofu's former British lover and the mother of his son, gave lawyers a statement alleging harassment from Winnie Mandela. She said she had received a death threat. 'She is believed to have instructed lawyers that the contents of her statement should be made public if she or her child come to any harm,' said the *Sunday Times* in its report of 16 June 1991.

*

Meanwhile, Andrew Ikaneng, victim of attempted murder by Winnie's MUFC in January 1989 just three days after Stompie's death, was the victim of a third MUFC assassination attempt.

On 6 May, before Winnie's trial had ended, Ikaneng was mown down by automatic fire outside his Soweto house. He and two witnesses identified his assailants as three MUFC members named Matthew, Theo and 'Marlboro' living in Winnie's old Orlando West matchbox house. Ikaneng survived the attack, but spent a week in hospital having bullets removed from his thigh and buttocks. 'The Football Club are still there,' Dudu Chili told me at the time. 'According to the community's demands, they should have been disbanded long ago. But they are still together and operating. They still take orders from their boss. Their boss is Winnie Mandela.'

*

Winnie's next attempt to strengthen her position came in July in Durban at the ANC's first legal congress on South African soil in more than thirty years. The congress elected Nelson Mandela as ANC President to succeed Oliver Tambo. But, against Mandela's will, it elected Cyril Ramaphosa as ANC Secretary-General, the second most powerful post in the organization. Ramaphosa was a determined enemy of Winnie Mandela: he was part of the group which had drafted the MDM/ANC statement of 16 February 1989 condemning the MUFC's 'reign of terror' and saying Mrs Mandela had 'abused

191

the trust and confidence she has enjoyed over the years'. He had also earned Nelson's anger by challenging his unquestioning right to be ANC leader.

Chris Hani, a Winnie ally who was chief of staff of Umkhonto we Sizwe and a leading member of the South African Communist Party, came top of the poll to elect fifty members to the ANC's National Executive Committee. Winnie stood for election and came twenty-sixth. It was a sop to her self-esteem after her humiliations in the Rand Supreme Court and at the hands of Albertina Sisulu. But she was still denied effective executive power: only the first twenty elected members on the list formed the full-time paid working committee, or ANC Cabinet, which would run the movement's affairs.

A month after the ANC Congress Winnie accompanied Nelson on a visit to Cuba. While she was away there was an internal coup by the new ANC Executive. Winnie was relieved of her post as Director of the Social Welfare Department, to be replaced by a bright young coloured (mixed-race) woman from the Cape, Cheryl Carolus. Cyril Ramaphosa ousted foreign secretary Thabo Mbeki as the ANC's negotiator in 'talks about talks' with De Klerk's government. Nelson Mandela was furious and on his return he demanded that Winnie be reinstated: she got her job back, but Ramaphosa was not dislodged from his new role as chief negotiator. 'He [Nelson] ignored reports that the [Social Welfare] department was in chaos under her [Winnie's] rule,' wrote Emma Gilbey. 'He ignored the protests of many who felt she was incompetent and he asserted his own authority by giving Winnie her position back.'

*

Winnie's personal drama was taking place against the background of a country in violent transition. South Africa was
readmitted to the Olympic Games and world cricket in 1991,
but the townships continued to burn as black-on-black
violence continued. In just six days in mid-September, for
example, more than 120 people were shot, blown up or hacked
to death in the townships ringing Johannesburg and countless
others were hideously wounded. South Africa was passing
through a kind of puberty. Black people who for so long had
been treated as minors were experiencing growing pains as
apartheid's iron grip was relaxed. The streets of black South
Africa were being bloodied as the battle for power in the post-
apartheid era intensified.

White on black violence persisted too. The worst case I expe-
rienced was the one my newspaper sent me to investigate at
Messina, on South Africa's northern border with Zimbabwe.
Fifteen-year-old Frank Mokwathe was alleged to have stolen a
TV set from an Afrikaner holiday resort. A local farmer, Jan
van der Westhuizen, picked up Mokwathe, took him to his
farm workshop, laid metal strips across his wrists on top of a
steel workbench, and proceeded to bond the boy to the table
using an arc welder. Mokwathe's clothes caught fire and he
was burned hideously. I found him in a local black hospital
and interviewed him and photographed him. Shortly after I
left police raided the hospital, threw the terribly wounded
Mokwathe into a van, manacled him by his scorched wrists to
a handrail and drove him to a prison hospital seventy miles
away. Mokwathe was subsequently sentenced to five years in
borstal; Van der Westhuizen walked free from court after opt-
ing to pay a Rand 5,000 (£1,000) fine in lieu of a two-year jail
sentence for attempted murder. Nothing, it seemed, had yet

prepared the Afrikaner farmers for democracy, for government in the name of a peasantry they believed could be controlled only by the lash and the torch.

Against this background it was perhaps hardly surprising if in the course of 1991 Katiza Cebekhulu, a mere Zulu teenage roughneck from Natal, had been virtually forgotten in South Africa since going missing ten months earlier.

CHAPTER FOURTEEN

Katiza in Exile

FEBRUARY–NOVEMBER 1991

Back in February 1991, Katiza Cebekhulu, faced with an unpalatable choice, had elected to leave South Africa. Two men, assigned to take him into exile, directed him from the Director of Social Welfare's office in the sky to the ANC's underground car park in Bree Street, just a stone's throw from the Rand Supreme Court in Pritchard Street. They drove into the night towards Nelspruit in the Eastern Transvaal.

'We slept in a house outside Nelspruit that night, and the next day I asked them when I was going to get my things [promised by Winnie],' Katiza told me. 'They said I would get them in Swaziland. The next night we drove to the Swazi border and they pushed me over the fence where another man was waiting who drove me to Mozambique. I was handed to a man called Tete in Maputo [the Mozambique capital]. I asked again about my things. He said I would get them in Angola. Next he and others put me on to a small passenger plane by myself: I had no ticket, no passport and no bag, just the clothes I was wearing when I left John Morgan's house.

'The plane landed in Luanda [[capital of Angola] and I was met by a man who called to me in my language [Zulu] and said: "Katiza, how are you? I was waiting for you. How is

Johannesburg?" As though I was just an old friend. He told me not to worry. Winnie had told him about me and he had instructions to keep me until I was able to go to another place. He took me to a house and introduced me to a man called Desta. They put me in the house for one week and then they put me on another plane to Lusaka [Zambia's capital].'

A black South African called Tbhoko met Katiza inside the immigration area at Lusaka Airport and took him through immigration without any of the normal formalities. Tbhoko drove him to a house in the suburb of Chilanga. 'The man called Desta turned up,' said Katiza. 'He said he had instructions from Winnie about me and there was no way to escape because this was an ANC house. He asked me if I knew Sizwe Sithole. I said yes. Then he asked me how Sizwe died. I said we had heard from the police that he hanged himself. Desta said: "Do you know I'm the one who trained Sizwe [as an Umkhonto guerrilla]?" I said I didn't know and Desta said: "Because we received information that you're the one who sold him. You know that is not good?" I said: "Yes."'

Katiza was now as frightened as at any time in the entire saga of his troubled life. As far as he was aware, only one person, Winnie, knew he had tipped off the police about a planned attack by Sizwe Sithole. Now Winnie had obviously been in communication with this man Desta, an ANC guerrilla instructor.

'They left, but I suspected I would be killed since Desta asked me about Sizwe,' said Katiza. 'There was something deep going on, so I ran into the bush and slept under the trees for three days without eating. I drank water from a stream. Then some woodcutters saw me.' The woodcutters must have alerted the police because a group of them came and arrested Katiza. 'They didn't know who I was. I was dirty and still wearing my clothes from Johannesburg. The police were confused by me and kept asking whether I had been planning to hang myself: the wood-cutters must have told them I was acting as though I wanted to commit suicide. I said: "No, my name is Katiza and I was brought here [to this country] by the ANC by force."

'They took me to Chilanga police station and an ANC man called Boy came and said I should be handed to the ANC. I refused and Boy said to me in Zulu that I should go because I was confused and I was embarrassing the ANC. I should return home, nobody would touch me, it was not good what I am doing. "Come with me, nothing will happen," Boy said. I said: "I want nothing to do with you. I don't want even to hear you people." I told the police they [the ANC] will kill me. The policeman on duty said this was too serious for him and he drove me into the centre of town to see a senior officer.'

The officer took Katiza to an intelligence official, Roy Mkanda, in State House (the Zambian President's official resi-dence). Mkanda told Katiza that the President's office had given instructions that he be taken to the Fairview Hotel, a cheap, rundown establishment in central Lusaka, and be given security protection. Mkanda said he would himself keep a constant eye on Katiza until his future was settled.

'By now I was smelling too badly,' said Katiza. He was still wearing the clothes in which he had left South Africa many days earlier. He had not washed in all that time. Now he bathed and rinsed his clothes and after a few days introduced himself to a trainee hotel worker, Linda Malik. 'Linda was so kind to me,' said Katiza. 'She never undermined me although I was so unpresentable and shabby. From then, I was falling in love with Linda.' They began taking strolls together through the streets around the Fairview. 'One day we were going to buy some peanuts when I saw Roy Mkanda pass by in a car with Desta. I felt my blood run cold and I said to Linda: "Let's go back." I was so afraid and didn't know what to do, so I telephoned the Zambia *Daily Mail* and they sent a reporter, Austin Nyasula, to see me. I told Austin how they smuggled me out of South Africa. He asked me if I was Inkatha or ANC. I said neither.'

Nyasula's report was picked up the next day – Friday 17 May 1991 – by the *Sowetan*, a mass-circulation newspaper aimed at South Africa's black population. The *Sowetan* said that Katiza was being held in protective custody in a Lusaka hotel and had confided that he 'was smuggled out of South Africa by certain people whom he did not wish to name. He said he now feared for his life . . . His "kidnappers" had promised him education, clothing and money . . . "My family still lives in Mpumalanga township but if I go back the police will arrest me and if I run away those same people who brought me here will arrest me."'

That same Friday a police party came to collect Katiza from the Fairview Hotel. 'They said they would give me a house, but they took me to Kamwala Prison,' he told me. 'I thought I was going crazy. The conditions were terrible.' After a short time in Kamwala he was transferred to Lusaka Central Prison. 'Ah, things there they were even worse. The first day when I enter inside, shit, I find people they were so thin and so weak they can't even brush off the flies. They were sick and they smelt.'

There were fifty or sixty men to a cell, sleeping on the concrete floor without blankets and sharing one bucket as a latrine. Often men died in the night and their corpses were not removed until morning. Some cells were for convicts; some for remand prisoners; a few were for those who had contracted diarrhoea, TB or other infections. There was one special cell for gang chiefs.

'I was new and I had no plate, just a sheet of plastic,' said Katiza. 'I joined the queue for the first time to get rations. There were hundreds in the line. The man gave me such a small portion that I was thinking maybe he made a mistake. I asked him. He gave me a slap, and my food fell down to the floor and the other prisoners stood on it.'

Katiza was put in cell 15, which had a mix of convicts and remand prisoners. They beat him up when the boss prisoner said he was ridiculing them by insisting he had committed no offence and had not been tried. 'They laughed and said: "Yes, there's not a single guilty man in this prison." I screamed when they beat me. When the warder came, he said: "It's time you learned about life in prison." So they beat me again until I was bleeding.

'The next morning I went to see the duty sergeant to complain. We were so many in the queue: inside the prison we are about a thousand. The sergeant didn't even look up in our faces when we complained. When he said: "What is your problem?" he don't look at you. When I gave my complaint, he said: "If your friend has beaten you, what is wrong there?" I said I had been beaten until my eyes were swollen. He was busy writing and not looking at me, and he said: "So? You like to fight. Bugger off. Next." The boy in front of me said he wanted to complain that he had been sodomized at night. The sergeant said: "What do you expect? Don't you know you're in prison now? You don't want them to sodomize you, then don't come to prison. Next."'

Back in the cell, Katiza was beaten again for complaining. The inmates removed his shirt and beat him with their fists over his kidneys until he collapsed.

There were sometimes searches of the cell, said Katiza. 'The officers were looking for drugs, cigarettes, knives, spoons, money, magic charms. They stripped us all naked. Then they made us drink soapy water so we go and shit in the toilet before they see if we were hiding things in our anuses. Me, I had nothing to hide. No money, no cigarettes. Nothing. Once I refused to drink the soapy water. I said I had done nothing wrong and had not been tried. The officers beat me and locked me in the "peanut" [punishment] block for two days. I was put in there naked.'

Katiza demonstrated to me the half-crouch he had to maintain all the time he was in the punishment cell. 'I was alone and the cell was so small I couldn't stand straight. I couldn't sit either because the floor was flooded. I was so cold.'

In August two African journalists visited Katiza in prison. 'They weren't really interested in how I got there. All they wanted to ask about was Winnie Mandela and the killings in South Africa. I gave them stories which confused them. I told them they had to get me out of prison if they wanted the real story.'

Jowie Mwiinga, of the Zambian *Weekly Post*, was smuggled into the prison by a warder to conduct his interview. Details Katiza gave Mwiinga matched some of those he would give me years later. He denied that he was being held as a prohibited immigrant, as Mwiinga had been told by the prison authorities, and said: 'I was kidnapped and brought here by Winnie Mandela's men. She promised me everything – a car, a house, money and education.' But, wrote the Zambian reporter, Katiza no longer believed in the promises. He believed he had been betrayed so that Winnie's neck could be saved.

Barney Mthombothi of the Johannesburg *Star* also managed to get into the prison in August. He found Katiza having a furious argument with a warder. Mthombothi was unable to speak to Katiza but managed to leave a list of questions with him: the written answers were smuggled out by another visitor. Katiza said that both the Zambian government, who put him behind bars, and the ANC, whom he accused of forcing him out of South Africa, refused to take responsibility for his predicament. The *Star*'s man reported that Katiza complained he was being denied privileges granted even to convicted prisoners. 'I want people to assist me to be released,' said Katiza. 'I want to be taken out of prison to any country where my life will be safeguarded.' Mthombothi wrote: 'He said the truth did not come out during Mrs Mandela's trial [which by now had ended in Johannesburg] and he would reveal everything he knows about the death of Stompie after his release.'

*

Quite by chance, I too found Katiza Cebekhulu.

I was sent in October 1991 to Zambia to report Presidential and Parliamentary elections in the central African country. The Parliamentary contest was to be the first multi-party election since independence. After twenty-seven years in power President Kenneth Kaunda, who had ruled since the end of British colonial administration, was tipped by some journalists to be ousted if the polls were fair. Kaunda had systematically destroyed the economy in the name of creating a 'humanistic paradise on earth' and had been forced by the international financial community to abandon the one-party state. Annual inflation was 100 per cent; the average wage was £7 a month; spending on education was only a third of the level it had been fourteen years earlier; 25 per cent of pregnant mothers were HIV-positive. Fierce government price controls had caused a collapse in commercial production of the people's staple food, maize; a country which experts agreed was so fecund in soils, water and space that it should be feeding most of Africa had become a mendicant for world food aid.

In short, Zambia was a disaster caused by massive incompetence. The worse things got the more bizarre Kaunda's proposed solutions became. His latest pre-election idea was to let the Maharishi Yogi – once spiritual adviser to the Beatles – take over one-quarter of Zambia's land surface and divide it into neat squares designated for the development of residential areas, agriculture, forestry, industry and mining. In a letter to the Maharishi's company, the Maharishi Heaven on Earth Development Corporation (Mahedco), Kaunda wrote: 'You kindly outlined your proposal to create a Heaven on Earth in Zambia. We aim to achieve, in the long run, a perfect society in Zambia. I therefore see the project by Mahedco as a necessary catalyst to what we are trying to do here.'

The Zambia *Weekly Post* described Kaunda's plan as 'defying description'. However, Kaunda never got the chance to put the Maharishi to work. In the 30 October election he was crushed in the presidential race by his opponent, Frederick Chiluba, and Kaunda's own United Independence Party (UNIP) was nearly wiped out in the Parliamentary elections by Chiluba's Movement for Multi-Party Democracy (MMD).

From the moment the co-accuseds and witnesses in the Winnie Mandela trial began disappearing I had doubted that the South African justice system would provide us with many truths about the Stompie affair. So it crossed my mind, as I flew from Johannesburg across the Limpopo and Zambezi Rivers to

Lusaka, that I might try to reach Katiza Cebekhulu in his Zambian prison and hear the story he would have liked to tell in the Rand Supreme Court. I had no idea how I would reach him, but in Zambia I laid the groundwork: the means of access surprised me and the journey to an eventual meeting was to be long and nerve-racking.

Observers from many parts of the world came to monitor the Zambian presidential and general elections. There were observers from the European Community, the United Nations, the Commonwealth, the Carter Institute in Atlanta, Britain's Electoral Reform Society and sundry other outriders from organizations devoted to ensuring that others behaved democratically. At a pre-election press briefing I met the British MP Emma Nicholson who was the Westminster Parliament's representative observing the election. With former Bangladesh Foreign Minister Fakruddin Ahmed, a Commonwealth observer, she was about to head 650 miles overland to observe the elections in Northern Province, a vast underdeveloped region crisscrossed by tributaries of the mighty Congo River.

I asked if I could join her and Ahmed on their adventure and Emma agreed with alacrity – a decision that would have far-reaching consequences for both of us and for Katiza Cebekhulu. Travelling with Emma through a province the size of England I had as much fun as at any other time in Africa. She worked prodigiously hard, crossing rivers by canoe, trundling along dirt-tracks and broken pot-holed roads, dropping in at police stations, polling booths and candlelit drinking dens straight out of *Heart of Darkness*. She talked to people day and night, at river crossings, roadsides, forest glades, political rallies. I estimated that something like 99 out of 100 told her they were voting for the opposition MMD rather than UNIP: it enabled me to forecast a landslide for Chiluba before the first vote had been cast.

'Nicholson of the River' returned each night to the government-owned Kwacha Relax Hotel in Kasama, the provincial capital. The name Kwacha Relax meant what it said: it was a formidable drinking establishment-cum-brothel. Emma's room was appalling. It was behind the main public bar where heavy carousing went on into the early hours. It had been painted in dark ochre years ago and was infested by mosquitoes and giant cockroaches. As Emma curled up on her rickety iron bedstead it was my job to smash as many of the cockroaches as possible with my shoe before retreating to my own area of discomfort. Emma survived each night and I would find her bright, breezy and early in the breakfast room ordering two boiled eggs, the only food available, and a copious supply of boiling water, allowing her to indulge in her only home comfort – Earl Grey tea (a cup with breakfast and a flask for the day).

We returned to Lusaka for the count. On 2 November Chiluba was sworn in as the new President of Zambia. He and his MMD had achieved a crushing victory – 'We are like a country awakening from a coma,' he told tens of thousands of people who gathered for the inauguration ceremony in front of the Lusaka High Court. 'We are weak and ill, but still alive and determined to get well again.'

Emma phoned me that morning to say she had been granted an audience with the new President. She had met him while we were in Northern Province and he had told her he felt he was going to lose. Emma, on the basis of her own observations, told him he was wrong. 'You're going to win,' she said. 'I'll be your first appointment when you're President. I'll see you early next week.' He shook her hand and said: 'Yes, come straight in. It's a promise.'

When Chiluba's victory was confirmed, Emma telephoned him and he said he would send an official car to collect her. Emma, a professional politician through and through, told me she felt it was not worth seeing people of power unless important matters were raised with them. Was there anything I felt should be taken up with her new friend?

Yes, as a matter of fact there was. How about asking him about a man named Katiza Cebekhulu, who was rumoured to be in one of Zambia's prisons? Was the rumour true? I would like to speak to Katiza – very much. It was a very important matter.

Emma had never heard of Katiza. She asked me to brief her. So, before she departed to meet the President, I described to her as fully as possible in the short time available the Winnie–Stompie saga, Katiza's unexplained disappearance on the second day of Winnie's trial and the press reports that he had been spotted inside Lusaka Central Prison.

Emma met Chiluba in a modest house: he had not moved into State House, having allowed Kenneth Kaunda to continue living there for two or three weeks to clear up his affairs and arrange a new home for himself. They began discussing the grave economic and social problems Chiluba was inheriting after Kaunda's twenty-seven-year Presidency. They discussed Zambia's human rights record under Kaunda and then Emma asked, as a personal favour, whether Chiluba would investigate the fate of an 'invisible political prisoner' called Katiza Cebekhulu, who, coincidentally and unwittingly, she had learned had been put in jail by Kaunda. She gave Chiluba her outline of Katiza's story: 'He didn't believe at first that Zambia had political prisoners from other countries. But he said he would investigate and contact me immediately if he discovered anything.'

Emma left for a series of other meetings. But in the afternoon the President telephoned and said: 'Come back, Emma, at once! I've found your man. You've got to come and listen to what he's got to say.' Chiluba had contacted the Director of Prisons and ordered the jails to be scoured. To his astonishment, Katiza Cebekhulu had been found. Chiluba ordered Katiza to be brought to him immediately and for the Director of Prisons and the Chiefs of Police and the Army to attend in full uniform.

Katiza was escorted in by the Director of Prisons. Emma observed that he was thin, his cheeks sunken – as a result of his back teeth being removed in Baragwanath Hospital – and was poorly dressed in borrowed pyjamas. 'He was like Lazarus – a corpse raised from the dead, but with hardly any life in him,' Emma told me afterwards. 'He looked like a man from a grave, very thin and with that pallor that comes with imprisonment under harsh conditions. He was, frankly, effectively dead but was struggling to stay alive because he felt he had something of large importance to say.

'The story he told President Chiluba over the next hour or two was indeed dreadful.' Katiza described the stabbing of Stompie beside the jacuzzi behind Winnie Mandela's Diepkloof house. 'He said he was in the wrong place at the wrong time with the wrong people. He told Chiluba he woke up and saw a youth being stabbed to death. With graphic illustration, raising his arm in the air, he brought it down with thrusts, saying, "I saw Mrs Mandela do that to Stompie."

'And the room went silent. It was clear that it was true. Everyone believed him. This was a cry from the heart, with no anticipation of it being answered. I know from my work with refugees that people tell the truth under those circumstances. This was not a man making something up for dramatic effect. This was someone who thought he had disappeared off the face of the earth for ever, who hadn't anticipated being brought to life again and who now had this chance while on his last legs of telling his story how it was. And he went on with other details implicating Winnie Mandela in other murders.

'The President turned to me and said, "This is extraordinary. We've got to talk. What is to be done?" Together we recognized the absolute seriousness of what Katiza was telling us, its immensity, its scale, its misery. His story was like the proverbial stone. It sank through many depths. But it touched the heart, apart from anything else, because why should another human being be hounded like that, chased by other men to extinction? Katiza had a right to be alive.

'I didn't feel I was the proper person to take down detailed evidence of this complex crime. I knew police needed to see him rather than myself. But the centrality of Mrs Mandela's involvement was very clear from what Katiza said. He said that if he gave evidence "that would be it" for her – her guilt would be wholly understood. He named names and his implication was that it was Mrs Mandela personally who organized his kidnap.'

Chiluba's aides, however, had meanwhile searched state papers and found there what purported to be the full story of Katiza's abduction from South Africa and his imprisonment in Zambia. The official papers suggested a surprising possibility: the mastermind behind the kidnap of Katiza Cebekhulu was claimed to be Nelson Mandela. 'It was clear to President Chiluba immediately from the government records that his predecessor had acted in the belief that Nelson Mandela had authorized the kidnapping and transportation of Katiza Cebekhulu to Zambia,' said Emma. 'The records told him that Kenneth Kaunda was requested to take Katiza Cebekhulu out of circulation when he [Katiza] arrived in Zambia.' Six years later Kaunda would admit to Emma, before a television camera, that the state papers revealed the possibility, albeit without formal proof, of Nelson Mandela's involvement.

After Katiza had left Chiluba's office – to return to Lusaka Central Prison, where Chiluba felt he would be safest for the time being – Emma and the President discussed at length how to secure his safety prior to making longer-term arrangements for him. Chiluba said Katiza had committed no crime in Zambia and should not be in jail. Emma felt that if he was released into a vacuum he would be a dead man. 'His situation was bleak indeed if no one would listen,' she said. 'I had no knowledge of whether his evidence was accurate, but I believed he deserved the chance to have it tested in a court of law.' Meanwhile, it was important that his safety should be guaranteed. Chiluba and Emma agreed she should make an immediate approach to London for Katiza to be allowed into Britain under some form of guardianship. They felt that the United Kingdom, as the Mother of the British Commonwealth, remained one of the world's most tolerant countries and would react with under-standing and discretion to the Katiza conundrum.

Emma briefed me on the Chiluba–Cebekhulu meeting. We made plans to fly to London with Katiza – I would interview him *en route* and obtain his exclusive story for my newspaper. With hindsight, we were naively optimistic. Emma went to the British High Commission and top-security telegrams whizzed to and fro between Lusaka and London about Chiluba's pro-posal. In the end it was quashed firmly by the British government in a classic exercise of *realpolitik*. The British Embassy in Pretoria was playing a discreet but highly influential role in helping the National Party government and the ANC move towards full constitutional negotiations. Both Mandela and De Klerk had 'hot lines' to the UK's ambassadors – Robin Renwick until June 1991, and thereafter Anthony Reeve – of which they made frequent use, especially when tensions between the two sides threatened breakdown. The British Embassy's mediating role almost made the ambassador a *de facto* member of the South African Cabinet. Imaginative British arbitration was one of the main reasons Nelson Mandela paid such high tribute to the British people when he made a state visit to London in July 1996.

Churchill described the smuggling of Lenin back into Russia in 1917 with German help as acting 'like a typhoid bacillus'. The Foreign Office and its Pretoria Embassy considered Katiza Cebekhulu's arrival in London would have a similar destructive effect on its endeavours to change the course of South African history. Deliberations went right to the top of Britain's government. 'I talked to the Prime Minister [John Major],' said Emma. 'I stalked him. I ambushed him in the passages at Westminster and begged him to help when I realized the final decision rested with him. But he wouldn't play ball.' Emma Nicholson was told by Major there could be no admission to Britain for the man from Mpumalanga.

Emma, herself a Conservative MP, was distressed by the decision. It deepened her disillusion with her own party's increasingly harsh 'little England' xenophobia and its paranoia about refugees: it helped shape her later decision to resign the Conservative whip and cross the floor of the House of Commons to join the Liberal Democrats.

Emma decided to begin a series of approaches to other countries and to the United Nations High Commission for Refugees (UNHCR) to secure help for Katiza. She returned to London but told Chiluba she would stay in touch. I flew back home to Johannesburg, instead of London.

CHAPTER FIFTEEN

The Mandelas Separate

1992

South Africa entered 1992 on a note of high hope. In the final days of 1991 constitutional negotiations had at last begun between twenty delegations representing political parties and black homelands. The Convention for a Democratic South Africa (Codesa), meeting on 20–21 December 1991 in Johannesburg's cavernous World Trade Centre, agreed the general principles for the establishment of an interim all-race government. It would, if all went well, lead to the first all-race general election in the country's history. The details were to be fleshed out in 1992.

For a while the Codesa accord seemed threatened by a string of victories in whites-only by-elections for the pro-apartheid Conservative Party over De Klerk's Nationalist Party. De Klerk, sensing his negotiating stance at Codesa was being undermined by the gains of the Conservative Party, which was boycotting the constitutional talks, consequently called a whites-only referendum for 17 March 1992. The country's 3.3 million white adults were asked to vote on whether or not they backed the reform process and negotiations for a new constitution. The choice was a simple one between 'yes' and 'no': they were, in effect, being asked to emancipate the country's twenty-six million black people after 350 years of white rule.

Political violence continued throughout the transition period, punctuated by explosions of particularly terrible force. The referendum triggered one such eruption, with more than 300 people dying in township fighting in the two weeks before the whites went to the polls. If the whites were to vote 'no' to reform there were widespread fears that the consequences would be catastrophic.

De Klerk's gamble paid off. Sixty-nine per cent of whites voted to pursue reform, 31 per cent voted against – virtually destroying the Conservative Party as an effective force in South African politics. It was an historic watershed. Never before in Africa's history had a white minority voted to give up power to a black majority: whites in Algeria, Kenya and Rhodesia had voted 'no' in similar referenda. 'Today we have closed the book on apartheid,' said De Klerk when the result was announced.

*

Though the political wind was turning in Nelson Mandela's favour, his personal life was in deep crisis. On leaving prison, Nelson had moved with Winnie into a third house that had been built for her in Soweto. Known as 'Winnie's Palace', because it had fifteen rooms and luxury fittings and was reputed to have cost about Rand 1 million to build, it was situated in an area of Orlando West known as 'Beverly Hills', because it was where Soweto's rich and famous lived. American singer Harry Belafonte made a donation towards the building costs.

But in November 1991, a month before Codesa began, Nelson moved out of Winnie's Palace to a house in Johannesburg's leafy northern suburbs, the refuge under apartheid of rich whites. He was particularly distressed and angered by two expensive official trips Winnie made as ANC Director of Social Welfare to the United States, accompanied by her deputy, Dali Mpofu; among the expenses charged to the ANC were transatlantic Concorde flights for Winnie and her lover from London. Nelson would never again live with Winnie.

When rumours of the separation first surfaced in newspapers ANC spokesmen dismissed them as untrue. The official ANC line was that there had been threats to the lives of both Nelson and Winnie. As a security precaution man and wife were being kept apart: they were not travelling in the same car or attending the same functions. The myth might have been sustained longer had there not been fresh violence in the back rooms at Winnie Mandela's Diepkloof Extension house.

Xoliswa Falati, convicted with Winnie in the Stompie trial a year earlier and still awaiting the appeal hearing, had been staying in the room where Katiza Cebekhulu had lived near the jacuzzi. In late March Falati was told by her lawyer, Kathy Satchwell, that because the London-based International Defence and Aid Fund was being wound up (following the revelation that it had been funding Winnie's defence) there was no longer any money available to cover legal expenses, estimated at more than Rand 70,000 (£14,000), for her appeal. Satchwell was withdrawing her services because she could not afford to represent Falati for nothing. Without representation at the Appeal Court in Bloemfontein, said Satchwell, Falati would have to serve her six-year prison sentence.

Falati had always been under the impression that some of the costs, including her own, were met in the Stompie trial by a Rand 1 million (£200,000) contribution by Libyan leader Muammar Gaddafi to Nelson Mandela. She contacted Nelson that same day, 27 March, asking for help. He set her mind at rest by assuring her he would look after the problem.

In the early hours of Monday 29 March Winnie Mandela barged into Falati's back room wielding a gun. Rousing her sleeping friend, she told her to get out of the house. Falati fled barefoot in her nightdress into the street. Winnie began tossing Falati's possessions into the back yard while shouting at her that she would be going to prison. Falati shouted back that she had spoken to Nelson, who had told her she could stay in the room. 'Who do you think you are? Who are you to speak to the [ANC] President?' Winnie stormed before locking the room, leaving Falati stranded outside.

Falati went to a neighbouring house and made two telephone calls – one to Nelson Mandela and the other to Ruth Bhengu, a *Sowetan* reporter, telling them what was happening. Mandela and Bhengu turned up at Winnie's house within a short time of each other in the early-morning darkness. Neither had expected to meet the other. Bhengu had walked into an extraordinary scoop. Mandela had brought a locksmith with him who was changing the lock of the back room so that Falati could get back in. The ANC President told Bhengu he would rather she did not write about the affair despite his belief in the need for a strong and free press: this particular story, he said, would only cause trouble.

Bhengu told her editor, Moegsien Williams, about Nelson Mandela's warning. Williams told her to write the story, but before it went to press he received a call from Mandela checking that the story would not appear. He told the editor it was important for the incident to be played down: Winnie's lawyers had advised her to keep a low profile until her appeal was heard, and the story would wreck her chances of success in the Appeal

Court, where he believed she had a good chance of being acquitted.

Williams was in a tough situation. If an assertion Falati now made to him was true, that she had perjured herself in court to protect Winnie Mandela, then it was apparent there must have been some kind of cover-up and here was an international hero wrestling with the dilemma and apparently endorsing the deception. Williams courageously decided to publish, running two separate stories incorporating Bhengu's material on different days.

In one article the *Sowetan* reported that Falati, in interviews with Bhengu, had threatened to 'spill all the beans' and reveal damaging information about Mrs Mandela, including circumstances surrounding the death of Dr Abu-Baker Asvat. Falati had told Bhengu that Winnie was breaking their relationship 'now that I've served my purpose . . . I can't believe that she is dumping me after all I've done for her.'

*

The Falati affair unleashed an avalanche of electrifying stories. The London *Guardian*'s Johannesburg correspondent reported Nelson Mandela's attempted cover-up, and worse followed. The *Sunday Times* of London said ANC intelligence men had interrogated Falati for four hours to discover what she knew about Winnie and what she might tell journalists. Her revelations had confirmed Nelson in a decision he was moving towards already – to separate from his wife. The *Sunday Times* said the parting would be announced soon.

John Battersby, the *Christian Science Monitor*'s Africa correspondent, waded in with new revelations about Abu-Baker Asvat's murder which were widely reported in South Africa.

Battersby had been given a copy of the statement made by Nicholas Dlamini to police Lieutenant Gert Zeelie after he was arrested and charged, with Cyril Mbatha, for the 27 January 1989 murder of Dr Abu-Baker Asvat. In his statement Dlamini had said Mbatha was to have received a payment of Rand 20,000 (£4,000) once Abu-Baker Asvat was dead.

Battersby had also found Jannie van der Merwe, the state prosecutor at the trial of Dlamini and Mbatha, at which both were sentenced to death for Asvat's murder. Van der Merwe, who had since moved from Johannesburg to another job in Cape Town, said the police had not produced Dlamini's statement in court for the extraordinary reason that 'it was at odds with the police investigation'. Van der Merwe told the *Christian Science Monitor*'s man he did not believe the true motive for Asvat's murder had been revealed – the police had argued persistently and unemotionally that the doctor's death was a straightforward case of robbery.

Van der Merwe said he was convinced the police had not explored every possible avenue of inquiry. He believed a link did exist between Mrs Mandela and the gunning down of Asvat: 'My gut feeling all along was that there was something very strange. It was just too much of a coincidence . . . I just had the feeling that this was not an armed robbery or a murder, but an assassination.' Battersby wrote that Van der Merwe was not alone in believing Winnie could be linked to Asvat's death: 'Two lawyers close to the Mandela trial (but not on her team), anti-apartheid activists, former friends of Mrs Mandela and the Asvat family are among those who say they believe she had a hand in the murder.'

Dr Ebrahim Asvat, Abu-Baker Asvat's brother, reacting to the new reports, said he was urging the South African Police to reopen inquiries into his brother's murder: 'We have never accepted robbery as the motive and we were never satisfied with the result of the trial . . . We have always believed Abu-Baker was assassinated.' And Abu-Baker Asvat's political party, AZAPO, issued a statement saying it was convinced a conspiracy existed to cover up the truth about the killing.

Battersby's article also quoted from John Sangwa's November 1991 taped interview with Katiza in Lusaka Central Prison. Picked up by South African papers, it revealed for the first time to the public Katiza's claim that he was taken out of the country at Winnie Mandela's request at the beginning of the Stompie trial. Mrs Mandela had offered him life or death, the *Christian Science Monitor* quoted Katiza as saying.

Winnie Mandela responded, in a statement issued by her lawyer Ismail Ayob, to Falati's insinuation that she was in some way involved with Abu-Baker Asvat's death. Denying complicity, Winnie said the allegation was inconsistent with the evidence Falati herself had given under oath in the Richardson trial and subsequently in Falati's own trial alongside Mrs Mandela.

A string of startling revelations quickly followed the *Christian Science Monitor* report. First, Pelo Mekgwe, the state witness kidnapped fourteen months earlier as Winnie's trial got off to its limping start, reappeared. The *Weekly Mail* revealed that Mekgwe had returned to South Africa after being taken out of the country by 'the usual ANC underground routes' on 10 February 1991, six days after Winnie's trial for Stompie's kidnap and assault had begun in the Rand Supreme Court. Two ANC Youth League members, Patrick Moloi and Salivi Molapsi, told the newspaper Mekgwe had left 'because he did not want to "betray" the ANC by giving evidence that would contribute to the state's case against [Winnie] Mandela'.

While it was Moloi and Molapsi who physically took Mekgwe out of the country, the *Weekly Mail* said it had been told by several informants, including senior ANC members, that the organizer and co-ordinator of Mekgwe's abduction was a top member of the ANC's National Executive Committee and of Umkhonto we Sizwe. But no one was prepared to name him.

Moloi and Molapsi claimed no physical force had been used in 'persuading' Mekgwe to leave, but they told the *Weekly Mail* 'that the consequences of being a state witness in her [Winnie's] trial were explained to him by the ANC'. (Tokyo Sexwale's startling revelation that his Special Projects Unit of the ANC had organized Mekgwe's original abduction followed two days later.)

Police told the newspaper that Mekgwe was not likely to be charged for absconding: they were not even investigating what they described as his 'departure' because no one had alleged that he left under duress – an astounding conclusion, given that Judge Stegmann had sentenced Mekgwe's fellow witnesses, Kenny Kgase and Thabiso Mono, to potential life sentences on pain of failing to give evidence at Winnie Mandela's trial.

*

There had been little time to digest the *Christian Science Monitor* and *Weekly Mail* disclosures before John Morgan admitted that he too had lied in court to protect Winnie Mandela. He said he had arrived early one morning, 1 January 1989, at Winnie's Diepkloof house and he had seen Stompie lying on the ground – 'I knew he was dead because he had already been stabbed and had blood on his neck,' Morgan told the *Sunday Times* of Johannesburg. 'I was told by Winnie to pick up the dog and dump him . . . I told Winnie I would never do something like that and went inside the house.'

Morgan, who had spent eight days sequestered in a Pretoria hotel with *Sunday Times* reporter Dawn Barkhuizen going over his story many times, said his original police statement on 21 February 1989 was for the most part true; it had not been fabricated as a result of police torture, as his defence advocate had argued before Judge Stegmann.

Nor, Morgan told the *Sunday Times*, had Mrs Mandela been in Brandfort from 29 December 1988 onwards, as he had asserted at her trial. She had been in her house at Diepkloof Extension, Soweto, and led the assault on Stompie Moeketsi, Kenny Kgase, Thabiso Mono and Pelo Mekgwe after they had been kidnapped. He said that on the evening of the kidnap and assault he drove Mrs Mandela's minibus to Paul Verryn's Orlando West manse for the kidnapping. Jerry Richardson had told him: 'Mummy said you must go.' Mrs Mandela at that moment was in her living room watching a soap opera on television, said Morgan. (Mandela asserted at her trial that at that time she was in the same minibus on her way to Brandfort.)

He added that testimony about the subsequent assault given by Kenny Kgase and Thabiso Mono during Mrs Mandela's trial – which conflicted with that given by Mrs Mandela and Mrs Falati – was essentially correct. Stompie Moeketsi and the other kidnapped youths were put into a back room at Winnie's house, where a chair had been placed and reserved for 'Mummy' by Richardson. Expanding on his original police statement, Morgan told Barkhuizen: 'Mrs Mandela came into the room and started asking the boys: "Why do you sleep with a European, a reverend . . . Do you let him fuck you, you dogs?"'

Morgan said Winnie struck the first blows. She slapped Stompie's face three times. Next she punched Stompie and Kenny Kgase. 'Then everybody started to hit them,' he said. 'Xoliswa, Nompumi [Nompumelelo], Jerry and the guys from the soccer club joined in. They were in a circle around the boys. Winnie hit them with a sjambok, not choosing one target but hitting whoever was in front of her. They started doing "breakdown". Before they hit the ground there were already many kicks in their faces.' The beating, Morgan estimated, lasted about forty-five minutes. Winnie left the room before the assault ended and was not there when Richardson ordered the boys to wipe their own blood from the walls.

Morgan returned to the house to carry out his customary driving errands the following day, 30 December. Winnie was preparing to go to her office at Community House and the beaten youths were sitting in the back courtyard. (Winnie, according to her trial testimony, was in Brandfort on 30 December.) 'Stompie's face was like a pumpkin and his hands so swollen that he could not lift a cup of coffee,' Morgan said.

Morgan was subsequently arrested, charged initially with the murder of Stompie and held in prison for about seven months in 1989. He said Mrs Mandela visited him in prison, brought him 'a couple of rand' and told him not to tell anyone what had happened. 'She said she would see me right later.' When Morgan was released from prison, after Winnie paid his bail, she hosted a big party at her house at which a sheep was killed and roasted. 'Throughout the day she kept telling me to say she was in Brandfort on December 29. She never threatened me, but I knew what happened to the other boys. I was afraid if I didn't lie.'

Morgan said he decided to tell his story after Winnie turned down his request to fund his appeal against his kidnapping con-viction. 'She refused and directed me to see Dali Mpofu. He said my case was not important and refused to give me money.' Morgan then received a letter from his lawyer – Kathy Satchwell again – saying she had been unable to raise money for his appeal and could no longer give him legal representation.

'I want to clear my name,' Morgan told Barkhuizen. 'People call me a child-beater. I am battling to feed my daughters and two grandchildren. Winnie used me and dumped me.' In a live interview on South African television Morgan repeated his account of his perjury.

Barkhuizen was sent to a secret hideaway after she had writ-ten her story. Her newspaper placed armed guards at her house. What triggered the alarm was a call she received within hours of finishing writing her story on Friday 10 April. She had loaded the story in mid-afternoon from her computer disk into her news editor's terminal. In the early evening she received a call telling her that Winnie Mandela had a copy of her story and was 'absolutely enraged, ranting about its contents to anyone in earshot'.

Barkhuizen was stunned. She could not understand how the story had reached Winnie so swiftly, given the security sur-rounding it. When her informant quoted extensive extracts, she promptly realized that Winnie must have a copy of the com-plete article. The *Sunday Times* management was informed and Barkhuizen was sent away on a long holiday. When she returned she found that the padlocked cupboard in which she kept all her files and notebooks had been opened: all had disappeared.

*

Who knows what finally made Nelson Mandela decide to separate from Winnie? But after John Morgan admitted lying in the Stompie trial, Nelson's old friend Walter Sisulu and the ANC Secretary-General Cyril Ramaphosa went to see Mandela to argue that the time had come for him to announce that his marriage was over. To persist with the illusion would be to damage himself and the movement.

Nelson was left to decide for himself. On Monday 13 April 1992, the day after the *Sunday Times* article was published, Nelson Mandela called a press conference and said he was leaving his wife after thirty-four years of marriage. I watched, at the ANC's Johannesburg headquarters, as Mandela, speaking softly and with dignity, but under clear strain, told the throng of reporters that his love for his wife remained undiminished. But they had agreed to part 'in view of the tensions that have arisen owing to differences between ourselves on a number of issues in recent months'.

Mandela, then aged seventy-three, was flanked by his lifelong friends in the fight against apartheid and white minority rule, staunch Walter Sisulu and the visibly ailing Oliver Tambo. Seeking to soften the impact on Winnie, Nelson said: 'My action was not prompted by the current allegations against her in the media. I deeply regret the role the media has assumed in this regard and would once again urge that the issue of her guilt or innocence be left to the judicial system to determine.' He added that 'Comrade Nomzamo', as he referred to his then fifty-seven-year-old wife, could continue to rely on his support 'during these trying moments in her life'.

Recounting the great pressures they had endured from 1961, when he was forced to go underground less than three years after their marriage, the ANC leader said he had no regrets about the life he and Winnie had tried to share: 'During the two decades I spent on Robben Island she was an indispensable pillar of support and comfort to myself personally . . . My love for her remains undiminished. Circumstances beyond our control, however, dictated that it should be otherwise. I part from my wife with no recriminations. I embrace [her] with all the love and affection I have nursed for her inside and outside prison from the moment I first met her.'

Mandela declined to take questions, but as he stood wearily to leave he paused and said: 'Ladies and gentlemen, I hope you will appreciate the pain I have gone through and I now end this press conference.' He walked out with bowed head.

Winnie did not attend the press conference, but the man who stood next to me at the back of the densely packed room was Dali Mpofu.

*

Two days later another press conference was called in the same room. Winnie Mandela, after twice refusing Cyril Ramaphosa's demand that she resign as Director of the ANC Social Welfare Department, was virtually frogmarched into the room to announce that she was quitting. In the wake of recent events, even she could not persist. Ramaphosa had called an emergency meeting of the ANC's 'inner cabinet', the national working committee, which gave him the authority to tell Winnie she could either go graciously or be publicly sacked pending an inquiry into Rand 400,000 (£80,000) which had not been accounted for by her Department of Social Welfare. Already the ANC's Treasurer-General had frozen the Social Welfare bank account.

Winnie, with her back against the wall, decided to go,

unwillingly and unapologetically. The conference room was packed once again as she said: 'The step I am taking is not because of the false allegations being made against me but because of the devotion that I have for the ANC and my family ... I have taken this step because I consider it to be in the best interest of the ANC whose cause and policies I will support to the end of my life.'

Winnie was flanked at the press conference only by second-tier ANC leaders. Her husband was notably absent, as also were Oliver Tambo, Walter Sisulu and Cyril Ramaphosa. Obviously determined to go out in style, she wore voguish ANC colours – a bright green silk blouse with black leather waistcoat, a yellow bead necklace and emerald-studded gold earrings. Reading from a statement, parts of which had been prepared for her by Ramaphosa, she said: 'I have had an overwhelming compassion for the suffering of my people under oppression, which has been so strong that it has overcome any fear that I may have had for my personal well-being or interests ... Nothing can make me waver in my commitment to my organization, my husband and to the oppressed and impoverished people of South Africa.'

She went on: 'False allegations have been made against me. I have always maintained my innocence and there is an appeal pending. My request that the matter should be left in the hands of the courts has not only been ignored but appears to fuel the desire of those who wish to destroy me and to discredit the ANC. Their campaign of vilification has created a difficult situation for the ANC, my husband as its President, and myself. I have asked the ANC to relieve me of my duties as the appointed head of the Department of Social Welfare as soon as a successor can take my place.'

Winnie, overcome by emotion, paused several times towards the end of her statement and tears welled in her eyes as she said: 'Finally, I would like to express my gratitude to those who have stood by me during the long struggle even at the price of victimization, harassment, imprisonment and death.'

Winnie Mandela, however, was only temporarily bowed. Just eleven days later she appeared on television, unabashed and unrepentant, and said: 'As far as I am concerned my political career goes on as if nothing had happened.'

*

Nora Moahloli, the primary schoolteacher who had testified – crucially – at both Jerry Richardson's trial and Winnie's trial that Mrs Mandela was in Brandfort from 29 to 31 December 1988, now admitted she did not know the precise date. 'It was in the late '80s, but I can't remember when,' she told Johannesburg *Star* reporters who visited her in Brandfort. Three times the reporters repeated to her the statements she had given in court, including the dates she had given Judges Brian O'Donovan and Michael Stegmann; three times Mrs Moahloli replied she could not recall the day or the date of Winnie Mandela's visit.

Whatever the date, Winnie had told Mrs Moahloli she would not return to Brandfort again. 'She said next time I would have to come to Johannesburg to see her,' said Moahloli. 'But I can't remember when she was here.' When she was asked if 'the late '80s' could be taken to mean Winnie was in Brandfort on the evening of 29 December 1988, Nora Moahloli said: 'I am not saying she was here. I can't remember.'

*

The saga of Winnie Mandela had still not run out of steam. In September 1992 a four-page letter written by Winnie to Dali Mpofu was leaked to the *Star* and other newspapers. The letter, in Winnie's handwriting, was believed to have come from ANC headquarters after Nelson had read it.

Winnie told Mpofu in the letter that she had put her love for him before her marriage to Nelson. She warned Mpofu: 'I will never be used by you for *ukufeba kwakho* [Xhosa for 'your promiscuity'] and you use our things we acquired together for running around fucking at the slightest emotional excuse.' She said she was not another Teresa Oakley-Smith, to be used and discarded when it suited him:

> *Ndoze ndibe sisibanxwa sakho mina* [I won't be your bloody fool], Dali. Before I'm through with you, you are going to learn a bit of honesty and sincerity and know what betrayal of one's trust means to a woman!
>
> You lie to me and suggest that in order to preserve our relationship you have to have a relationship as a cover to defuse our problem? I understand and know how difficult it was for me to accept that reality but it eventually dawned on me that because I love you so much I had to agree with you even though I shuddered at the thought of you lying and pretending to love this other woman . . .

Winnie's letter gave a number of names as Mpofu's 'other women' – one she named as Imogin; another she referred to as 'Miss X'; another as 'the woman you were sleeping with on the 21st floor' (of the ANC's HQ).

Recalling February 1991, the month her trial began at the Rand Supreme Court, Winnie wrote: 'Do you remember how in love we were then?' But now she said he was treating her shabbily and when he had come to her the previous weekend he was already 'emptied up' physically by another woman.

The letter was dated 17 March 1992, less than a month before Nelson announced he was leaving his wife. It went on:

> You think you can just wish away certain things Dali. Not with me. I tell you I'm in trouble with the Simmonds Street a/c (one of her department's bank accounts) which reflects over Rand 160,000 [£32,000] drawn over a period for you.
>
> You don't even bother to check how we can overcome this. I tell you that [Ismail] Ayob has been sent by Tata [Nelson's affectionate family name] to get a lawyer to investigate my account. I tell you Ntombi [an employee of the ANC's Department of Social Welfare] is gossiping about the cheques we used to ask her to cash for [us] in the name of the Dept and how I gave you all that money and you and I are now being investigated.

Winnie returned to their affair. Referring to Oakley-Smith as 'your white hag', she said Mpofu had lied to the mother of his child about his involvement with the Mother of the Nation. She continued:

> The only time you have time to talk to me is about women *ofeba nabo* [you are having sex with], as you are doing right now. You are supposed to care so much for me that the fact that I haven't been speaking to Tata for 5 months now over you is no longer your concern.
>
> I keep telling you the situation is deteriorating at home. You are not bothered because you are satisfying yourself every night with a woman you are 'involved' with and you are not in love with her. How long did you think I will buy this?

Winnie signed off: 'It's me.'

In another leak from ANC HQ, reports of fights between Winnie and Mpofu were said to be numerous. In one fracas security guards in the ANC's underground car park said they saw on their closed-circuit television sets Winnie's wig being knocked off by Mpofu.

Following publication of the letter, Winnie Mandela resigned from all her remaining ANC posts, including her position on the National Executive Committee.

*

All this took place against a background of increasing violence in South Africa in 1992 and the breakdown of negotiations between the National Party government and the ANC. Forty-five people were killed in fighting between residents and Zulu hostel dwellers in the tiny township of Boipatong, near Sharpeville, on 22 June. Aaron Mathope, a nine-month-old baby, was found dead with a Zulu assegai (stabbing spear) through his head: the hacked and slashed body of his mother, Rebecca Mathope, lay next to him.

On 7 September twenty-eight ANC supporters were shot dead and more than 200 wounded when soldiers opened fire on a column of thousands of protesters marching across the border into the 'independent' black homeland of Ciskei. Cyril Ramaphosa, who was at this Battle of Bisho (the Ciskei capital), said: 'The clear intention was to shoot and shoot and kill and kill. It was the most horrific day of my life. I saw a man near me have his entire head blown away.'

CHAPTER SIXTEEN

Lusaka Central Prison

1992–1993

Katiza Cebekhulu went back to his prison cell from his meeting with President Chiluba with his hopes high that soon he would be released and on his way to London. 'At the time I didn't know the British woman who was with the President, but now I know it was Emma,' Katiza told me years later. 'After I told the President everything, he and Emma were discussing how I could go to Britain.

'The President said I was going back to prison because I would be safe there. At first I was happy to wait. Linda tried to send me clothes, soap, shoes and food. The prisoners used to steal from me, but I had a new friend, Kambaranja, who used to look after me and shared some of the things his family brought him. He even gave me a watch.'

Kambaranja Kaunda, the youngest son of President Kaunda, had been sentenced to death two weeks before the October election for murdering a woman. Now he was sharing a cell with Katiza and three-score others pending his ultimately successful appeal against the death sentence.

After Emma flew out, John Sangwa, a local human rights lawyer, twice visited Katiza in Lusaka Central Prison and on the second occasion took with him a hidden tape machine to record the conversation, without Katiza's approval. Katiza had no idea who Sangwa was. He was suspicious and constantly interrupted the flow of the interview to express his unhappiness. When Sangwa asked him to sign an affidavit confirming details of the meeting, Katiza signed but added a sentence saying it had happened without his prior consent.

Sangwa briefed Jowie Mwiinga of the Zambia *Weekly Post* about the first visit and released a transcript of the tape secretly recorded during the second to a correspondent of the *Christian Science Monitor*. Years later I managed to get hold of the transcript: the conversation was very confused and disjointed, but parts corroborated what Katiza would in due course tell me. Katiza told Sangwa that Mrs Mandela had poured boiling water over him because he knew 'all the scandal about Winnie'. He explained how he was taken to Winnie on 8 February 1991 and was asked: 'Katiza, do you want to die now or do you want to go into exile? If you go into exile I will give you a car, house, money and everything and education.'

Katiza explained to Sangwa how he and Winnie made a plan 'to destroy this priest [Paul Verryn]'. He said two men had killed Dr Abu-Baker Asvat 'because Dr Asvat was checking Stompie before he died and Dr Asvat was telling Mrs Mandela that Stompie any time is going to be died . . . Mrs Mandela was telling Dr Asvat to write in the book this white man is raping me. And this white man didn't rape me.'

Several times Katiza told Sangwa he felt he was being harassed and was unhappy with the interview. Neither the Zambian government nor the ANC had explained why he was in prison; he felt weakened from his harsh imprisonment, he told Sangwa, and would prefer to give his evidence in court. He was annoyed with some of the questions, particularly one alleging that vehicles stuffed with cocaine and mandrax had been delivered from Port Elizabeth to Winnie Mandela's home in Soweto. It was not true, said Katiza.

Jowie Mwiinga quoted Katiza as saying that the evidence presented in Winnie Mandela's trial was only the tip of the iceberg and that he was convinced the ANC would do 'anything' to stop him testifying: 'If they give me security, I will gladly return to South Africa to testify against Winnie . . . I would like to return home but I am afraid that the ANC could get me.'

*

After her failure with Britain, Emma Nicholson next approached the Danish government. 'I'd had a lot of contact with Denmark when I was a director of the Save the Children Fund [a London-based charity], and knew it had an excellent human rights record,' said Emma. 'It was on the verge of taking Katiza on a private basis when the press stories based on Sangwa's tape recordings were published. Denmark lost its nerve and pulled back. Sangwa's recordings condemned Katiza to continuing imprisonment.'

Emma next tried the United States and Sweden. They declined to open their doors to a man who was technically a fugitive from justice in South Africa. 'I approached every country in the world that was a signatory of the United Nations human rights agenda. Sometimes I went alone. Sometimes I knocked on the door of a ruler of a country and begged them to take Katiza. Mainly I worked through the UNHCR, but all turned me down. The last to refuse was Ireland.

'Every government caught the virus that if they accepted this particular refugee they would be destabilizing the fight against apartheid. So he was a mere pawn that could be discarded.'

*

In early September 1992 Katiza was taken from prison to the office of Zambian Foreign Minister Vernon Mwaanga. 'He told me Nelson Mandela was coming to Zambia and my case would need to be discussed,' said Katiza. 'Mwaanga said he needed to go through my story with me. So I told him Winnie had killed Stompie and was working with the police. I told how Dr Asvat was killed. I told Mwaanga about Winnie's order to me to call the police about Sizwe. I told how Paul Verryn had not raped me. I told him how Winnie always looked so smart and sophisticated that you couldn't believe she could do these things.'

Mandela visited Zambia in the third week of September 1992. He had some major fence-building to do with Chiluba: before the election ten months earlier the ANC leader had openly expressed support for Kenneth Kaunda. He was asked in a newspaper interview what he was going to do about Katiza. 'We never asked that Cebekhulu should be detained,' said Mandela. 'If he is released so that he comes back to his country I will be happy about that . . . We will do everything we can do to get him out. He has nothing to fear from us now or in the future.'

During the Mandela visit Katiza was taken from prison and driven to meet the ANC President: 'There was Mandela and two other ANC officials – I don't know who they were – in a big room. It was a long meeting. I hid nothing, I told everything. He [Mandela] promised to work on my case and release me soon so that I could come home. He said the problem was that the South African government wanted to arrest me. It was the only time I have met Mandela. I can't say he was good or he was bad, he just listened.

'I went back to prison but was called again to the Foreign Affairs office and told by men there not to speak to anyone about Winnie or my meeting with Nelson; it would put me in trouble. But they promised to release me within a few days.'

The release, however, did not come. Instead Katiza was called again to the Foreign Ministry to meet two white officials from South Africa's Department of Foreign Affairs. 'They said I was a citizen of South Africa and I should return. I would be a free man and they would not put me in prison. They wanted me to return with them. I said: "No, I don't think it's a simple matter."'

*

What the South African government and police really wanted to do about Katiza at this time is difficult to establish. Department of Foreign Affairs official Stephen Grundlingh told a *Weekly Mail* reporter the government had 'lodged no formal requests' for Cebekhulu's return. But I discovered by chance that in February 1992 an attempt had been made through South Africa's Embassy in Lilongwe, the capital of Malawi, to kidnap him from Lusaka Central Prison and take him back to South Africa.

In September 1995 in Johannesburg I met the agent the South Africans recruited to help them in the kidnap. Sipho Sibanda had been in Lilongwe in early 1992 trying to get help from the South African Embassy to return home after deserting from Umkhonto we Sizwe in Zambia. A Major Boere and two white police captains said if Sipho helped them with an important mission he would be given papers to return to South Africa, which he had left nearly twenty years earlier to join the ANC in exile.

Major Boere told Sipho his contact in Lusaka would be a top Zambian official in charge of liaison between the ANC and the Zambian government. His name was Roy Mkanda – the intelligence officer who had met Katiza in State House, Lusaka, back in May 1990!

Sipho was told to rendezvous with Mkanda in Lusaka's Capital Hotel. Mkanda would arrange for Sipho to be arrested as a prohibited immigrant from Malawi and put in the same cell as Katiza. Mkanda would eventually smuggle them both out of prison and drop them on the road to Chipata, near the Malawi border. Some new clothes would be waiting there and then they would cross the frontier and make their way to the South African Embassy in Lilongwe.

Sipho spent ten days in Katiza's cell – 'He was in a terrible situation. His clothes were ragged and dirty. He wasn't bathing. The toilet was one bucket shared between fifty and eighty people in the cell. The food was terrible – rotten *kapenta* [dried fish] and boiled maize. While I was there two illegal Senegalese immigrants died near us. Katiza was intelligent. He kept asking me where I came from, and when I said Malawi he looked doubtful and asked if I'd been to Soweto. I asked what he thought his future would be if he was released. He said he would be very reluctant to go back to South Africa – he knew what the outcome would be.

'I was ready to take Katiza out. But then we were joined by another "illegal" immigrant, a guy called Amon who was really a courier. Amon passed a message to me to drop the mission. Roy Mkanda got me out and I went back to Lilongwe. The two police captains said orders had come from South Africa to abandon the mission. They didn't say why, but I got my papers and went back home to South Africa.'

*

By February 1993 the ANC and the National Party had hammered out the broad outlines of a deal to hold South Africa's first all-race general election by May 1994. Talks between the two protagonists had begun behind closed doors in mid-November the previous year. Both sides, mindful of the 1992 massacres, realized that efforts had to be redoubled to get negotiations back on track or the country would retreat into total chaos. The main element of the deal was that there would be some kind of power-sharing in the life of the first all-race Parliament to give time and space for reconciliation between the races. Now the ANC and the National Party had to take the proposals to reconvened multi-party talks to obtain wider agreement on a new constitution.

Fundamental though the agreement was, it seemed unreal. The Johannesburg *Star* felt it necessary to spell out the reality. 'The shilly-shallying is over,' the newspaper said. 'The real thing that you prayed for – or dreaded – is about to happen because the men with power have decided it is going to happen.'

Disgraced and cast into the wilderness by the ANC, Winnie Mandela had begun a political fightback by early 1993. In a series of speeches to the downtrodden poor in squatter camps around Johannesburg, she seized on the power-sharing deal and accused the ANC leadership of being out of touch with the wretched of South Africa and being in the pocket of the National Party. 'This will plunge the country irrevocably into yet another vortex of mass violence and protest,' she said in an article which infuriated Nelson and the ANC leadership. 'This time not against the National Party but against the new government, which the masses will have discovered to be representing the same class interest as the National Party it fought so bravely.'

Free of responsibilities to the ANC's National Executive and determined not to be gagged, she went on: 'The ANC belongs to the people. It belongs to me just as much as it does to the leadership. I am not about to abandon the ANC to the mercies of elitist politicians . . . It was people's power that drove the National Party to negotiate with the ANC, and there is no need or justification for abandoning people's power to be co-opted into the Nationalist regime.'

That ANC 'elite', argued Winnie, was 'getting into bed' with the National Party 'to enjoy this new-found luxury [of] its silken sheets'.

*

Katiza, meanwhile, was beginning another year in Lusaka Central Prison without the luxury of silk sheets – in fact, without any sheets at all, not even a blanket on the floor of the cell he shared with fifty or more inmates. All the best continuing efforts of Emma Nicholson and Frederick Chiluba had failed to find a country willing to give him shelter and protection.

Chiluba still believed Katiza was safer in prison than out. On his first state visit to Britain he met Emma. Chiluba said he would ensure Katiza's safety, and she said her search to find him a safe haven was continuing: 'I assured President Chiluba that my commitment hadn't wavered, and we renewed our joint resolve.' But after long incarceration without any charge against him Katiza was longing to be free. He began a hunger strike and ate nothing and drank very little for ten days – 'After five days I was unable to stand. The prison commander, Chris Tembo, came to see me and asked why I was on hunger strike.

I said everybody was cheating me and I was ready to die. Everybody, including Mandela, wanted to hear my story but did nothing for me.'

When Katiza ended his strike he was devastated to learn that his friend Kambaranja Kaunda had been transferred from Lusaka Central. Kaunda's sister had brought jeans to replace the tattered and worn trousers Katiza had been wearing since Winnie had kidnapped him two years earlier; she had brought him food and drink too to provide relief from the appalling prison diet.

Katiza wept for days after Kaunda left. Not only had Kambaranja acted as his protector against the more psycho-pathic of the prisoners, but he had persuaded the Zambians that this strange foreigner, this Zulu from a township in a foreign land, could be embraced socially – 'The criminals in prison eventually liked me, because I persuaded each of them to stand up and tell his own story, how he got inside. I said don't talk about films and things outside yourself, tell us your own life story.' With a chuckle, Katiza remembered: 'When I told my story they assured me I was a great criminal.'

Displaying the chutzpah with which he had won the tradi-tional story-telling competitions arranged by the Zulu elders back in Mpumalanga, Katiza assured his fellow inmates that Zambian criminals were not fit to tie the shoelaces of South African criminals. He cited a murderous attack by a criminal gang on a retired British Army officer living in Zambia who was alleged to have shot dead ANC exiles who invaded his property. The gang comprised three South Africans and one Zambian. 'I told them the Zambian was such a lousy criminal that he had only been allowed by the South Africans to shoot the dog. The South Africans had killed the white man and his servant and they had removed their eyes. I asked them to look at the kind of South African criminals they met in Zambian jails. The South Africans were in for big crimes like forgeries and bank robberies. I made them laugh when I said you Zambians are in for stupid little crimes like stealing car wheels.'

But the times of laughter could not permanently suppress the pain. More hunger strikes followed, and in October 1993 a human rights commission, appointed by President Chiluba, visited Katiza in jail, finding him 'barefooted in a prison cell he is sharing with hordes of convicts'. The commission chairman, Bruce Munyama, told reporters afterwards that he would press for Katiza's release: it was wrong to continue his imprisonment without a charge being laid. 'I told the commission I was fed up and wanted to go back and die in my own country and stop suffering in Zambia,' said Katiza. 'I said everyone was listening to me but doing nothing. I preferred to die.'

He began yet another protest hunger strike and for the first time the local representative of the United Nations High Commission for Refugees (UNHCR), Abou Moussa, visited him in prison. Moussa pleaded for an end to the hunger strike. After twelve days Katiza began eating again, but only when he had demanded that the UN man get him out of prison within twenty-four hours. 'Moussa said they would need seventy-two hours, and when that had passed he said it was not enough. I got so angry and demanded to be taken back to South Africa to tell everything about Winnie. Moussa said I'd be killed outside and he called some black South Africans to try to calm me down. I'd never seen them before. I warned the ambassador [Moussa] that he had persuaded me to begin eating and he couldn't just sit in his office and do nothing. He promised to release me after a week, but nothing happened. I was so angry.'

Katiza began another hunger strike, which inspired a number of visits by Zambian government ministers, including Home Minister Newstead Zimba, who attempted to persuade him to eat. He refused to speak to them. After fifteen days a doctor was called. 'He said they should release me or I would die in prison. I wasn't able to talk, stand or see clearly. I wasn't using the toilet. My body felt very hot.' In anticipation of his release Katiza was given a special diet of fruit and milk. 'To begin with I could only drink one cup of milk a day; the rest I gave to the other prisoners. In the evening I'd drink a cup of tea with sugar.'

On 15 December 1993 Katiza Cebekhulu was released, thirty months after he had been imprisoned for no offence and nearly three years after his abduction by Winnie Mandela.

He was taken to Solwezi, in the remote north-west of Zambia. There the UNHCR gave him a house in a village where the American charity Care International was teaching Angolan refugees cookery and other practical skills. It was here, 1,250 miles north of his home in Mpumalanga, that he passed New Year's Eve – the fifth anniversary of the death of Stompie Moeketsi.

*

Full constitutional negotiations had resumed on 1 April 1993 between the ANC, the National Party and twenty-four other political parties. Before the end of the year final agreement was reached. In the early hours of the morning of 18 November De Klerk, Nelson Mandela and other party leaders consigned white minority rule to oblivion when they put their signatures to a new draft constitution guaranteeing equal rights to people of every race and colour and paving the way for the first all-race

general election on 27 April 1994. The Nationalists' chief negotiator, Roelf Meyer, and the ANC's Cyril Ramaphosa danced
together at the party which followed to the slow rock refrain
'He ain't heavy, he's my brother'.

In the week beginning Monday 20 December 1993 South
Africa's last white-dominated Parliament debated the new constitution and voted the reforms on to the statute book, thereby
legislating itself out of existence.

But the months between January, when the outline of the
deal first emerged, and December, when it was sealed, had been
as rocky as any in South African history. On 10 April Chris
Hani, the fifty-year-old head of the South African Communist
Party, widely touted as Nelson Mandela's successor as leader of
the ANC, was assassinated outside his Boksburg home by a
Polish immigrant, Janus Waluz, who had links to the pro-
apartheid Conservative Party.

Violence erupted in the townships as the news spread that
the former chief of staff of Umkhonto we Sizwe – probably the
most popular black leader next to Mandela – had been cut
down by a white gunman. The paradox was that because of his
militant past, and his consequent revered status among radical
township youths, his peace calls in recent months had had a
greater impact than those of Mandela. No leader articulated
better the fears and hopes of South Africa's poor than Hani. No
leader, bar Mandela, drew bigger crowds at rallies.

As the killing and burning spread Nelson Mandela warned
that the country teetered on the brink of disaster. Urging an end
to the carnage, he appeared on state television and said: 'This is
a watershed moment for us all. We must not let the men who
worship war and lust after blood precipitate actions which
would plunge our country into another Angola.'

Within a week of Hani's murder two other giants of the South African struggle saga were dead. Oliver Tambo died from a stroke. Andries Treurnicht, leader of the Conservative Party, known as 'Dr No' because of his unbending opposition to any reform when he was a Nationalist minister in the 1970s, died of complications following a heart operation.

Hani's, Tambo's and Treurnicht's sudden passings marked a South African turning point. Cyril Ramaphosa said the country had looked over the precipice at potential chaos: he hoped constitutional negotiations would proceed faster and more purposively. A fortnight after Hani's assassination everyone was back around the negotiating table.

*

Drama never exhausted itself in South Africa. On 17 March 1993 five judges at the Appeal Court in Bloemfontein began hearing Winnie Mandela's appeal against her sentencing in May 1991 to six years' imprisonment for kidnapping Stompie Moeketsi and three others and for being an accessory to their assault. No new evidence was introduced before the court. The original testimony of the trial witnesses was taken at face value. Neither John Morgan nor Xoliswa Falati, who had since admitted they had lied to protect Winnie Mandela, was called to explain their perjuries.

On 2 June Chief Justice Michael Corbett gave the verdict. Winnie Mandela would not serve all six years in prison. In fact, she would not go to prison at all. Her conviction for being an accessory to assault was quashed, thus eliminating one year of her six-year sentence.

Her conviction on the charge of kidnapping Stompie Moeketsi two days before he was murdered was upheld. It carried a sentence of five years' imprisonment, but Judge Corbett said: 'In appropriate cases the Court should always consider the possibility of alternative sentences to imprisonment.' After 'careful and anxious' consideration the Appeal Court had concluded that Winnie Mandela's was just such a case. She was fined Rand 15,000 (£3,000) and given a suspended sentence of two years. One newspaper suggested she sell her white Mercedes, in which she drove to township political rallies; the money from that alone would pay the fine seventeen times over.

That same day Winnie celebrated her reprieve by giving a champagne party in Johannesburg for her daughters and friends.

In Tumahole, the small Orange Free State black township where Stompie Moeketsi was born and spent the early years of his short life, his mother Joyce told a Johannesburg *Star* reporter she was surprised by the Appeal Court decision. But after agreeing to be interviewed she was warned by local ANC officials not to talk: they took her to the local ANC offices, banished her to an adjoining room and told the reporter they would not allow journalists near her because their motives were to gather 'negative news' detrimental to the ANC.

In an editorial on the Appeal Court verdict, the *Star* said the precedents for commuting a prison sentence for kidnapping to a fine must be rare. 'The Appeal Court finding will not allay feelings of disquiet,' it said. '[Winnie] Mandela has never seemed to have difficulty in raising sums of money, so the sums she has been ordered to pay in fines and compensation cannot rank as serious punishment. We cannot accept that this penalty, as the Chief Justice believes, will "achieve a measure of social justice and fit the crime".'

Dennis Davis, a lecturer in law at the University of the Witwatersrand, writing in the *Weekly Mail,* commented: 'The Appellate Division's decision was politically correct and Stompie is still dead . . . Kidnapping is an extremely serious offence and a Rand 15,000 fine hardly seems suitable punishment for such a repulsive deed . . .'

Mrs Mandela, in a press statement, said she would have welcomed a judgement absolving her of all blame, but she was glad her claim that she would 'never lift a hand on to a child' had been finally vindicated. She declared that she had been victimized by the press and by some of her ANC colleagues. But she said her involvement with Stompie Moeketsi and the other youths brought to her house from Paul Verryn's manse on the fateful evening of 29 December 1988 had stemmed from her belief that they were being sexually abused – 'This was a social problem which I saw as my duty to solve.'

John Morgan's one-year sentence for kidnap was upheld, but it was suspended for five years on condition that he committed no similar offences in that time and in view of the fact that he had already been detained for seven months in 1989 while police investigated Stompie Moeketsi's murder.

Xoliswa Falati was less fortunate. Judge Corbett upheld her sentences for kidnap and assault and could spare none of the 'careful and anxious' consideration he devoted, in Winnie Mandela's case, to 'the possibility of alternative sentences to imprisonment'. For Falati 'an effective sentence of imprisonment is imperatively called for', said Corbett. Falati, he said, would go to prison for four years: he suspended two of them.

Falati, speaking to reporters as she was taken into Soweto's Diepkloof Prison to begin her sentence, repeated her assertion that in the Stompie trial she had falsely supported Winnie's alibi that Mrs Mandela was in Brandfort, 200 miles from the scene of the crimes, from 29 to 31 December 1988. Asked if she would fight the Appeal Court decision from jail, Falati said: 'The truth will soon all come out. But don't forget that people like me are underdogs. We are dealing with a super-being who is the most feared person in South Africa who is capable of doing anything.'

*

The 'most feared person in South Africa', now free from the threat of imprisonment, was quickly back in the headlines. Having lost all her national ANC posts, Winnie, as a convicted criminal, was suspended in June 1993 from the executive of the ANC Women's League in the Johannesburg region. Members of the executive were subsequently subjected to a number of unspecified death threats and one very senior member had a severed pig's head dumped in her back yard with a message pinned to it which read: 'This is what will happen to your head.'

But by the end of the year Winnie had achieved a comeback. On 9 December she was unexpectedly re-elected President of the ANC's Women's League by 392 votes to 168 over her old rival, Albertina Sisulu. She had garnered votes by persistent hard work at grassroots level in the teeming, fetid squatter camps of the big cities – and by other means. Winnie arrived at the conference with a group of ululating supporters, some of whom carried knives, guns and *muti* (traditional medicine, or witchdoctors' charms), according to a Sunday newspaper. A report exposing irregularities at the conference was written for the ANC's official publication, *Mayibuye*, but was never published.

Several people resigned from the Women's League in

protest. Among them was Dudu Chili, who had been a member of the League for a quarter of a century, through times when it was banned to when the ban was lifted and the Winnie controversies erupted. 'I cannot be led by a criminal who burned down my home and killed my niece,' Mrs Chili told me. 'A lot of people feel the same way, but at the moment too many are frightened to speak out.'

But Winnie Mandela was unfazed. As 1993 drew to its close on the fifth anniversary of the murder of Stompie Moeketsi the ANC leadership decided it could not deny someone elected to the Women's League Presidency the right to be one of its Parliamentary candidates. By the end of April 1994 Winnie Mandela would walk into Parliament in Cape Town as an MP while Xoliswa Falati sat in Diepkloof Prison, Katiza Cebekhulu waited in lonely exile in Zambia and Stompie lay a-mouldering in his Tumahole grave.

CHAPTER SEVENTEEN

Freedom

1994–1996

South Africa's first all-race general election was held from 26 to 28 April 1994. Archbishop Desmond Tutu, voting for the first time in his life, said: 'It is an incredible feeling, like falling in love . . . It's like a new birth. We are going to be the rainbow people of the world.'

The ANC, after an eighty-two-year struggle for universal emancipation, swept to an overwhelming victory with 252 of the 400 seats in the new Parliament. And on Monday 9 May when the new legislators – nearly 300 of them black – gathered in Cape Town for the first time they chose Nelson Mandela as State President. Winnie Mandela, elected an MP on the ANC list, was there too. But the honour of proposing him as the country's first black President went not to his wife but to Albertina Sisulu, Winnie's rival, who still, more than five years on, maintained her silence about the murder of her friend and employer Abu-Baker Asvat.

Winnie was sworn in by Chief Justice Michael Corbett, the man who the previous year had quashed her six-year jail sentence, thus making it possible for her to become an MP. She walked down from her bench near the back of the National Assembly to take her oath. Afterwards she sat down, uninvited, next to Nelson on the new State President's front bench to the right of the Speaker. Nelson frowned and declined to acknowledge her; after a minute or two she rose disconsolately and walked back up to her own allotted seat.

Winnie was banned from the VIP podium the next day in front of the Union Buildings in Pretoria when, in the presence of 150 monarchs, princes and heads of government, Nelson Mandela was inaugurated as State President.

Only the most bitter of men or women could have failed to be moved by the sheer joy and majesty of the event, a coronation, a national rebirth, a wrenchingly stirring climax of a legendary struggle in an epic country. It had been a close-run thing though. In the months preceding the election South Africa had been on the brink of civil war as the Zulu Inkatha movement, diehard white right-wingers and 'independent' homeland governments in Bophuthatswana and Ciskei threatened the use of force to stave off inevitable ANC rule. But somehow the country got through and Winnie Mandela MP was given a small role by her estranged husband in his government. She became Deputy Minister of Arts, Culture, Science and Technology – and for a while maintained a low profile.

*

Her period of comparative withdrawal came to a surprise end on 9 August 1994 when, during a debate on women's issues, she rose in Parliament and made an extraordinary speech about Stompie Moeketsi, dead by then for nearly five years and eight months. She told astonished MPs: 'My deepest regret is that I failed Stompie – that I was unable to protect him from the anarchy of those times and he was taken from my house and killed, adding his life to the hundreds, perhaps thousands, who

fell victim to the terror of intolerance and injustice of the kangaroo courts.' She did not spell out whether by 'kangaroo
courts' she meant the white government's courts of justice or
'people's courts', like those she conducted with the MUFC,
beyond the state system.

The opposition, at first stunned into silence, began to taunt
her with shouts of 'Stompie!' She replied: 'I do not defend the
anarchy of those times, but I understand its roots in the terror
of apartheid, which had reached its zenith.' Here it was not clear
whether or not she was trying to explain her own aberrant conduct in the years following the end, in the mid-1980s, of her
internal exile in Brandfort.

Winnie again retreated for a while into the obscurity of her
minor government job. But then at the ANC's triennial congress in Johannesburg on 19 December her old enemy,
Secretary-General Cyril Ramaphosa, launched a broadside
against her, in her role as Women's League President, saying
her organization did 'not adhere to financial control'.
Ramaphosa's attack stemmed from a report – based on leaks
from ANC HQ – in a Johannesburg newspaper a few days
earlier that Winnie had reneged on payment of a £10,000 fee for
a Lear jet she hired to fly from Johannesburg to Luanda in June
1993. Court papers showed that she had hired the jet in the
name of the Co-ordinated Anti-Poverty Programme (Capp),
the non-profit charity she ran ostensibly to provide poverty
relief to slum dwellers, but that its mission was actually to pick
up a package of diamonds from Angola State President
Eduardo dos Santos. The report stated that Mrs Mandela was
being sued for non-payment.

Two months later eleven executive members of the ANC's
Women's League – of which Winnie was still President –

resigned in protest against a business venture she had established, without consulting her colleagues, between the League and Hollywood film star Omar Sharif. The new venture, to be called 'Road to Freedom' tours, would encourage Afro-American tourists to visit historic South African 'struggle' sites, including Nelson Mandela's birthplace, at Qunu in the Transkei, and his Robben Island prison cell. The profits would be shared between the Women's League and Sharif, whose photographs alongside Winnie adorned South African newspapers in early February 1995.

Oliver Tambo's widow Adelaide, who was the Women's League Treasurer, led the mass resignation on 11 February. Among the others who resigned were Nelson's Health Minister Nkosazana Zuma, Women's League spokeswoman Lindiwe Zulu, League Secretary-General Nosiviwe Mapiso and ANC MP Baleka Kgosistile, later to become a government minister. 'We had no option,' said Ms Zulu in a statement. 'We feel we've been humiliated for a very long time.'

Nelson Mandela, bowed by the prospect of yet another Winnie controversy, met with Adelaide Tambo and the other dissidents all the following day, Sunday 12 February, in an attempt to persuade them to withdraw their resignations. They were adamant: they would definitely leave unless Nelson agreed to several demands, including the calling of an emergency Women's League Congress to enable them to attempt to overthrow Winnie from the League Presidency. Mrs Tambo and her allies issued a statement declaring that at an emergency conference they would charge Winnie with undemocratic behaviour, lack of accountability and an inability to unite women.

That same Sunday Nelson gave Winnie an ultimatum: in a letter he told her she must apologize for stinging criticisms she had made of his government or resign from it. The demand followed a speech she made at the graveside of a black policeman shot dead on the orders of white officers during a demonstration by black constables in Soweto. Winnie said the ANC-led government of national unity had not addressed 'apartheid imbalances' in society and had not removed racism from the workplace. She attacked Nelson's 'overindulgence' in seeking reconciliation with the white minority and challenged ANC leaders to demonstrate whether 'we are in power or just in government'.

On Monday 13 February Winnie was accused by the Women's League dissidents of pilfering half a million Rand donated to the League by Pakistani Prime Minister Benazir Bhutto. Adelaide Tambo and Baleka Kgosistile said in a joint statement that Bhutto, while attending Nelson's Presidential inauguration in May 1994, had given the cheque to Winnie but it never found its way into the Women's League bank account. Winnie issued a counter-statement saying the Bhutto money had not been intended for the Women's League, but 'was specifically given for upliftment projects in disadvantaged communities'. By this she seemed to mean her own private charity, Capp.

That same Monday Winnie also responded to Nelson's ultimatum with a letter which contained no apology for her graveside attack on the government or for her scorn at his weakness in seeking accommodation with whites. She said it had not been her intention to insult the President or embarrass the government – 'I was merely trying to assure the masses that the government and the ANC are aware of and concerned about the flaws that the government must deal with . . . The impression of the people is that we neither care nor know about these things. I was trying to correct that perception. If in doing so I created a different impression, that was not my intention.' The coldness of the couple's relationship was illustrated by the way she signed off: 'Yours faithfully, N W Mandela'.

Nelson made no immediate move over his Deputy Arts Minister's intransigence. This was coupled with a reluctance to act against another leading ANC figure, the Reverend Allan Boesak, a Calvinist cleric with a taste for fast Lancias and high-powered blondes, who was accused by a Danish donor Danchurch Aid of 'enriching himself substantially' at the expense of an anti-apartheid charity he had founded with foreign funds. It all gave an impression of weakness and vacillation. Recalling Archbishop Tutu's rapturous celebration of South Africans as 'the rainbow people of God' at the time of the first all-race election, the *Sunday Times* of Johannesburg warned: 'We are in danger of becoming known as the rainbow nation of gangsters.'

There was a brief lull in hostilities, until on 1 March the chief of the Commercial Crime Unit of the South African Police Service, Colonel Antonie Botha, led raids on Winnie's Soweto home and ten offices connected with her public activities. Botha said one allegation against her was accepting a bribe of Rand 75,000 from a construction company, Professional Builders Ltd of Pretoria, to construct low-cost houses for Capp to the exclusion of other companies which had tendered. In addition to the initial kickback, Winnie was alleged to have demanded a monthly retainer of Rand 32,000 and that Zindzi be given shares in the white-owned Professional Builders. Forty police raided Winnie's Palace, her luxury split-level house in Soweto's 'Beverly Hills'. Thirty heavily armed riot police took up stations outside. As the operation proceeded a minibus packed with American tourists, on one of the now daily excursions by foreign tourists to 'historic' Soweto sites, drew up outside the Palace. 'Wow,' exclaimed one camera-laden American, 'it's a real-live police raid.'

Accounts subsequently released by the Capp board showed that Winnie had claimed Rand 168,000 from the charity for repairs, maintenance and other expenses connected with her personal vehicles, including her Mercedes-Benz. 'Why is a non-government organization supposedly aimed at poverty relief funding repairs of its chief executive officer's Mercedes?' asked a columnist in the *Business Day* newspaper. The Capp accounts further showed a total of Rand 549,888 owed to 'W Mandela' for various services and expenses.

Four days after the police raid on her home Winnie launched a public attack, extraordinary even by her standards, on President Mandela. She accused him of depriving her of the right to free speech after she had devoted her life, during his long imprisonment, to achieving precisely that right for him. Her blitz against Nelson was contained in private letters she wrote to him and which were obtained by the Johannesburg *Star*.

One letter said her resignation statement as head of the ANC's Department of Social Welfare in 1992, after sums of money went missing, had been written by Nelson. And although she had written her 13 February 1995 'letter of apology' herself, she said it had been done under duress applied by Nelson. Another of the *Star* letters referred to Nelson's twenty-seven-year imprisonment and went on:

As you will know, when you were forcibly prevented from exercising your inalienable right to free speech I and the children

[Zindzi and Zenani Mandela], with others, spoke up for humanity.

Circumstances forced me into becoming a political activist. The children and I suffered for refusing to succumb to the oppression of the apartheid regime. We were banned and banished and were also jailed and physically manhandled.

Winnie said she had received reports that Nelson had encouraged Adelaide Tambo and the other Women's League dissidents 'to keep up their media campaign against me so as to enable you to dismiss me as deputy minister and to remove me from Parliament ... I shall very much appreciate a disavowal by you of the same.' She added that she objected to signing one document he had prepared for her because it implied that 'in certain respects I no longer have the right of free speech'.

Nelson, by now exhausted by disputes with his wife, handed the 'Winnie affair' to the country's Deputy President, Thabo Mbeki. Mbeki began by summoning her from Soweto to Cape Town on 6 March to discuss her crisis-ridden public life. She refused to go and issued a statement containing the text of a letter she had posted to Mbeki saying she saw no reason why she had to meet him. The tone suggested she was prepared to see only the organ grinder, not his monkey. 'The issue under discussion has assumed the proportion of a national crisis which requires the intervention of the President,' she said.

Meanwhile, Zindzi Mandela was telling the Johannesburg *Star* that her parents were now likely to divorce. 'I sense pressure on him to distance himself definitely from her,' she said. 'It's people within the ANC who consider that to be better.' Zindzi described her father as 'very lonely' while her mother felt 'she has been sacrificed'. Winnie was especially bitter about being allocated a seat among lesser dignitaries at the May 1994

Presidential inauguration, Zindzi said. Her parents had never had a fair chance:

> When my father was free at last he did not have any time for normal family life. He was under constant strain. They had been separated for 27 years and all that time they remained devoted to each other. But after such a long time you must get the opportunity to build something together, to get used to each other anew. They didn't get this . . . Everything my mother does is magnified beyond all proportions by the press. She is supposed to have had lots of lovers, she has stolen funds belonging to the party and so on.

Zindzi said her parents now had no relationship worth speaking of. 'They don't see each other any more. They never visit me at the same time. They don't speak to me about their problems. It's as if they don't exist for each other any more.'

A small but significant problem now arose. Britain, whose system of government had long been admired by Nelson Mandela but whose governments had, by and large, regarded the ANC as a terrorist organization, was toying with the idea of knighting the State President in advance of an official visit to South Africa in late March 1995 by Queen Elizabeth. The South African press tied itself in knots for days wondering whether Nelson Mandela would go for a quick divorce to prevent Winnie becoming Lady Mandela. In the end the British, with elegant sleight of hand, solved the problem by conferring on Nelson an even higher honour, the Order of Merit, which gives no title to the wife of the recipient, and inviting him to pay a state visit to Britain in 1996. The only other foreigner to have been awarded the Order of Merit was Mother Theresa of Calcutta.

*

Britain's Queen Elizabeth duly arrived in South Africa for a visit redolent with imperial nostalgia and memories of a stirring history – the first by a reigning monarch in nearly half a century. The event honoured the return of South Africa to the British Commonwealth after an absence of more than thirty years: it had been expelled because of its apartheid laws. There were a number of protocol problems of a particularly South African nature. King Goodwill Zwelethini of the Zulus, whose spear-wielding ancestors had killed a record 1,400 British Redcoats and their allies in one day at the Battle of Isandhlwana on 22 January 1889, wanted to pay the Queen the highest possible Zulu compliment – the gift of a white bull descended from the herd established by the founder of the Zulu nation, Shaka Zulu. Tradition demanded that the recipient of such a special gift respect the honour by taking the bull back to his or her home kraal – in Queen Elizabeth's case, London's Buckingham Palace – and there wrestle it to death. British diplomats worked out a compromise: it was delivered to a Natal stud cattle farm. One of the thirteen other South African tribal kings wanted to bring 235 advisers as part of his royal entourage to a glittering official banquet. 'We had to firmly dissuade him,' said a British diplomat.

Then there was the Winnie problem. That was solved by not inviting her to any of the British monarch's official engagements in Cape Town, Port Elizabeth, Johannesburg, Soweto, Pretoria and Durban during her week-long visit. Winnie responded with a boycott of her own. When Elizabeth addressed the South African Parliament on Monday 20 March and said she had come to see 'what is little short of a miracle, one of your own making', only one of the 400 MPs was absent. A sign on Winnie Mandela's office door in the corridors of Parliament read: 'This office will be closed until Wednesday. The queen is out of town.' Staff members insisted it was a joke.

*

On the penultimate day, 24 March, of Elizabeth's visit, 'queen' Winnie launched a tirade against Nelson, criticizing his government for spending Rand 2.5 million (£500,000) 'to entertain a British queen'.

After the British monarch's departure, President Mandela, after weeks of controversy and personal agonizing, fired his wife from his government on 27 March. Visibly pained, he told reporters in Cape Town: 'I hope this decision will help the former Deputy Minister to review her position and seek to improve on her own conduct in positions of responsibility so as to enable her to make the positive contribution to society her talents would enable her.' He declined to detail what precise events had triggered his decision, but said he wanted his coalition government to work effectively and every member of it to make a successful contribution.

On 17 August 1995 Nelson's lawyer, Ismail Ayob, said his client was to divorce Nomzamo Winifred Zanyiwe Madikizela Mandela. Nelson said he wanted the divorce handled sensitively and amicably. Winnie insisted on fighting it publicly, taking it all the way to the Rand Supreme Court. She sought a settlement of Rand 20 million from her estranged husband, approximately half of his estate. She wanted a share of royalties from his autobiography *Long Walk to Freedom*, which was on bestseller lists around the world for many months, and a share of his Nobel Peace Prize. She also demanded that he pay the outstanding

Rand 400,000 mortgage on their third Soweto home, 'Winnie's Palace'.

On 19 March 1996, at the end of a two-day hearing, Judge Frikkie Eloff pronounced one of the world's most celebrated and myth-laden couples divorced, their union having irretrievably broken down. Nelson Mandela closed his eyes and a faint smile crossed his austere face as his marriage came to an end after thirty-eight years. His affidavit had cited Winnie's adultery, which had left him humiliated and lonely; her 'hypocritical' expressions of affection for him at public gatherings; and her lavish spending on make-up, clothes and parties she could not afford – 'It appears that she earns some Rand 16,000 per month but leads a luxurious lifestyle which costs Rand 107,000 per month.'

Nelson said a copy of a love letter to Dali Mpofu from Winnie had been given to him in 1992. He recognized her writing, the tone and style of the letter: she had, after all, written him countless letters during the twenty-seven years he had been in prison. He also recognized the accuracy of some of the statements in the letter which had been published in newspapers. It caused him much pain and acute personal and political embarrassment. 'The contents of the letter were incompatible with a marriage relationship and, even if there was the possibility of reconciliation, it confirmed my decision never to reconcile with the defendant,' he told Judge Eloff.

In probably the most painful revelation of his life, President Mandela told Eloff how, since his release from prison more than six years earlier, his wife had not once entered their bedroom while he was still awake. 'I was the loneliest man during the period I stayed with her,' he said. 'If the entire universe persuaded me to reconcile I would not.'

During cross-examination Nelson three times warned Winnie's lawyer, Ismail Semenya, not to push him to damage her character. 'I appeal to you not to put any questions to me which may compel me to dent the image of the defendant and bring a great deal of pain to our children and grandchildren,' he said. Winnie attempted to postpone the hearing on the ground that no attempt had been made at reconciliation through customary tribal law. She said there were only 'slight tensions' between herself and Nelson and that the main cause of the separation was her conviction for kidnapping Stompie Seipei Moeketsi. Judge Eloff rejected the postponement request.

It transpired during the divorce hearing that George Bizos, who had defended Winnie in the Stompie trial, had been despatched by Nelson as an emissary to his wife to confirm whether reports of her affair with Dali Mpofu were true. Bizos reported back that they were true, something he could have discovered five years earlier if Katiza Cebekhulu had not been kidnapped on the second day of Winnie's trial and had been able to give evidence.

Winnie sacked her lawyer towards the end of the hearing and then Eloff threw out her claim for a share of Nelson's assets when she failed to turn up for a financial settlement hearing. She issued a statement describing the divorce proceedings as a 'travesty of justice', and went on: 'I have fought all my life against this kind of injustice, my ex-husband has fought all his life against this kind of injustice. That such injustice happened in his presence undermines everything our marriage was all about.'

When the hearing ended the *City Press* newspaper said Nelson had been physically attacked several times between 1990 and 1992 by Winnie before he finally left her. A 'family member' said Winnie had assaulted him more than once after he moved in with her following his release from prison. 'A body-guard stepped in on one occasion and drew a firearm, saying he would not allow Mr Mandela to be humiliated,' *City Press* quoted the family member as saying. After one such attack a 'well-known cleric' was called to mediate, but he was thrown out by Winnie, who told him to go back to church.

A revival of *Sarafina*, a musical based on the 1976 Soweto student uprising, opened at Johannesburg's Market Theatre soon after the Mandela divorce became final. The musical, as usual, ended with Hugh Masekela's anthem, 'Bring Back Nelson Mandela', but Masekela's famous line, 'I want to see him walking down the street with Winnie Mandela', was omitted.

*

On 8 May 1994 Katiza flew out of Zambia to a secret location thousands of miles away in one of the most unstable countries in the world where, nevertheless, the UN offered him a measure of protection until his situation could be resolved.

Towards the end of 1994 Emma received from Katiza, through the UNHCR, a notebook in which he had attempted to write his story. 'With it was a heartrending letter saying he'd been very ill and had had enough and wanted to die,' Emma told me. 'No one wanted him, but would I get his notes published so his story would be known?

'For Katiza the truth mattered more than his life. I didn't agree. I thought, given time, I could find an education and a future for him and get his story told. Everybody seemed to have conspired to destroy the hope and the very life of this unimportant Zulu boy from South Africa, but I was determined not to throw in the towel myself. He was in no position to publish anything himself, but I didn't want his story to be told in such a flimsy way that nobody would read it and that he would, if you like, die for nothing. I telephoned him several times and urged him not to give up.'

Emma now persuaded Katiza to grant her power of attorney so she could act and speak on his behalf. She sent him regular sums of money so he could buy clothes, food and books: he had begun studying English at a college. She also had one last throw at the British government, from which she now felt significantly alienated. 'By dint of pulling in every single favour that anybody owed me on everything, I got [Home Secretary] Michael Howard's very unwilling agreement for a slender, quick visit by Katiza to the United Kingdom, which I managed to expand.'

Emma alerted me in May 1995 that she had at last secured a limited entry right for Katiza into Britain. I flew from Johannesburg and waited until, on 2 July, Katiza flew into London's Heathrow Airport, where Emma and I greeted him.

The first thing I noticed was how small he was. His legs were very short and his arms were thin. His face was haunted and his cheeks sunken, reminding me of Edvard Munch's *Scream*. He was wearing a cheap brown bush jacket and trousers. We took him first to the Heathrow Hilton, where Emma, whose lonely campaign for his freedom was now well into its fourth year, wanted to speak to him alone for a while. I watched them from across the Hilton's breakfast lounge. Suddenly their conversation stopped. Katiza was overcome by some great emotion. Tears dropped like big raindrops and seeped into his bush jacket. Emma told me later he had been trying to explain to her how he had at one point on 29 December 1988 held down Stompie Moeketsi's leg while Winnie beat the boy. Then he had described how Winnie had used a whip until it broke and

Stompie's head had gone soft, 'like flesh on the meaty part of a forearm'.

The first few nights Katiza stayed with Emma at her London home near the House of Commons. 'He was in a high state of tension because he wanted to unburden himself of his story very fast now that we'd found a way it could be done. Great sheets of tears fell on to his lap as he talked further about what had happened to Stompie and Lolo Sono, as he talked about what had happened to other people I didn't know and had never heard of. He almost died of sorrow that first night as he told me his story fully after the gap of four years since I last saw him in Chiluba's office. It was in his heart. He had to get it out. But his sadness was profound.'

I collected Katiza from Emma's house and we drove to a secret location on the British Atlantic coast. The following morning he said he had dreamed about Winnie Mandela and had confronted her in South Africa with a grenade in his hand. He had forced her to confess she had killed Stompie after threatening to blow up both her and himself.

We began several weeks' work, with Katiza telling me the details of how he became involved with Nomzamo Winifred Zanyiwe Mandela, Stompie Seipei Moeketsi, the President of Zambia and Nelson Rolihlahla Mandela. But the story began where Katiza Cebekhulu was born in the troubled township of Mpumalanga, in Zululand, a region of rippling grassy hills, precipitous mountains and rivers tumbling to forests and swamps alongside the Indian Ocean.

Conclusion

Two people would perhaps be serving life sentences in Leeuwkop Prison, near Pretoria, for the murder of Stompie Moeketsi if Katiza Cebekhulu's evidence had been given in South Africa and accepted by a Supreme Court judge. He is the only person to claim to have watched the fatal stabs being inflicted to Stompie's neck and throat. The individual he saw stabbing the fourteen-year-old boy was not Jerry Richardson, chief coach of Winnie Mandela's Mandela United Football Club, who was convicted of Moeketsi's murder purely on circumstantial evidence.

No one saw the chief coach kill Stompie. Richardson has always maintained his innocence. During his trial, and subsequently, several people intimately involved in the Stompie saga argued that Richardson, a grown man of low intelligence so devoted to Winnie Mandela that he called her 'Mummy', had perjured himself to safeguard his boss. 'He was protecting people,' Richardson's defence advocate, Henti Joubert, told me some seven years after his client was tried. Who was he protecting? 'Well, the only one that was involved in the affair was Winnie Mandela – more deeply so than anybody admitted during the trial . . . I was convinced that he lied to protect others.'

CONCLUSION

The enormity of that lie, and of other fabrications, is self-evident if the truth of Katiza's story is accepted. His account sheds new light on an important and tragic part of South Africa's history. He provides a logic – however crazy – which has been missing from the events which led to Stompie's murder and the consequences which flowed from it. For those of us who reported them, those events seemed random, irrational and at times preposterous. We were puzzled about how, if at all, they meshed. Katiza's evidence threads them together and stands the trials of Jerry Richardson, for Stompie's murder, and that of Winnie Mandela, fined Rand 15,000 for kidnapping Stompie and his companions, on their heads.

His testimony raises immense questions about South African justice and politics and compels a major re-examination of the Stompie affair and the murders of Lolo Sono, Siboniso Tshabalala, Finkie Msomi and others whose cases have not been explored in this account. Katiza's views are not simplistic. I had expected him to argue that Winnie Mandela should be in jail instead of Jerry Richardson. But, no, he argued: 'He should be in jail for the murder of Stompie because when Mrs Mandela killed I saw Richardson. Even if he didn't kill, once you are with the killer you are taking part. You need to be charged for murder.'

I calculate that since January 1989 Katiza has told at least sixteen people, including Nelson Mandela, Frederick Chiluba, Emma Nicholson, former Zambian Foreign Minister Vernon Mwaanga and myself, that he saw Winnie Mandela stab Stompie Moeketsi – enough material for any truly open society to justify setting up a major commission of inquiry.

That commission of inquiry would need also to investigate the sting operation against Paul Verryn, in which Katiza was used as the bait to entrap the Methodist minister in a homo-sexual relationship – an enticement that failed. The revelation of the sting means that a substantial slice of Winnie Mandela's defence arguments was a sham, based on fabrication and deception.

Xoliswa Falati was a player in the sting, and she has since admitted she was a key actor in a much wider subterfuge. In 1993 she was visited in prison by Democratic MP Lester Fuchs and she told him that the evidence she gave at Winnie's trial was 'a tissue of lies'. Fuchs told the South African Parliament that Falati 'now admits that not only did she perjure herself, but she did so with the knowledge of one of Mrs Mandela's lawyers, Dali Mpofu'. She said Mpofu had told her what she should, and should not, say at the trial. Falati said Winnie never went to Brandfort and was in Soweto when the assault on Stompie was launched.

With a television team led by independent film-maker, Nicholas Claxton, an Emmy Award-winner contracted by the BBC's *Inside Story* documentary unit, I sought out Falati in Soweto in the final days of research for this book to ask about her reference to Dali Mpofu, now an advocate practising in Johannesburg. She said she was told by Mpofu before Winnie's trial: 'You have to protect Mummy by all means . . . It's better for your commander to lose a unit [private] than to lose the commander.'

The Brandfort alibi was explained to her by Mandela and Mpofu. They also explained it to Nora Moahloli, the teacher who testified that Winnie was in Brandfort's black township from 29 December 1988, throughout the crucial day of 30 December, until the 31st. 'Nora was moulded into the lies and fit into this jigsaw,' Falati told me. 'This was a jigsaw which had so many pieces . . . I was there when Nora came [from Brandfort] to Diepkloof. I was there when Nora was taken to one of the hotels here in town.' Falati said Winnie Mandela and Dali Mpofu would meet together to refine the alibi before briefing her and others on the story – 'Ours was not to reason why, ours was just to do and die.'

I considered Falati's testimony to be particularly important, for I did not tell her I had met Katiza Cebekhulu and had heard from him a similar story alleging that Dali Mpofu had manufactured the Brandfort alibi.

She also confirmed, without knowing it, another vital part of Katiza's then as yet unpublished story, for which there had been no previous supporting evidence: 'Katiza was taken into the boot of a car to be assassinated, until somewhere the boot got opened and he jumped out. He was taken to Baragwanath and he survived the assassination.'

There is now a mass of evidence suggesting that the Brandfort alibi was a chimera, an invention, a deliberate obstruction of the truth. A commission of inquiry would need to examine how it came about and how it came to be rejected in one trial, Richardson's, but accepted by Judge Michael Stegmann in Winnie Mandela's trial.

Judge Stegmann, in his summary, said: 'I am not going to spend much time on Mrs Mandela's alibi.' And yet this was at the very heart of the whole tragedy, as Katiza Cebekhulu has described.

The medical card filled in for the visit by Winnie Mandela to Abu-Baker Asvat's surgery in late December 1988 to obtain confirmation from the doctor that Katiza Cebekhulu had been homosexually raped was date-stamped 30 December 1988 – the day Winnie said she was 200 miles away in Brandfort.

The medical card was produced briefly during the trial by state prosecutor Jan Swanepoel. But it was passed over with amazing laxity. Judge Stegmann's sole observation on the card during his summary went: 'Mr Swanepoel showed Mrs Mandela a card, which apparently purported to relate to Katiza Cebekhulu. However, Mrs Mandela was unable to state whether or not the card was Dr Asvat's. There was in fact no evidence to identify any card completed by Dr Asvat when he examined Katiza Cebekhulu.'

The whole trial turned on this moment. It remains a mystery why the state failed to call Albertina Sisulu and Ebrahim Asvat as witnesses to give evidence about the card. Ma Sisulu, Abu-Baker's surgery nurse and the wife of Walter Sisulu, Nelson Mandela's lifelong friend and comrade, could have destroyed the Brandfort alibi with simple answers to a few simple questions. She could have verified as accurate the 30 December 1988 date-stamp of Katiza's medical card and identified her own and Abu-Baker's handwriting.

Nicholas Claxton and I decided to ask those simple questions of Ma Sisulu, which should have been asked at the trial, in front of the *Inside Story* cameras at the Shell House HQ of the ANC in Johannesburg. I believe the interview we conducted, without informing her we had met Katiza, will become important evidence should any commission of inquiry or similar body be convened, so it is worth reproducing in part here.

I showed Ma Sisulu a copy of Katiza's 30 December 1988 card from Abu-Baker's surgery and asked her if it was her writing across the top showing Katiza's name, age, card number – K 569 – and other details.

'That's my handwriting,' she replied.

And was it Abu-Baker's handwriting below describing

Katiza's symptoms and recommending certain drugs?

'Yes, it's his writing.'

And was the date – '1988.12.30' – the one she stamped on the card? Was that part of her job?

'I should think so because I wouldn't just put any other date if it's not the right day. You would query it or correct it.'

So you're certain that's the correct date?

'That was the correct date if it's stamped there.'

*

In front of the TV camera, I put the same card before Dr Ebrahim Asvat, Abu-Baker's brother, who arrived at the surgery shortly after Abu-Baker was shot dead on 27 January 1989. 'I am quite sure that the date depicted here is correct, because I verified it against the record book [kept by Abu-Baker]. That also stated it was 30 December 1988.'

The record book was a double-entry system maintained by Ma Sisulu. Ebrahim said the logbook was collected from him by Captain Fred Dempsey of the Soweto Murder and Robbery Squad. The logbook was not produced at Winnie Mandela's trial and Captain Dempsey did not return it to the Asvat family.

Thabiso Mono too says he wants to be called before South Africa's Truth and Reconciliation Commission to testify that he saw Winnie Mandela at her Soweto house on 30 December 1988. 'There is no way Winnie Mandela was in Brandfort unless there are two Winnie Mandelas,' he told me. 'On 30 December I was sitting in the courtyard [of her house] and we saw her working in the kitchen in her nightdress. I saw her standing right at the window of the kitchen. I know that in my heart, and she knows that.'

I asked Mono if any lawyer asked him during Winnie Mandela's trial whether he saw her on 30 December. 'No, that question was not asked to me,' he replied. 'If they could have asked me that particular question, I would have said, "I saw her on that day."'

The whole saga is a sorry one, leaving unanswered a host of questions and raising the suspicion of a cover-up. Or, as my fellow foreign correspondent in Johannesburg, David Beresford of the London *Guardian*, wrote: 'Perhaps two cover-ups – one by the state, the other by the ANC. If the feeble efforts by the state to destroy Mrs Mandela's alibi during her trial were any indication, they [the state authorities] would have been perfectly happy to avoid a prosecution altogether.'

Since the trial much new evidence has accumulated and key participants, including John Morgan and Xoliswa Falati, have admitted that they perjured themselves. Now Jerry Richardson also has admitted perjury. 'I lied to save Winnie Mandela,' he told a reporter from the black-oriented Sunday newspaper *City Press* who managed to visit him in Leeuwkop Prison. 'They must let me give evidence and I will tell all. I will tell that Winnie ordered the kidnappings and was present for much of the time when he [Stompie] was tortured because she wanted him to confess that he was a sell-out.'

City Press said Richardson had made a submission to the Truth and Reconciliation Commission implicating Winnie Mandela in four murders – those of Stompie Moeketsi, Lolo Sono and Siboniso Tshabalala and also that of a young woman named Kuki Zwane. Richardson made his submission when TRC investigators visited him in his cell. Richardson named the members of the Mandela Crisis Committee as knowing the facts he was sharing with the TRC. 'I feel betrayed because since

I was jailed Mrs Mandela paid me a visit only once, in 1994,' he told *City Press*. 'Even if I am killed for telling the truth, I'll rest in peace.'

David Beresford raised the questions of complexity and conspiracy in the Winnie Mandela affair. The complexity is self-evident. The problem with conspiracy is that there appear to have been so many conspirators as to make the ultimate nature of the intrigue elusive. But on the basis of Katiza's evidence the South African Police were certainly part of it. Why, to take just one example, have the police never questioned, let alone charged, Winnie Mandela in connection with the MUFC assault on Dudu Chili's house, where little Finkie Msomi was shot and burned to death? The severest test they surely face now is whether they bring charges in connection with the death or disappearance of Lolo Sono: Katiza Cebekhulu has submitted a signed affidavit to the South African authorities saying he witnessed Winnie Mandela beating Sono with a heavy whip in the garage of her Diepkloof home on the last day he was seen alive in November 1988.

It also needs to be asked why Jan Swanepoel, widely accused of 'under-prosecuting', began working full-time on the Winnie Mandela case only a week before the trial commenced when there had been two years available to prepare.

One reason is that Transvaal Attorney-General Klaus von Lieres, who originally was to lead the prosecution, decided at the last minute to withdraw. I sought him out, after he had resigned to return to the bar, to ask why, but he declined to give a full interview. He gave me only a carefully worded statement. 'In the Winnie Mandela prosecution we faced wholesale and unprecedented intimidation of witnesses and the co-accused,' he said. 'We also laboured under the handicap that for two decades beforehand the criminal justice system had been misused by politicians. It meant that the bona fides of our prosecution was heavily questioned.'

David Beresford noted: 'Mr Mandela has repeatedly criticized the press for subjecting his wife to "trial by media". But as one local columnist commented tartly: the press had to, nobody else was trying.'

And the conundrum of Nelson Mandela was the subject of my final piece of investigation before completing this book. Kenneth Kaunda's government records apparently indicated that Kenneth Kaunda himself believed that Mr Mandela might have been the mastermind behind Katiza's abduction from South Africa to a prison cell in Zambia. This needed to be checked with Kenneth Kaunda, the President of Zambia at that time.

Emma Nicholson, Nicholas Claxton's *Inside Story* team and I approached Kaunda and requested a TV interview. Emma knew him from the early days of Zambian independence, when she was an adviser on computer systems to the government, so we decided she should question the former President.

Kaunda recalled the Cebekhulu case, and Emma asked him whether Nelson Mandela had told him why he 'wanted Katiza Cebekhulu here and out of South Africa'.

'He didn't give me any reason at all,' replied Kaunda. 'What I did was to work on trust.'

But how did he get the message from Mandela to give 'safe haven' to Katiza in Zambia?

'That came through Oliver Tambo [the ANC's leader-in-exile]. And he said that Nelson Mandela wants this man out of South Africa . . . He said we must go by what Nelson has said about him. And so we took that on trust, and that's how the young man found himself in trouble.'

How did he know the message came from Nelson Mandela?

'I trusted Oliver Tambo very much indeed.'

And Tambo spoke to him claiming to be talking on behalf of Nelson? That was how the message came?

'Exactly.'

*

This leaves South Africa with a dilemma. Oliver Tambo is dead. So it is left to Nelson Mandela, now the State President, to explain whether he engineered the abduction and imprisonment without trial of one of his own citizens or that Tambo was acting without authority. My guess is that Mandela was involved. He will argue he did it to protect Katiza. But to protect him from whom? And why was it left to a British backbench MP to save Katiza from the horrific conditions in Zambia's prisons where he could have died without the outside world knowing? If he was involved, how, given the huge international support Mandela received when he was cruelly incarcerated for so many years, could he justify having consigned his fellow countryman to apparent oblivion? If he was not involved, how many other unauthorized activities was Tambo author of? Or could he have been covering for someone else?

Katiza luckily, and happily, survived. He says he knows who killed Stompie Moeketsi and of the plot which led to the fatal stabbing of the little boy from Tumahole. Is he telling the truth? 'Now that I have told my story, people must make up their own minds about the truth,' he said. 'Who is the big liar? Is it Winnie Mandela or Katiza Cebekhulu? Ordinary people who read this book should ask this question and decide for themselves.'

Notes

Prologue

page 1. Alan Paton, *Cry, the Beloved Country* (first published by Jonathan Cape, London, 1948; Penguin, Harmondsworth, in numerous paperback editions).

Chapter 1

page 4. Aggrey Klaaste, *Sowetan*, 26 October 1987.

page 5. Sandile Memela, *Sunday Independent* (Johannesburg), 8 October 1995.

page 11. Paton, *Cry, the Beloved Country* (Penguin 1988 edition), p. 11.

Chapter 2

page 15. Based on a passage from Paton, *Cry, the Beloved Country* (Penguin 1988 edition), p. 16.

NOTES

page 18. Allister Sparks, *Tomorrow Is Another Country* (Mandarin, London, 1996), p. 16; Joseph Lelyveld, *Move Your Shadow* (Michael Joseph, London, 1986), p. 211; Mary Benson, *Nelson Mandela* (Penguin, Harmondsworth, 1994), pp. 169 and 188; Ellen Kuzwayo, *Call Me Woman* (Ravan Press, Johannesburg, 1991), p. 247.

page 18. Rian Malan, *My Traitor's Heart* (The Bodley Head, London, 1990), pp. 272–3.

page 18. Tony Allen-Mills, *Independent*, 24 September 1987.

page 19. Nomavenda Mathiane, *Frontline*, April 1987.

pages 20–2. Case number 41-1743-88, Johannesburg Regional Court; *Citizen*, 20 and 22 September 1988; *Star* (Johannesburg), 22 and 27 September 1988; *Weekly Mail*, 23 September 1988; Emma Gilbey, quoting interviews with lawyers and police, in *The Lady: The Life and Times of Winnie Mandela* (Vintage, Random House, London 1994), pp. 164–6.

page 23. Gilbey, *The Lady*, p. 156, 216–17.

page 26. In a later interview with the author Katiza estimated there were about eight photos.

Chapter 3

pages 28–9. 'Richardson the Monster', *Drum*, October 1990; Gilbey, *The Lady*, p. 162.

page 29. Henti Joubert, from the transcript of case number 184/89, *The State* v. *J. V. M. Richardson*, Rand Supreme Court.

NOTES

Chapter 4

page 43. Gilbey, *The Lady*, p. 184.

page 44. Verryn's friends, interviews with author.

page 45. Among those giving Mrs Mandela funds was the British government's Overseas Development Organization. It donated money for a nutrition project run by Mrs Mandela for destitute shack dwellers in the bleak Winterberg area north of Pretoria. A senior British diplomat told the author that London's Pretoria Embassy knew the money had gone towards the building of a wall around Mrs Mandela's new £250,000 twenty-two-room mansion, known locally as 'Winnie's Palace', just down the hill in Orlando West from Winnie's fire-gutted matchbox house and Paul Verryn's manse.

page 46. Gilbey, *The Lady*, p. 174.

page 46. In fact, no other accounts refer to rapes by both sides. Authors/journalists refer either to the rape by the MUFC or to that by the Daliwonga High School. Emma Gilbey, in *The Lady*, p. 173, refers to a rape of an MUFC girl by Daliwonga High School. Rian Malan, in *Frontline*, December 1989; David Beresford, *Guardian*, 27 January 1989; Spencer Reiss, *Newsweek*, 13 February 1989, all refer to rape by the MUFC of a Daliwonga pupil.

page 47. Malan, *My Traitor's Heart*, p. 273.

page 48. Verryn's friends, interviews with author.

page 49. Nomavenda Mathiane, *Frontline*, March 1989.

pages 49–51. Interview with author.

page 51. Gilbey, *The Lady*, p. 182; *Observer*, 29 January 1989.

page 51. Interview with author.

page 52. After Nelson Mandela was elected President of South Africa in April 1994 he appointed Arthur Chaskalson to be the first President of the new Constitutional Court.

pages 52–3. Friends of Paul Verryn, interviews with author; Gilbey, *The Lady*, p. 183.

page 55. Case number 184/89, Rand Supreme Court.

page 56. Evidence given by another manse resident, Sello Dendwe, on 16 January 1989 at a Soweto community meeting called by the Mandela Crisis Committee.

page 56. *Frontline*, March 1989.

Chapter 5

pages 58-60. Interview with author, 9 April 1992.

page 63. Gilbey, *The Lady*, p. 50.

page 67. Case number 184/89, Rand Supreme Court, 3 May 1990; *Business Day*, *Weekly Mail* and *Star* (Johannesburg), 4 May 1994; *Daily Mail* (Johannesburg), 25 May 1990; case number 644/91, *The State* v. *John Morgan, Xoliswa Falati and Nomzamo Winifred Mandela*, Rand Supreme Court, 2 June 1993.

page 67. Thabiso Mono, interview with author, 8 January 1996.

page 69. Richard Maponyawes, a millionaire supermarket and BMW car-sales franchise owner who was a friend and benefactor of both

Nelson and Winnie Mandela.

page 69. Case number 184/89, Rand Supreme Court.

page 70. John Morgan, interview with Dawn Barkhuizen of the *Sunday Times* (Johannesburg), 12 April 1992.

Chapter 6

pages 71–2. Independent, 21 September 1990. Other source materials for the Seheri affair include various public statements by Andrew Ikaneng; Gilbey, *The Lady,* pp. 167–73; transcripts of case number 39/88, *The State* v. *Oupa Seheri and others,* Rand Supreme Court, November 1988; *Sowetan,* 22 May 1990.

page 72. Andrew Hogg, *Sunday Times* (London), 19 May 1991.

page 73. Gilbey, *The Lady,* p. 179–80; case numbers 183/89 and 184/89, Rand Supreme Court, May–August 1990.

page 75. Interview with author.

page 76. Kenny Kgase, evidence to the Rand Supreme Court in case numbers 183/89 and 184/89.

pages 76–7. Case numbers 183/89 and 184/89, Rand Supreme Court.

page 78. Gilbey, *The Lady,* pp. 188–91.

page 78–9. Friends of Paul Verryn, interview with author; case number 184/89, Rand Supreme Court; medical report on Kenneth Kgase by Dr Martin Connell, 7 January 1989.

pages 81–2. Gilbey, *The Lady,* p. 191.

page 83. Secret report to Oliver Tambo from the Mandela Crisis Committee, late January 1989 (copy in author's possession).

page 83. Gilbey, *The Lady*, p. 194.

Chapter 7

pages 89–91. *Guardian*, 10 February 1989 and 27 January 1989.

pages 92–96. Asvat family members and Reggie Jana, interviews with author, from April 1992 and June 1997 onwards; Gilbey, *The Lady*, pp. 200–1.

pages 98–101. Asvat family and friends, interviews with author; *The State* v. *Cyril Mbatha and Nicholas Dlamini*, Rand Supreme Court, October–November 1989; *Weekly Mail*, 20 October and 16 November 1989; Gilbey, *The Lady*, pp. 203–4.

page 102. NBC, 1 February 1989.

pages 102–3. Translation from the Afrikaans in the *Star* (Johannesburg), 8 April 1992; Gilbey, *The Lady*, pp. 205–6.

page 103. Interview with author.

Chapter 8

pages 104–7. Dudu Chili, interviews with author between 1991 and 1997; Andrew Hogg, *Sunday Times* (London), 19 May 1991.

pages 112–14. Case number 183/89, *The State* v. *Sibusiso Chili and six others*, Rand Supreme Court, March–April 1990.

NOTES

Chapter 9

page 115. *Sunday Star,* 12 February 1989.

pages 115–17. Testimony of Dr Patricia Klepp, case number 184/89 and 167/90, Rand Supreme Court.

pages 117–18. *Guardian,* 16 February 1989.

pages 118–19. *City Press,* 17 February 1989.

pages 119–20. As reported in *Independent,* 21 February 1989.

pages 120–2. Author's interviews with Miranda Harris, Katiza Cebekhulu and friends of Fink Haysom. Miranda Harris left Johannesburg soon afterwards to run a guest house near Port Alfred and lecture part-time in journalism studies at Rhodes University. I met her eventually in September 1995 in Mama's Pizzeria, in Rocky Street, Yeoville – Johannesburg's equivalent of London's Soho or New York's Greenwich Village. She defended Winnie Mandela stoutly. She dismissed Katiza Cebekhulu as a practised liar, but confirmed his account of his visit to her and his making of the tape on her property.

pages 122–3. Author's interviews with friends of Satchwell who asked not to be named.

page 123–4. Extracts of the statement taken by Captain Dempsey from Katiza Cebekhulu first appeared in the *Star* (Johannesburg), 8 April 1992. They appeared also in the *Weekly Mail,* 10 April 1992, and the *Sunday Times* (Johannesburg), 14 August 1994.

pages 123–5. Katiza Cebekhulu, interview with author, 29 July 1995.

page 125. *Guardian*, 27 February 1996.

pages 126–7. Interview with author.

page 128. *Christian Science Monitor*, 6 April 1992.

page 128. *Weekly Mail*, 20 October 1989.

Chapter 10

pages 130–1. TV address to the nation, 24 August 1989.

pages 131–2. Sparks, *Tomorrow Is Another Country*, p. 36.

page 132. *Business Day*, 12 February 1990.

page 133. *Washington Post*, February 1990; *Sunday Telegraph*, 25 February 1990.

page 134. See, for example, Rich Mkhondo, 'The Fall and Rise of Icon Winnie', *Star* (Johannesburg), 27 January 1990, and 'Fairytale Marriage to Winnie', *Sunday Times* (Johannesburg), 11 February 1990. The love letter was published in an official biography of Winnie Mandela, *Higher Than Hope*, by Fatima Meer (Madiba Publishers, Cape Town, 1990).

pages 137–8. *Sunday Times* (Johannesburg), 26 July 1992 and 2 August 1992; *Guardian Weekly*, 6 August 1992.

pages 135–40. *Star* (Johannesburg), 13 February 1993, 1 August 1992. Gilbey, *The Lady*, p. 228. See also ibid., pp. 226–9; the report of the Commission of Inquiry into the death of Clayton Sizwe Sithole; and case number 184/89, Rand Supreme Court.

NOTES

Chapter 11

pages 143–4. Interview with author, July 1995.

pages 144–51. Sunday Times (Johannesburg), 27 May 1990; case number 184/89, Rand Supreme Court.

page 147. Gilbey, *The Lady*, p. 231.

page 150. Independent, 16 May 1990.

page 151. Star (Johannesburg), 24 June 1990.

pages 151–2. Star (Johannesburg), 1 July 1990.

page 152. New York Times, 23 June 1990.

page 152. Gilbey, *The Lady*, p. 238.

page 153. Star (Johannesburg), 2 June 1990.

pages 153–4. Sunday Telegraph, 22 July 1990.

page 155. Weekly Mail, 21 September and 30 November 1990.

page 155. Mark Gevisser, *New York Times*, 14 May 1991.

Chapter 12

page 159. Observer, 23 September 1990.

page 161. Independent, 21 September 1990.

pages 164–5. Gilbey, *The Lady*, p. 249.

pages 170–4. Independent, 2 and 4 February 1991.

NOTES

page 175. *Star* (Johannesburg), 18 February 1991.

pages 177–8. Ray Kennedy, *The Times* (London), 8 February 1991.

Chapter 13

pages 179–80. *Star* (Johannesburg) and *Guardian*, 13 February 1991.

pages 179–89. The Winnie Mandela trial continued for almost four months, producing prodigious volumes of evidence and argument. Therefore no account in a chapter this size can pretend to be comprehensive. Anyone wanting to retrace all the twists and turns in the courtroom saga would need to get hold of the trial transcripts of case number 167/90. Otherwise, the detailed reporting of London *Daily Telegraph* crime correspondent Neil Darbyshire and the then *Weekly Mail* correspondent Emma Gilbey, who both covered the entire proceedings, are first-class reference material, as also is Gilbey's account in chapter 15 of *The Lady*.

page 190. *City Press*, 9 June 1991.

pages 190–1. *Sunday Times* (London), 16 June 1991; Gilbey, *The Lady*, p. 272.

page 191. *Star* (Johannesburg), 11 May 1991; *Independent*, 8 May 1991; *Daily Telegraph*, 21 May 1991; *Scotsman*, 21 May 1991. The author has no record of whether Ikaneng's assailants were charged or tried.

page 192. Gilbey, *The Lady*, p. 272.

NOTES

Chapter 14

pages 200–1. Zambia *Weekly Post,* 2 August 1991.

page 201. Star (Johannesburg), 28 August 1991.

Chapter 15

pages 213–15. Sowetan, 30 March and 7 April 1992; *Sunday Times* (London), 5 April 1992; *The Lady,* pp. 274–5.

pages 215–17. Christian Science Monitor, 6 April 1992.

pages 217–18. Weekly Mail, 10 April 1992.

pages 218–21. Sunday Times (Johannesburg), 12 April 1992.

page 225. Carte Blanche, M-Net TV, 26 April 1992.

pages 225. Star (Johannesburg), 19 April 1992.

pages 225–8. Sunday Times (London), 6 September 1992; *Star* (Johannesburg), 6 September 1992; *Scotsman,* 7 September 1992; *Daily Telegraph,* 7 September 1992; Gilbey, *The Lady,* pp. 291–4.

Chapter 16

pages 229–31. Jowie Mwiinga of the Zambia *Weekly Post,* writing in the *Weekly Mail* of South Africa, 15 November 1991; transcript of the interview between John Sangwa and Katiza Cebekhulu, recorded 15 November 1991.

pages 232–3. Zambia *Weekly Post* and *Weekly Mail*, 18 September 1992.

pages 233–4. A pseudonym. 'Sipho's' real name is known to the author.

page 235. *Star* (Johannesburg), 16 February 1993.

pages 235–6. *Sunday Times* (Johannesburg), 24 January 1993.

page 238. *Times* of Zambia, 14 October 1993.

page 242. Montshiwa Moroke, *Star* (Johannesburg), 3 June 1993.

page 242. *Star* (Johannesburg), 3 June 1993.

page 243. *Weekly Mail*, 11 June 1993.

page 243. South African Press Association report, 3 June 1993.

page 243. Case number 644/91, Supreme Court of South Africa, Appellate Division, 2 June 1993.

pages 243–4. South African Press Association, 9 June 1993.

page 244. *Sunday Times* (Johannesburg), 10 October 1993.

page 244. *Sunday Times* (Johannesburg), 19 February 1995.

pages 244–5. *Sunday Telegraph*, 10 December 1993.

Chapter 17

page 246. *Sunday Telegraph*, 10 April 1995.

pages 247–8. *Star* (Johannesburg), 10 August 1995.

page 248. *Sunday Times* (Johannesburg), 14 December 1995.

pages 248–9. Scotsman, 13 February 1995.

pages 249–50. Sunday Times (Johannesburg), 12 February 1995.

page 253. South African Press Association report, 7 March 1995.

pages 253–4. Star (Johannesburg), 7 March 1995.

pages 255–6. South African Press Association, 9 March 1995; *Scotsman*, 10 March 1995.

pages 256–9. City Press, 24 March 1996; Associated Press, 24 March 1996; Reuter, 25 March 1996; Carolyn Dempster, *Scotsman*, 19 and 21 March 1996; *Sunday Times* (London), 24 March 1996.

Conclusion

page 264. Lester Fuchs MP in the South African Parliament on 14 June 1993, as reported in the *Star* (Johannesburg), 16 June 1993.

pages 267–8. Thabiso Mono, interview with author in Johannesburg, 8 January 1996.

page 269. Klaus von Lieres, telephone interview with author in Johannesburg, 7 September 1995.

pages 270–1. Interview with Kenneth Kaunda in Lusaka, June 19.

INDEX

INDEX

INDEX

INDEX

INDEX

INDEX

INDEX

INDEX

INDEX

INDEX